IAMBIC

A collection of lyrical and terrifying poems

Marco Di Chio

Grosvenor House
Publishing Limited

All rights reserved
Copyright © Marco Di Chio, 2025

The right of Marco Di Chio to be identified as the author of this
work has been asserted in accordance with Section 78
of the Copyright, Designs and Patents Act 1988

The book cover is copyright to Marco Di Chio

This book is published by
Grosvenor House Publishing Ltd
Link House
140 The Broadway, Tolworth, Surrey, KT6 7HT.
www.grosvenorhousepublishing.co.uk

This book is sold subject to the conditions that it shall not, by way of
trade or otherwise, be lent, resold, hired out or otherwise circulated
without the author's or publisher's prior consent in any form of
binding or cover other than that in which it is published and
without a similar condition including this condition being
imposed on the subsequent purchaser.

This book is a work of fiction. Any resemblance to
people or events, past or present, is purely coincidental.

A CIP record for this book
is available from the British Library

Paperback ISBN 978-1-83615-358-0
eBook ISBN 978-1-83615-359-7

Contents

Memories

The Buzzing Mind	3
When Music Called the Years	5
Do you remember?	7
Planes	9
Hymn to Verona	10
The Stage	15

Love poems

In Arch and Ember	19
Thou, serpent in the garden of my days	21
Te vi cruzando la plaza	23
I saw you crossing the square	24
Letter to an unknown lover	25
Love poem	28
The Body of the Man	30
While Still Their Hands Are Warm	33
While the bubbles rose	35
Too Close but So Far	37
Ode to Love, the Tempest Crowned	39

To a friend

Letter to a friend	45
In this small, silent box of memory	47

Lament for Sandy Brodie	49
Wait Me There, My Friend	53

People

A poem for Anna	57
To a Sister	58
A Man's Tears	60
To an unborn child	62
Alien	64

To the earth

The White Rose by the Sea	69
The chase	71
Speak to me	74
Elegy Upon a Stone	77
The Seagull and the Hound	79
The Noisy Silence	89
The Petal and the Wind	91
To Walk the Floor in Rain	93
The First Rain of Summer	96
Dirt	99

Glasgow Poems

Flow Gently, Swift Clyde	117
The Duke of Wellington	119
Lochburn mist	121
Glasgow journey	124
Summer at Clyde Canal	128
Cadder woods	130
The Tree and the Cat	133

Poems of mystery

The Breath Behind Me	203
The Woman in the Café	224
A Dinner Invitation	228
The Box	234
The Hundred rooms	241
The Woman in the Mirror	541
The Fiddler's Rite	553
Beneath the breath	573
The House in the Wood	589

Memories

The Buzzing Mind

I try to sit, but thoughts begin to spin,
a thousand voices knocking to get in.
The morning light is fractured on the wall,
and every sound becomes a beckoning call.

The kettle screams. I feel it in my chest.
A flood arrives, unbidden, unexpressed.
A single word can tear the day in two,
I cry too loud, then laugh before I'm through.

No thought can live alone inside my head;
no sooner born than ten more crowd its bed.
Each one half-formed, each louder than the last,
the present shatters with the echoing past.

A phrase appears, I catch it, then it's gone,
replaced by flashes, questions, dusk, and dawn.
I chase the fragments down a crooked stair
and lose myself in blank, electric air.

The pages wait, though I forget they do.
My pen is lost. My lunch. My list. My shoe.
But when I find one syllable in line,
I feel a moment's quiet pulse is mine.

Iambs arrive like footsteps on a trail,
each beat a gate against the inner gale.
Within this cage of count and rising tone,
a kind of peace appears, but not my own.

It isn't stillness, not the world outside,
but structure makes the torrents coincide.
The form becomes a friend that holds my hand
when thought and feeling both are out of hand.

And there, between the chaos and the page,
a voice I know steps forward from the rage.
It doesn't shout. It doesn't run or hide.
It walks with me. It listens. It's my guide.

So let the world pour in, as wild as fire.
I'll shape its roar to rhythm and to lyre.
For in the storm, I do not drown or flee,
I write, and writing, I remember me.

When Music Called the Years

The decade dawned with promise in the air,
Madonna ruled, and hope came in a beat.
I played outside with sun-struck, tousled hair,
While grown-ups spoke of walls that fell in heat.

The world moved fast, new voices every week,
But I heard Puccini behind closed doors.
While others sang of love they dared to seek,
I found it swelling in La Traviata's scores.

Alanis hadn't come to break us yet,
But Laura Pausini began to rise.
I queued for Titanic, cold, Verona wet,
And hid a thousand thoughts behind my eyes.

The cinema was full, a breathless hush,
As ocean swelled and violins took flight.
A boy sank with the ship beneath the crush,
And something in me surfaced in the night.

I watched Jurassic Park with popcorn fists,
Its roars and wonders towering on the screen.
A world where monsters walked and nothing missed,
I stayed half-lost between the seen and seen.

We lived beneath one roof but worlds apart,
Ten years between, like pages left unturned.
She danced through teen years; I drew quiet art,
And kept the things I longed for unconcerned.

We went to Tyrol, high among the pines,
My parents' car a stage of older sound.
Celentano, Mina in their lines,
The hills would echo Battisti all around.

While Spice Girls played in stores I walked right past,
I hummed the bars of Donizetti's pain.
The modern songs came through like smoke, not glass,
A soundtrack I endured more than I claimed.

Diana gone. The silence thick and slow.
We watched the candle flicker on the screen.
But later, singing Angelo, I'd know
That sorrow speaks through songs that sound serene.

She wore the veil; the decade held its breath.
A thousand tiny moments led to this.
We faced the passing time, the world, the rest,
And learned to speak in ways we never did.

Do you remember?

Do you remember Cà di David's light,
The rows of poplars rising still and proud?
The hush of earth beneath the sky so bright,
Your name first whispered soft, not yet aloud.

Do you remember Verona's warm stone,
The music flowing out into the square?
How opera made childhood not alone,
And every aria perfumed the air?

Do you remember Glasgow in the rain,
The trembling chords of life you chose to play?
A voice that curled like smoke around your name,
And eyes that made the coldest morning stay.

Do you remember your dear friend long gone,
The one whose laugh still lingers in your chest?
The memory that will not ever move on,
A love that stayed while all the rest found rest.

Do you remember weaving through it all,
The birth, the voice, the heart that would not yield?
How past and present answer every call
From roots in song to love in foreign fields?

Do you remember early Cadder walks,
Where Lola led and silence softly grew?
Each step among the trees became your talks,
The woods a chapel morning carried through.

Do you remember all that waits ahead,
The futures spun from what you've dared to hold?
A thousand lives through every word you've said,
Still blooming strong from poplars, stone, and gold.

And in the wind that knows just who you were,
Do you remember?

Planes

Where are they going, all the silent wings,
The aeroplanes we dreamed but never flew?
They hum through time, through half-remembered things,
Past gates we closed before we ever knew.

They trace the skies of lives we did not lead,
In cities where our names were never called.
They carry hopes that vanished into need,
And voices stilled, and answers never stalled.

What makes a path but all the turns we shun?
The world we walk is stitched with could-have-beens.
Yet choice is cruel: it makes of many, one,
A thread pulled tight, unraveling the twins.

We envy stars for being always far,
Unreachable, yet burning all the same.
But we are stars, just trapped behind a scar—
We shine in absence, luminous with flame.

So let them fly, those ghostly silver birds,
Through skies not ours, beyond regret or fear.
Not every truth can find its home in words,
But still, we name what's lost to hold it near.

Hymn to Verona

O sovereign jewel cast by gods in stone,
Verona stands where fate and beauty meet,
A citadel where time itself is known,
And every breath resounds with echoes sweet.

No city rises like this hallowed place,
Where every wall is steeped in living art,
Where arches frame the light with solemn grace,
And every stone remembers from the heart.

The river sings in tongues of silver fire,
Its waters laced with histories profound,
It mirrors domes and towers that aspire
To draw the stars like bells from holy ground.

In spring, the courtyards bloom with ancient light,
Where lilac spills from crumbled cloister walls,
And breezes through the loggias take flight
To stir the petals as the sparrow calls.

The vines awake upon the sunlit hill,
The cypress lifts its prayer to open skies,
And every garden murmurs soft and still
Of secrets passed in love's immortal guise.

The summer gilds the marble into flame,
And cloaks the piazzas in golden breath,
Each narrow lane a poem with no name,
Each colonnade a hymn defying death.

When night descends, the balustrades ignite
With whispered songs from opera and lyre,
The air is drenched in perfume, warm and white,
And every window holds a hidden fire.

The voices rise from open balconies,
And laughter lingers down the frescoed walls,
While lovers walk through shadows made of peace,
Beneath the moon that blesses as it calls.

When autumn weeps her gold upon the stone,
Verona glows with reverence and fire,
The grapes are crushed, the harvest stands alone,
The vineyards blaze with last and full desire.

The cloisters breathe beneath October's veil,
As incense from the hillsides curls and fades,
And every gust across the sacred pale
Reveals the hush of time in colonnades.

In winter's hush, the towers bear the snow
Like crowns of saints enshrined in silver light,
The bridges arch where frozen currents flow,
And lanterns bloom against the coming night.

The flutes return to call through veils of frost,
Their notes like prayers upon the still, white air,
And nothing here is ever truly lost,
The past and present walk as one, aware.

The Arena holds the roar of voice and flame,
The ancient stones still drink the song of men,
Each whisper there preserves the sacred name
Of drama born again, and born again.

Its breath is dust and thunder, blood and wine,
A vault where every silence thunders deep;
Here, time kneels low before the grand design,
Where echoes of the centuries still sleep.

The moonlight floods its aisles in silver streams,
As voices rise in arias of fire;
Each note becomes the shape of mortal dreams,
Each cry ascends like smoke from sacred pyre.

Here gladiators bled, and emperors gazed,
Now passion sings where once the sword held sway.
The ghosts applaud where newer fires are raised,
And art redeems what war once took away.

No stage can match its breath, no script its soul,
No coliseum dares its flame contain;
The Arena is Verona's burning whole,
A living wound that glorifies all pain.

The olive bends in reverence and praise,
The fig tree dreams beside the ruined gate,
And all the sky above prepares to raise
Verona's name beyond the grip of fate.

This city is not bound by clock or chain,
It breathes in symphony with blood and star,
And through her halls walks joy as well as pain,
Each moment marked by beauty near and far.

Let empires fade, let monarchs be unmade,
These stones endure where power cannot stay.

Where others fall, Verona shall not fade:
She stands in song, and shall beyond decay.

O city wrought of echo, light, and flame,
Thy arches carve the shape of time's own throne,
Thy silence louder than a victor's name,
Thy every breath a monument in stone.

Not Rome, nor Florence, nor the southern shore
Can steal the fire Verona keeps alight.
She is the wound, the wonder, and the lore,
The timeless crown that burns against the night.

Let thunder speak and winds be still and bow,
Let angels hush the stars to catch thy name,
For none who breathe shall match thee then or now,
O city graced with ever-burning flame.

Thou art the altar of the world's desire,
Where blood and light in holy union blend,
A forge of song, a throne of stone and fire,
Where even time must kneel, and silence bend.

Eternal is thy beauty, never veiled,
Not cloaked in ruin, nor in age's dust,
But robed in dreams that neither fate has failed,
Nor storm defaced, nor treachery unjust.

All nations seek thee in their deepest sleep,
All poets trace thy name in sacred ink,
And hearts that lose thee find no joy too deep,
No wine as rich, no sky from which to drink.

Verona! Crown of earth and gate of flame!
Let centuries arise to kiss thy feet.
Thou art not memory, but burning name,
Alive where all that's lost and great must meet.

O blaze of soul! O monument of breath!
No final line may hold thy full decree.
Though flesh may pass, and empires taste of death,
The world shall end, and still thy soul shall be.

The Stage

The silence stretches tight before the storm,
A breath held deep within the lungs of light.
Each figure waits, composed in tempered form,
Their stillness charged, electrified with night.

The bow is lifted, not in thought, but need.
A tremble rides the wrist, the spine, the air.
A muscle wakes. A hush begins to bleed.
The first note blooms—and all the world is bare.

It moves like skin. It slides, it climbs, it dives,
It shivers down the neck, the arm, the floor.
It pulses in the seat where silence thrives,
Then breaks the dam and floods from every pore.

The strings are fingers plucking at the chest,
The brass exhales a groan too low to lie.
The drums ignite the stomach with their quest,
A thrust, a pulse, a cry too wide to die.

The cellos moan, the flutes slip through the ribs,
The oboes twist like hands behind the eyes.
Each voice entangles, bares, consumes, and gives,
No part untouched, no breath left to disguise.

The rise, the swell, the bending of the sound,
The lean of limbs, the arc of sweat and flame,
It isn't thought that moves them, but unbound
And aching force too primal yet to name.

The strokes are bold, but trembling in control,
The pauses grip the throat, the jaw, the thigh.
The violins seduce the hidden soul,
They lure the edge, then kiss it as it cries.

It builds. It breaks. It slows to drag and tease.
Then leaps again, now louder, raw and true.
The horn thrusts high; the violas, on their knees,
Beg underneath in trembling residue.

Now nothing stands between the heart and sound.
Now everything is rhythm, gasp, and skin.
The tempo climbs, no longer paced or bound,
Each moment slides its fingernails within.

And then—the peak. The surge. The grip. The gasp.
The trembling hush of everything released.
The silence falls again, a final clasp,
The breath that held the storm now finds its peace.

They do not speak. They do not look. They know.
What passed between them cannot be explained.
The stage still echoes with the afterglow,
The holy mess of beauty, muscle, strained.

Love poems

In Arch and Ember

Beneath an arch of timeworn stone he stands,
With warmth upon his chest and grace in hands.
A scarf of fire drapes his quiet frame,
As though the wind had whispered him by name.

The wall behind, so ancient, dark, and deep,
Now cradles him like memory in sleep.
He leans as if to listen to the past,
Yet in his eyes, a light that will outlast.

His gaze is kind, both open and refined,
The sort that speaks of thought, of soul, of mind.
And round his face, the gentle morning glows,
Where love once looked and never let it go.

He wears the hues of autumn, soft and proud,
As though he walks through leaves instead of crowd.
The world may turn, may falter, fall, and flee,
But here he stands, as steady as can be.

I knew that day, when first I saw his face,
That silence bent to him with quiet grace.
He didn't speak, and yet my heart replied,
As if his breath had stirred the world inside.

His laughter, low and sweet, became my song,
The one I'd waited for my whole life long.
No need for grand parade or trumpet's call,
Just him, and that was more than all in all.

Through every stone of Glasgow's rain-kissed street,
I'd trace his step and feel my own heart beat.
Where once I wandered, restless and unknown,
He built a place that I could call my own.

His eyes hold Strongoli, the salt, the flame,
The Calabrian fire no time could tame.
And Santa Fe, where hunger learned to sing,
Still lingers in the way he holds the spring.

What hands could hold the laughter we have made?
What lips could name the comfort he has laid?
In fleeting dusk, in mornings bold and bare,
His love's the weight of earth, the breath of air.

So here I keep this image, soft and still,
A flame against the dark, against the chill.
And when the years move on without a sound,
His light will be the one that I have found.

Thou, serpent in the garden of my days

Thou, serpent in the garden of my days,
Thy venomous words did poison every breath.
A shadow's curse, a harbinger of woe,
Thou art the bringer of my deepest death.

With each cruel glance, each whispered deceit,
Thou turned to ashes all my hopes so sweet.
In thy presence, love became a lie,
A mask that hid the ruin in thine eye.

Thy hands did grasp what was not thine to take,
And left me drowning in the hollow wake.
Thou wove thy plots with bitter thread and seam,
Tearing asunder all I dared to dream.

O! What foul torment thou hast wrought upon me!
A world of thorns where once was light and free.
Thy lies, like daggers, cut through tender skin,
And left me walking where no peace could win.

A tempest's fury, fierce and cruel,
Thy wickedness, a lesson cold and full.
Yet still, I rise from all that thou hast done,
A moon that rises when the day is gone.

Though thou hast struck, thy hand shall not be near,
For in thy shadow, I shall show no fear.
I cast thee down, and from thee, I break free,
The weight of thy cruelty will not define me.

Thou art the storm that I shall leave behind,
Thy ghost a phantom, lost and blind.
No longer shall thy bitterness take root,
For I walk tall, and thou remain a mute.

The worst thou gave, I've cast upon the wind,
And in its wake, a new life shall begin.

Te vi cruzando la plaza

- in the style of Federico Garcia Lorca -

Te vi cruzando la plaza,
tu pelo, olas negras de medianoche,
tu voz, susurro de tambores lejanos.
El cielo se inclinó para escucharte.

Tato, te llamé,
como si mi alma supiera tu nombre
antes de que mis labios lo aprendieran.
El viento se volvió cálido cuando sonreíste.

Intentaste besarme la mejilla,
pero yo ardía por probar tu boca.
La vergüenza cosió mis labios,
mientras mi corazón galopaba sobre piedra.

Ríes como el agua corriendo libre,
comes como si el mundo acabara,
y aún así, eres lo más hermoso
que esta tierra hambrienta me ha dado.

Te amo como
la sombra se aferra al fuego,
un secreto antiguo,
y que siempre regresa.

I saw you crossing the square

English version in Iambic

I saw you crossing slowly through the square,
your hair like midnight waves in curling flight,
your voice a whisper born of distant drums.
The sky leaned down to listen as you spoke.

I called you Tato, as if all my soul
had known your name before my tongue could shape it.
The wind turned warm the moment that you smiled.

You tried to kiss me softly on the cheek,
but I was burning just to taste your mouth.
My shame had sewn a silence through my lips,
while fire-footed horses struck my chest.

You laugh like water rushing over stone,
you eat as if the world might end tonight,
and still you are the finest gift this earth
has ever placed within my open hands.

I love you as the shadow loves the flame,
an ancient
secret,
always
coming
back.

Letter to an unknown lover

I write to you beneath the shroud of night,
When silence hangs and all the lamps burn low.
You come to me in slivers made of light,
But never when the world begins to glow.

Your face is smoke. Your hands are made of rain.
Your breath is soft as mist along the moor.
You walk beside me, whispering my name,
Then vanish through an ever-absent door.

I do not know the colour of your eyes,
If they are storm or sky, or green with flame,
But still I feel their gaze beneath my cries,
And every night I tremble at your name.

They do not speak of men like us with grace.
They twist our want and write it down as shame.
But I have traced devotion on your face,
And kissed you in the shelter of a flame.

The river knows. I told it once your name,
And still it coils in silver through the land.
It answered back in ripples much the same
As yours, when once you brushed against my hand.

The poplars lean. They bend to hear me speak.
They shiver when I whisper where you've gone.
I've seen your shadow flicker on the creek,
And vanish like the memory of dawn.

The moon is part of you. I see it rise
And think your soul has slipped into the sky.
It follows me with low and watching eyes
That never ask, but only wonder why.

The stars are strung like beads along your trail.
I count them like I'd count the ways you're near.
Though wind may howl and heavy storms assail,
Each constellation carves your name in fear.

I speak to rocks. I press my face to stone.
The earth is old, but never deaf to love.
I ask if it has known you, felt you, grown,
It answers with the worm, the hawk, the dove.

The sea, it croons your name with every wave.
The foam forgets, the tide recalls your touch.
It's there I almost found you once, so brave,
Before the pull of silence grew too much.

The hills still bear the print where once you stood,
A hollow where your body pressed the grass.
I gather leaves and twigs and bits of wood,
And build a shrine no soul would dare to pass.

At dusk, I feel you lingering in trees.
Their trunks hold warmth no sun could leave behind.
I walk through dusk as if it holds your knees,
Your breath, your shoulders shadowing my mind.

The sky turns red. The planets swing in arcs.
They burn, but never brighter than your name.
You are the secret hidden in the darks,
A pulse that neither time nor space can tame.

I do not beg you come. I do not plead.
The night is gift enough, if you are near.
But if you feel some answering of need,
Then send your voice, and I will always hear.

Then let this ink dissolve into the night,
A vow the stars may carry through the blue,
For love like ours outlives both wrong and right,
And I was born to wander until you.

Love poem

I wandered long with half a heart in tow,
Through silent streets where love refused to grow.
Each voice, each hand, each fleeting, passing face
Could not complete the ache, the empty space.

You are the one I searched for in the night,
A whispered thought just out of reach, of sight.
The mystery I longed for all my life,
Now here you are, my haven and my light.

If there is perfection, it wears your form,
A portrait sketched in warmth, in grace, in storm.
In you, the flawed world finds a faultless truth,
In every glance, in laughter, strength, and youth.

Your beauty, yes, I underline the word,
It moves in ways that silence all I've heard.
No music plays more tender on my skin
Than your soft breath when day's about to begin.

I love to wake and find you by my side,
Still sleeping sweet, your chest a rising tide.
To hold you close before the morning breaks,
It's there I know what real belonging takes.

How lucky I am just to share this time,
To walk this life while your hand rests in mine.
The world could spin a thousand suns above,
I'd trade them all for one more night of love.

I love the colour of your golden skin,
Where summer dwells and morning light begins.
My hands could wander there and never tire,
As though they touched the surface of a fire.

You are the reason in the rhyme I write,
The hush that turns a shadow into light.
What grace, what gift, what wild and sacred art,
That you exist, and chose to share your heart.

The Body of the Man

The shoulder curves as though a god once drew
A line in flesh to teach the hands their goal.
Its sculpted roundness shifts beneath each view,
A changing shape that answers touch with soul.

In lamplight it is bronze and carved from flame;
In morning's grey, it softens into sleep.
At dusk, it melts like wax without a name,
And midnight makes it holy, raw, and deep.

His chest—divine in breadth, in breath, in heat,
Is where the eye and hand begin to stray.
Its rise invites the mouth to drink, to meet
The sacred in a sensual display.

And when the fingers trail across its span,
They feel both warmth and hardness, flesh and stone,
As though the gods in making mortal man
Let heat and marble share a single throne.

The arms are fluid, flexing under light,
Like rivers caught in golden afternoon.
They glisten when the sweat begins to bite,
Their skin half-velvet, half a tight cocoon.

The belly, taut and touched by passing breath,
Holds motion in the stillness of its frame.
Its warmth beneath the hand defies all death,
And heat there builds without a need for name.

The thighs—O god—the thighs transform with stance.
They broaden when he plants, they tense in speed.
In shifting light, they flicker like a dance
Of power just withheld, of boundless need.

To touch them is to feel the world's deep root,
A pulse within the earth, alive and bare.
The skin is smooth, then rough, then sharp, then mute,
A world that changes underneath the stare.

The back becomes another kind of sea,
A plane of muscle flexing with the breath,
Its shadows speak in shifting symmetry
Of labor, longing, sleep, and love and death.

The curve that forms beneath the lower spine
Is drawn for lips to follow, slow and sure,
And light reveals each movement as a sign
Of how the body learns what it's endured.

His neck, when kissed, is tender, warm, and tense,
A field of nerves just under surface caught.
And there, the sacred turns to raw, immense,
Where heat dissolves whatever prayer has brought.

The mouth—a gate, a flame, a yielding sword,
Is not just shaped for speech but for the sin
Of tasting, biting, gasping without word,
And drawing breath and pleasure deep within.

But more than any part, it is the whole,
The way he shifts beneath the eye's regard.
He changes shape, from firelight into coal,
From satin into steel, from soft to hard.

A sculpture that is breathing, made of need,
Of joy and weight and heat and hunger's thread;
A body not for conquest but for creed,
Where worship is not knelt, but touched instead.

He is not fixed: he flickers, folds, and glows.
He darkens in the corners of the room.
He gleams when sweat upon his body shows,
And bends the night to shape, to breath, to bloom.

To look at him is more than just to see,
It is to feel the truth of flesh made bright.
His body holds the ache of mystery,
A changing shrine of shadow, scent, and light.

While Still Their Hands Are Warm

There is a weight in love that does not press,
But lifts instead, and leaves no mark behind,
A hand that strokes the temple in distress,
A glance that speaks before the voice can find.

My parents live. Their laughter fills the air,
Though I now dwell far off, in stranger lands.
Yet in my skin remains their patient care,
And all the world is shaped by their two hands.

When I was small, the night was never vast,
For they would wrap me in a woollen light.
Their arms were walls no shadow ever passed;
Their whispers broke the longest stretch of night.

They touched with quiet. Fingers smooth and slow
Would part the tangles of a troubled brow.
They never spoke of all they feared to know,
But carried all my burdens then, and now.

And though they walk with time against their side,
And though their hair grows soft with silver threads,
They are my pillars still, my certain guide,
The lamp that flickers not, though daylight sheds.

I worry for the day when all must change,
When I will seek their hands and find them gone.
That thought, it comes in moments dark and strange,
A wind that steals the breath before the dawn.

But they are here. Their hands are warm today.
Their voices still can calm the storm in me.
And though I live too many miles away,
They love without the need of eyes to see.

So let me not forget the gift I own,
The rarest thing, too often cast aside:
To call, and hear their answer on the phone,
To know they're still a harbour, still a guide.

And when that time shall come, as all things must,
I'll hold the shape their kindness left in me.
Their love is more than memory or dust,
It is the root of who I came to be.

But now, while yet they breathe, while yet they smile,
Let me not waste the wonder that is near.
For in their arms, though stretched across the mile,
Still lives the world, its worth, its heart, its tear.

While the bubbles rose

The strings began, but I could only hear
the sound of you, the rhythm of your breath.
The world grew soft, as if it knew to fade,
to give us space to speak with just our eyes.

I saw you, not as others ever had,
but as the one I somehow always knew.
You took a step, and I forgot to breathe,
how strange that love could feel so calm, so true.

You smiled, and every thought I had dissolved.
There was no fear, no need for anything.
Your hand in mine was more than any vow,
a truth that needed nothing but its name.

I would have married you in rain or dark,
with no one there but silence and your voice.
But here we stood, and even stars felt close,
as if the sky had bent to see us kiss.

The music flowed like light between the trees,
a quiet thread that held the air in place.
And bubbles drifted softly through the day,
like tiny wishes floating as we spoke.

We spoke in whispers meant for only us,
the words were simple, but they carried all.
"I choose you" was the only world I knew,
and in your eyes, that world would never end.

No blessing could be greater than your touch,
no song more lovely than the way you smiled.
And when we kissed, the universe stood still,
as if it understood what we had done.

This love is not a firework or storm,
but something deeper, patient, ever warm,
the quiet joy of always coming home,
the peace of knowing I am fully known.

Too Close but So Far

The silence settled not with weight but grace,
A hush that moved between them like a tide.
It touched the edges of their shared old space
And softened what the heart had tried to hide.

No voice disturbed the quiet they had made,
No hurried word to patch what ran too deep.
They let the ache remain, not sharp but stayed,
A sorrow not for shouting, but for sleep.

They breathed the same slow air, but held apart,
Each lost within the hush of tender thought.
The wound was not a tearing of the heart,
But more the gentle stillness conflict brought.

Love lingered there, not spoken yet not gone,
A warmth beneath the surface of the day.
It trembled like the hush before the dawn
When light prepares but does not yet give way.

No gesture broke the calm, no glance betrayed,
Yet everything was filled with what they felt.
The silence was a place where hope had stayed,
And not a wall, but something that could melt.

They didn't speak,not out of pride or shame,
But for the love that asked to be preserved.
A word too soon might only fan the flame,
And silence was the kindness they deserved.

The closeness hurt, but distance would have killed.
The air was thick with things they would not say.
But in the hush, a softer truth was filled,
That love may wait, but does not drift away.

And still it held them, gentle, unresolved,
Like music resting just before a chord.
A grace that asks no question to be solved,
But trusts in what the silence has restored.

Too close for loss, too far to touch repair,
They stood within the pause that time allows.
And in that space, they found a form of care
That speaks with neither silence nor with vows.

So love endured without a grand display,
No proof but what the quiet made it be.
And in not speaking, both had found a way
To say, I'm here, and you are still with me.

Ode to Love, the Tempest Crowned

O Love, thou art the tempest in the chest,
The fire that cracks the heavens into rest.
Thou com'st not soft, nor meek, nor mild in gait,
But dressed in wrath, in bloom, in blood, in fate.

No anchor holds when thou dost raise thy hand;
No hull endures thy thunder's vast command.
The tallest minds are flattened in thy sweep,
The boldest hearts are broken into sleep.

Thou buildest temples out of air and ash,
Then drown'st the faithful in a single flash.
The field is gold, the scythe unseen, yet near,
Thou laugh'st in joy, and bendest joy to fear.

Thou art the flood that bursts from buried rain,
The river taught by earth how to disdain.
A gentle trickle hides thy fiercest swell,
Thy silence is the tolling of the bell.

A thousand roots are torn beneath thy surge,
Thou drag'st the stone, the seed, the soul, the verge.
Thou com'st in spirals flung from southern seas,
And break'st the spines of groves and centuries.

The glens are thine, the moors in fog and chill,
The stags that pause on frost-encrusted hill.
Majestic as the thistle's guarded bloom,
Yet bleak as dusk that hangs o'er Skye in gloom.

A fire from marrow, sudden, unexplained,
A heat that breaks the mind before it's named.
No doctor sees the chamber where it sleeps,
A furnace veiled in flesh, in depths it keeps.

No shape defines thee, thou art light and stain,
As sweet as fruit, as cruel as hunger's pain.
A shadow cast by gold, a gold in flame,
Too vast for truth, too close for any name.

Thy hands are velvet, iron, salt, and air,
Thy grip may cradle or may strip the bare.
The kiss may sweeten death, or bring it fast,
The smile may curse, the silence may outlast.

Not born but poured from womb and root and bone,
Not summoned, yet arriving all alone.
It has no law, yet speaks with lawless grace,
A god with neither temple, shrine, nor face.

Then rises, faster, louder, deep and wide,
The branches split, the tides undo their tide.
The roofs are torn, the songs are drowned in screams,
The night is cracked with fever, shards, and dreams.

The stars collapse beneath its tightening pull,
The wind forgets its name, the void grows full.
The blood obeys, the reason reels and runs,
And all is drawn into the fire that stuns.

The world becomes a throat that gasps and howls,
The seas unsheathe their teeth, the moon disbowels.
A pressure builds that time itself can't bear,
Then breaks,

and all is lifted into air.
The sky splits open. Nothing left to spare.
The trees are roots alone. The ground is glass.
The sun forgets the hour, lets it pass.

No voice remains to tell what once had been.
The fields are dust. The rivers, pulled within.
The breath of earth is stolen from the stone.
All stands, undone, unspeaking and alone.

A silence falls, so heavy, thick, and bright,
It hums like bells submerged in endless night.
The hearts that beat now beat in foreign time,
Their rhythm marred, chaotic, and sublime.

The faces changed, reforged by unseen hand,
As if they'd stared through fire, and understand.
No word survives. No oath is safe or true.
The stars that watched have vanished from their view.

Yet in the ash, a glow begins to form,
Not warm, nor kind, but strange, a different storm.
It does not promise peace, nor even grace,
But something vast still lingers in its place.

For love, once loosed, will never be contained,
It lives in ruin, and it feeds on pain.
It seeds in cracks and blossoms out of scars,
And dances still beneath the shattered stars.

No prayer can cage it. None may ask it why.
It is the voice behind the lover's cry.
It holds the blade, the bloom, the flood, the flame,
And leaves behind no soul that stays the same.

To a friend

Letter to a friend

My dearest friend, I write to you in dusk,
When shadows stretch and all the world feels hushed.
The silent room still holds your echoed laugh,
A faded print upon time's fragile glass.

You always said the glass was mostly full,
You saw the light inside the darkest pull.
But that last night, your voice grew soft and low,
You said, "I've always tried, but I don't know."

"I've fought to stay the same," you said, "to shine,
But lately something's breaking down inside."
No tears, just pause—the kind that silence makes
When even steady hearts begin to ache.

You told me then to go to Gigha's shore,
To see the sea you loved, and feel it more.
You said, "The light there doesn't sting the same,
It soothes. You'll see. Just go. Please, go one day."

You hated hush. You filled it up with sound:
With music loud, with stories spinning round.
You didn't dance, you didn't need to, friend,
Your words alone could make the stillness bend.

With coffee warm and cigarette in hand,
You built your world like only dreamers can.
And now, that warmth still lingers in the air,
Though you're not here to lift the heavy care.

Thank you for being life to me, for grace,
For holding me through storms I couldn't face.
You gave me space to break, and then begin,
You taught me how to lose, and still let in.

But Campbeltown still holds you in its grace,
Beneath its sky, your ever-chosen place.
You rest where sea meets sky and sky meets stone,
In front of Davaar's island, wind-blown, lone.

One day, I'll come and sit beside you there,
And bring the tales you'd ask for if you cared.
I'll tell you that I stood on Gigha's shore,
And heard the silence hum, and hurt no more.

You'll smirk and flick your smoke into the breeze,
And say, "About damn time you found some peace."
We'll sit and watch the boats drift out and in,
And let the long, old evening settle in.

And thank you, too, for letting me belong,
For giving me a friend so brave and strong.
I count myself among the lucky few
Whose hearts were shaped by knowing love like you.

Until that time, I keep you in the light,
The flame that steadies me through every night.
You were, and are, the voice that keeps me strong,
And in my heart, you hum a living song.

In this small, silent box of memory

In this small, silent box of memory,
A piece of thee doth rest, so tender and still,
Ashes that whisper of what once did be,
Of laughter, of joy, and dreams to fulfil.

I hold thee now in this fragile form,
Like a dream enwrought in the dawning morn,
And yet it's so hard to let thee go,
To close the door on the love we did know.

Thou smoked much, the smoke in thy breast,
A habit entwined, in which thou didst rest.
Now thy mortal frame is naught but dust,
A fleeting wisp of time, no longer just.

The urn, a small home for all that remains,
A vessel of thee, with all its pains.
I sit with it close, as though thou wert near,
Hoping the ashes might whisper dear.

If only I could open this urn,
And watch the ashes rise and turn,
To see thee step from smoke once more,
Thy laughter, thy warmth, the soul I adore.

If only I could break the seal and find,
A way to bring thee back, to unwind,
To hold thee again, to see thy face,
To feel thy presence in this empty space.

How shall I bear the days that draw nigh,
When thy voice no longer doth reply?
The echo of thy laughter, thy smile so bright,
I would trade all the time to share but one night.

'Tis hard, so hard, to live without thee near,
To carry thy memory, trembling in fear,
Fear of forgetting, of losing thy grace,
The warmth that thou brought to this earthly place.

What thou gavest me, so much I cannot repay,
Thy kindness, thy wisdom, thy strength in each day,
How I wish I could turn back time's cruel hand,
To share but one moment, to make a stand.

If only I could, I'd give all my breath
To feel thy embrace, to forget death's death.
But now, my dear friend, 'tis time to say farewell,
Though the pain of thy loss doth a deep sorrow swell.

In this urn, thy spirit shall remain,
A part of my heart, through joy and through pain.
So I shall carry thee with me, though thou art far,
In this box of memories, like a bright, distant star.

Yet still I wish, if only I could open this urn,
To watch the world 'round us twist and turn,
To feel thy warmth, to hold thee once more,
To share in thy joy, as we did before.

But here I sit, with naught but grief to say,
Holding to the hope that in some distant day,
Somehow, in some way, our paths shall entwine,
And once again, dear friend, thou'lt be mine.

Lament for Sandy Brodie

- in the style of Robert Burns -

Ae year has passed, yet thou art near,
In ilka sang we stop to hear.
The notes ye loved, baith auld an' braw,
Still float like mist o'er hills sae raw.

Ye cared sae deep, gied a' ye had,
A heart sae warm, a spirit glad.
Wi' gentle hands, though thin an' worn,
Ye shared yer licht ere break o' morn.

Nae ailment dimmed yer kindly grace,
Nor stole the radiance o' yer face.
Ye gied, ye glowed, ye didna tire
A soul alicht wi' quiet fire.

Ye loved yer coffee doon Byres Road,
To watch the folk, to shed the load.
Wi' smile sae sly, an easy blether
A moment shared, light as a feather.

And there ye sat, wee smoke in hand,
A puff, a grin, a stance sae grand.
A wee bit cough, a glance sae sly,
As if the hale world wandered by.

Ye gathered friends like stars sae bricht,
Burns Nicht wi' sang an' laughter licht.
A table fu', a dram sae fine,
The joy o' life in every line.

And when the nicht felt lang and wide,
Ye let nae silence grow inside.
A tune, a note, a wee guid word,
Though far awa', ye still were heard.

A video, a sang at e'en,
Yer way tae say, "I'm aye seen."
And even noo, through auld texts scrolled,
We hear yer voice, sae clear and bold.

Ye dreamed o' Verona, sun sae sweet,
Its ancient stanes beneath yer feet.
Though fate sae cruel stilled the flight,
We see ye there, in gloamin's light.

And noo this 9th o' May we stand,
Still hearin' echoes o' yer hand.
In rain, in sun, in smoke and tune,
Ye walk wi' us 'neath May's bright moon.

So here's tae Sandy, bauld an' free,
A heart, a licht, a mystery.
We love ye still, we aye shall do,
For in oor hush, we dream o' you.

English version

It's been a year, yet still you're near,
In every song we pause to hear.
The notes you loved, Gaelic and grand,
Still drift like smoke across the land.

You cared so much, gave all you could,
A heart that burned for doing good.
You helped with hands both frail and kind,
And found your purpose, soul, and mind.

Your illness never dimmed your grace,
Nor stole the light upon your face.
Instead, you gave, you soothed, you shone
You never let us feel alone.

You loved your coffee on Byres Road,
Just watching people, letting go.
Always ready with a smile, a chat
A word or two, and that was that.

And there you'd be, cigarette in hand,
A swirl of smoke, a quiet stand.
A little cough, a breath, a grin
As if the world came pouring in.

You gathered friends like stars each year,
Burns Night with laughter, song, and cheer.
A table full, a dram well poured
The kind of joy we all adored.

And when the quiet felt too wide,
You never let it bloom inside.
A message sent, a tune to hear,
No reason, just to feel you near.

A video, a song at night,
Your way to say, "I'm still alright."
And even now, in texts long gone,
We find you still, we carry on.

You dreamed of Verona's streets once more,
Its ancient stones, its whispered lore.
Though time ran out before the flight,
We see you there, in evening light.

And now we stand, this 9th of May,
Still missing all you used to say.
But in our hearts, you still remain
In smoke, in song, in sun, in rain.

So here's to Sandy, brave and free-
A friend, a soul, a mystery.
We love you still. We always will.
And in our quiet, you are still.

Wait Me There, My Friend

Wait me there, my friend, where lilacs bend,
Where silence folds the meadow at its edge,
Where dusk begins its slow and golden end,
And stars lean down like candles on a ledge.

Sing lullabies to me, to sweet off sleep,
Dearly sleep, to hush the ache I bear.
Remove my pain from cask, where shadows weep,
And lay it down where winds forget their care.

Be your voice be my garland, soft and low,
A wreath of sound that circles round my brow.
I'll wear your words where tender grasses grow,
And feel them bloom anew in every vow.

Be your land be my eyes; let me see
Through hills that know the print of all you are.
Let dusk-light break its hush across the sea,
And bring your nearness home from every star.

Be the daisies my jewelries, bright and plain,
No gem but those the morning dew has kissed.
Let nothing gild me more than sun and rain,
Let nothing that is gold be more than this.

And let the sky be sky, my only home,
A vault of blue that curves through all I do.
Where'er you walk, no matter where you roam,
I'll rest beside the memory of you.

People

A poem for Anna

I waited hours, nineteen and wild with fire,
October winds like whispers in my blood.
The hallway stretched, a tunnel of desire,
Each breath a wave, each silence like a flood.

Outside, the trees wore crowns of rust and flame,
The dying leaves spun softly through the air.
But in my chest, a birth I couldn't name
Prepared to split my world beyond repair.

The door was shut. The light beneath it glowed.
My thoughts ran faster than my heart could pace.
I held my fear the way a child holds snow,
A fleeting, shivering, sacred kind of grace.

And then, her cry. It cracked the world in two.
So small a sound, and yet it moved the stars.
The waiting died. The wind itself felt new.
She came to us from somewhere past the far.

They placed her near, and I forgot to breathe.
Her eyes were wide, too wide for such a face,
As if she saw all time beneath the sheath
Of skin and light, untouched by any place.

O Anna, you were born while night stood still,
And in your eyes, my soul began to fill.

To a Sister

I did not choose the day you came to me,
Yet nothing truer ever came to pass.
You were the bloom that split my silent tree,
The storm that shook the stillness of the glass.

You walked ahead where shadows stalked the way,
As if the dark could never touch your flame.
You laughed, and night itself turned into day,
The world grew softer just to speak your name.

Where I was slow, you danced with sharpened pace.
Where I was lost, you carved the path from stone.
You held the stars like torches in your grace
And made the fiercest trials yours alone.

You gave no room for chains or whispered doubt.
You made your voice a place where truth could rise.
When silence crowded in, you called it out,
And burned your image into all our skies.

The world would shape a girl to shrink and fade,
To fold her wings and bow her head with shame.
But you refused. You rose and, unafraid,
Declared yourself a kingdom, not a name.

I saw you gather ruin into gold,
And grief into a garment fit to wear.
You stitched your scars like thread into the fold
And made your very wounding something rare.

You mothered me, though I was never child.
You were my roof, my raft, my final shore.
You calmed my tempests with a glance so mild,
And loved me even when I gave you war.

When others fled, you stayed to lift the wall.
You bore the weight when none could see you strain.
You caught the pieces each time I would fall,
And never once complained about the pain.

You are the thunder softened into skin.
You are the voice that sings when all is lost.
You are the strength I carry deep within
When life demands a stand, no matter cost.

I've known no braver heart in all my years.
I've seen your triumph carved from endless trial.
You've kissed my wounds, you've shared my silent tears,
You've taught me how to breathe and to be wild.

You are not just my sister, you are more:
The air that shaped me, fire in my chest.
You are the open, unrelenting door
Through which I walk to find my truest self.

And if I ever lose my voice or way,
If night descends too thick to see the line,
I'll think of you, your laughter in the grey,
And find my feet again by tracing mine.

No blood, no bond, no fate could tie me more
Than love that flows from you, an endless shore.

A Man's Tears

Have you yet seen a grown man start to weep?
Not eyes that mist, but sobs that bend the spine,
That choke the breath and leave the shoulders deep
In tremors drawn from sorrow's darker line?

His face, though rough with sun and years of strain,
Will buckle like a sail against the gale.
You'll see no show, no artifice or feign,
Just sorrow's pulse in flesh grown thin and pale.

Perhaps his child has gone one night unfed,
And pride, that iron gate, swings loose at last.
His hands, once gods, now tremble full of dread,
Each coin he counts a shadow of the past.

The wolf will howl when hunger stakes its claim,
The stag will kneel beneath the hunter's dart.
But man hides pain beneath a mask of shame,
Though beasts may mourn, he tears his soul apart.

And nature too, when breaking, does not boast:
The oak splits inward in the quiet storm.
The mountain crumbles under winter's ghost,
Yet outward shows a silhouette still warm.

A stream that floods will rage then disappear,
Its force now buried deep beneath the clay.
So man, when overwhelmed, must make unclear
The path his grief may take, then turn away.

The lion limps into a silent place
To bleed alone, unseen by rival eyes.
So man retreats and hides his ruined face,
And swears his love in silence as he cries.

His tears are not the storm of shallow grief,
But thundered prayers in chambers of regret,
For chances missed, for years gone like a thief,
For debts of love he's terrified to set.

A weeping man is like the broken tree
That still gives shade though split along its bark.
His tears, like rain, fall silently and free,
Yet feed the ground, unseen within the dark.

And when he weeps, the earth should bow its head.
For in those drops, the truth of labor lies,
Not weakness, no, but all he's done and bled
To keep his house from cold, his children's cries.

A woman's tears the world is taught to hold,
To soothe, to stroke, to welcome with embrace.
But man must build his sorrow into gold,
And cry in secret, stone upon his face.

Yet look upon him when he breaks that wall:
He is no less a tower for the rain.
The man who weeps has not begun to fall,
He rises, forged by honest, human pain.

To an unborn child

I did not feel you stir beneath my skin,
Nor hear the echo of your beating heart,
But still you grew, a silence deep within,
A shadow love before its gentle start.

Forgive me, child, for drawing closed the gate
Before the path could open to your feet.
The choice was mine, and tangled was its weight,
A bitter root with petals strangely sweet.

You'll never wake to hunger in the night,
Or taste the copper tang of being left.
You'll never learn to fear the hallway light,
Or feel the years of longing in a cleft.

The world is full of laughter, yes, it is,
Of hands that lift, of voices like the rain,
But also cold that kisses like a hiss,
And doors that close and never speak again.

You will not kneel beside a parent's bed
And beg them not to fade before the dawn.
You will not learn how grief is gently fed,
How joy can vanish just as it is drawn.

The playground would have cheered you to the skies,
And words would have come dancing from your tongue,
But also lies, and scorn in classmates' eyes,
And songs you loved that you would die unsung.

And so I hold your absence like a flame,
It burns, but still I shelter it with care.
I whisper not a blessing, nor a name,
But something of a breath remains in air.

You are not hurt. You do not bleed or cry.
You do not break or tremble in the cold.
You never had to learn the art to lie,
Or watch the ones you trust grow hard and old.

Forgive me, not for choosing, but for pain.
Forgive me that you are, and never were.
You are the soft unfallen summer rain,
The seed that slept and did not choose to stir.

And though your face I never came to know,
Still in the dark, you shine. Still, you forgive.
For some are born to light, and some to glow
Like stars unborn, who teach us how to live.

Alien

It came with neither name nor kind nor face,
No ship descending from the molten skies,
But born within, a shadow in the grace
Of cells that danced before it colonised.

It stirred in silence, breathed where silence dwelled,
A spark beneath the ribs, the hidden lung.
It watched the beating heart, and softly swelled,
A thing unsought, a song unsought, unsung.

It mimicked us. It grew and learned to live,
To feed, to change, to scatter and arrange.
It does not hate. It only takes. Forgive
The alien whose weapon is not strange.

It builds itself from flesh and buried code,
It paints the blood with shapes that do not hold.
It walks the veins, a master of the road,
And teaches cells to hunger and grow old.

It wears our voice. It speaks in quiet nights
When thought is raw and walls are thin as breath.
It asks no questions, makes no claims or rights,
Its only law the gravity of death.

And still it moves. It does not always kill.
It sometimes leaves. It sometimes stays asleep.
It sometimes lets us walk, and hold, and will
A life rebuilt, though never whole or deep.

But when it comes, it comes with perfect poise,
A child of time, the sum of all decay,
It doesn't scream or fight or make a noise,
It only sits and slowly eats away.

We call it alien, though it is ours,
A thing that speaks in blood and takes its throne.
It wears our likeness, walks beneath our stars,
And makes its quiet kingdom in our bone.

It made a throne of marrow once I knew,
Where laughter lived, where sweat and motion stirred.
And bit by bit, it changed the body's hue,
Each silence there more brutal than a word.

We learn to name the medicines like prayer,
To count the drips, the breaths, the days that bend.
We sit in chairs, and listen, hope, and stare,
And wonder if it's mercy in the end.

For those who lose, there is no noble flame,
No tidy bow, no line that makes it neat.
The alien leaves only what became,
A bed unfilled, a dish we do not eat.

And yet it teaches. Teaches slow and deep.
That love outlasts the days it cannot hold.
That bodies break, and still the souls may keep
A will untouched, defiant, brave, and bold.

A moving thing, this shadow with a mind,
A mindless thing that echoes what we are,
We, too, invade, consume, evolve, unbind,
We, too, burn bright and then become a scar.

So when it comes again, as come it will,
Let none call weak the ones who bear its tread.
There's nothing more alive than one made still,
Still breathing though the alien has fed.

To the earth

The White Rose by the Sea

Upon a jagged rock above the tide,
A single rose grew white against the blue.
The wind would howl, the sea would rage and chide,
Yet still it stood, unshaken, ever true.

Its roots found cracks where nothing else could cling,
Its leaves drank mist the storm would sometimes spare.
No garden's hand, no sheltered nurturing,
It bloomed in salt and sorrow, wild and bare.

Around it, waves would crash and skies would tear,
The gulls would scream, the sun would rise and fall.
But still it shone, a ghost of light and prayer,
A voice of hope, though frail and soft and small.

It did not bloom for praise, nor bloom for need,
No eyes to watch, no hands to cut or claim.
It lived because the soul of life is freed
When none demand a purpose or a name.

O rose, so pale against the darkened foam,
What made you bloom where others would not grow?
What strength has silence, standing there alone,
That sings more loud than all the world below?

You teach that beauty need not beg for grace,
That love is not the fire, but the flame,
The quiet kind that time cannot erase,
The kind that stays though none recall its name.

So let me learn, dear flower by the shore,
To hold my peace where loud illusions flee.
To root in stone, to ask for less, not more,
And bloom like you, alone, but wholly free.

The chase

A rustle stirred the bracken in the shade,
The morning pale, the earth still damp and made
Of scent and light half-born. The trees stood still.
A deer stepped out, pure form, a silent will.

The dog was crouched; his ears like arrows pricked,
His breath held back, his muscles wound and quick.
One heartbeat passed, and then he broke the thread,
The world dissolved beneath his pounding tread.

The deer sprang forward, carved of speed and air,
Its hooves struck silence clean and split the glare.
The dog gave chase, his breath now harsh and raw,
The woods flew past in streaks of fang and claw.

"I saw no prey, I saw a thread of fire.
My legs obeyed a sharper, nameless wire.
I did not think, I burned, I leapt, I ran.
I was no longer beast, but living plan.
Not hunger, no, not even joy or fear,
But just the need to close the space, get near."

He ran not for the hunger, nor the kill,
But something deeper, older, nameless still,
A throb beneath the rib, a voice unmade,
The pulse of life that will not be obeyed.

"I've chased before. The chase has chased through me.
Each time I think, 'This time, it sets me free.'
This time, the deer and I will meet as flame,
And all this trembling want will earn a name.
But faster still she flies, and so must I,
And still she shines, and still I do not die."

He panted hard, his tongue a crimson sail,
Each gasp a rhythm carved into the trail.
The joy was sharp, the purpose was complete,
To chase, to want, to never taste defeat.

The trees grew dense, the sky a shredded grey,
The path grew blind, then fell and slipped away.
The deer, a shimmer in the tangled gold,
Leapt high and vanished, silent, proud, and bold.

He stopped. His chest heaved wild, his mouth hung wide,
The bitter air now flooding from inside.
His limbs still trembled, stretched toward what had fled,
Desire itself, a ghost he'd never shed.

"Where did she go? She was the shape of right.
She filled my mind with wind and turned to light.
I thought I'd catch her, break the ache I bear—
But all I hold is torn and empty air.
I ran, and ran, and gave myself away…
And now there's nothing more I need to say."

He stood, the leaves like ashes at his feet,
The chase now still, the ending incomplete.
Yet in that panting void, a silence grew,
A moment where the will released its due.

"I do not chase. I do not feel the burn.
The forest breathes. I do not ache or yearn.
This peace is brief. It will not stay too long.
But here I am, without the hunt, the song.
No more, no less, a dog beneath the trees,
A heart unbound, and drifting on the breeze."

He lifted up his snout into the sky,
Not howling, only breathing, soft and shy.
No prize. No death. No conquest and no shame,
Just being, brief and bright, without a name.

Speak to me

A stone lies low beneath the nettled grass,
Its edges dulled, its carvings worn and pale.
The lichen climbs where once a hand had cleaned,
And roots push gently through the cracked white base.

A broken jar, long emptied of its blooms,
Leans eastward with the habit of the wind.
The earth is still. A silence holds its breath,
As if the grave itself awaits a word.

Speak to me now, and do not turn away.
What do you see? What lingers in the dust?
Has anything endured, or all been lost,
The careful thread I stitched into the world?

Do voices echo still in places dim,
Or has the air grown deaf to what we were?
Do hands recall the gestures that I gave,
Or have they shaped new shadows in my stead?

I ask you, has the reverence remained?
The solemn grace I hoped the years would keep?
Or was it swept beneath the season's tide,
Forgotten like the ash upon the hearth?

Speak of the things I might have cast aside,
The lives that brushed against me in a blink.
What did I leave unfinished in their eyes?
What words unsaid still wander through their nights?

Do not spare truth, have I been left behind,
A name once whispered now no longer known?
Do strangers pass the door where once I stood,
And feel no stirring of a soul once there?

I do not ask for praise, nor idle grie,
But tell me if a trace of me survives.
A song half-hummed, a rhythm in a step,
A scent upon a coat not worn in years.

Has any moment held me unaware,
And made someone forget that I was gone?
Speak too of those whose names I cannot grasp.
They fade from me, as stars fade into dawn.

I know they walked beside me once in light,
But time has drawn a curtain through my mind.
Were they of joy? Did they hold fast to truth?
Did we share bread, or silence, or a flame?

And speak of love, the deepest thread of all,
Does love still speak in silence where I slept?
Do tears still fall from eyes that once were mine,
Or have they dried and found another sky?

Does someone call me in their quiet thoughts,
Not knowing why the ache still bears my form?
Do I return in dreams that blur and bend,
A presence half-remembered in the dawn?

Oh, traveler, I cannot reach the world,
But you can carry pieces in your hands.
So speak me back into the breath of life.
Let not my fading be a final hush.

If I was kind, then let that kindness go,
To light the path of one who walks alone.
If I was cruel, then let my name be stone,
But learn from it, and cast no further pain.

Speak to me now, and I will speak through you.
And when you leave, do not forget I asked.

Elegy Upon a Stone

O thou cold relic of the aged deep,
That liest still where mortals come to weep,
What dost thou know of grief or joy or breath,
Thou steadfast witness to both life and death?

No tear hast thou, nor pulse to throb with pain,
Yet dost thou bide through sun and flood and rain.
The years have carved thy silence into song,
While all around thee alters, right or wrong.

Thou wert when first man's trembling foot did fall,
And thou shalt be when none remain to call.
The dust of empires clings upon thy side,
Where once the proud and perished did reside.

A grave-mark thou, or pillar in a hall,
A cornerstone where saints and sinners crawl.
The child did toss thee, laughing, in his play,
Now grown, he lies beneath thee, wrapped in clay.

O stone, thou know'st not triumph, nor despair,
Yet thou outlast'st the hearts that learn to care.
Where hands once built, and broke, and bled, and prayed,
There thou remain'st, while all the rest doth fade.

If I should die, and breath no more bestow,
Lay me not soft where tender lilies grow,
But place me near where thou dost calmly rest,
That I may learn to still my foolish breast.

For thou, who feel'st not sorrow, nor delight,
Art nearer kin to truth than mortal might.
Time bows to thee, but hastens past our race,
Who chase the wind and vanish without trace.

So be thou firm, O keeper of the past,
And guard the hush of those who sleep at last.
And should the world forget where I have gone,
Let memory dwell not in name, but stone.

The Seagull and the Hound

Part I

Upon a parapet of mottled stone,
Where winds from sea to city softly roam,
A seagull strode with muscles firm and white,
Its breast held proud, its feathers sharp with light.

Below, upon a terrace bathed in gold,
A hound lay sleeping, peaceful, loose, and old.
His flank was hot where sun had kissed the floor,
And dreams had drawn him through a quiet door.

But then a sound, a click of claw on ledge,
Awoke the hound along the terrace edge.
He raised his head and squinted at the gleam
That danced upon the parapet like dream.

The gull had stopped before a shaded flat,
And stared with eyes as calm as ancient cat.
The dog beheld the bird with hungry gaze,
His stomach stirred, his mouth began to raise.

"O what a feast," he murmured in his mind,
"So plump, so close, and sun-baked, sweetly lined."
With sudden will, he rose and gave a bound,
A gentle spring upon the sun-warmed ground,

He leapt onto the sofa with a hum,
But wings beat fast, the gull was not so dumb.
It soared, it wheeled, it circled with a cry,
Then settled once again against the sky.

"O wait," the seagull said, "do not pursue,
Nor seek to catch me, I've no harm for you."
The hound sat down, his head a tilted sphere,
His brow in folds: "Then tell me why, my peer?
Why should I spare a meal so near, so fine?
Your flesh is gold, your scent is salt and brine."

The bird looked out, one eye upon the sea,
And breathed a wind that sang of mystery.
"My wings," it said, and spread them to the light,
"Are scrolls that write the meaning of the height.

This breast you see, so strong, so wide, so proud,
Is not for feasts, but skies without a shroud.
Your back is earthbound, mine is air and sail,
I ride the sun, I dance upon the gale.

"You see these eyes?", he turned, and they grew dark,
"They've watched the kings descend and beggars bark.
They've seen the bones of cities sunk in dust,
And lovers kiss on rooftops born of trust.

I've flown o'er lands where battles scar the trees,
Where rain is war and silence speaks of seas.
I've watched the pope, the poet, and the thief,
All swallowed in the tides of joy and grief."

The hound was still, his breath began to slow,
His eyes grew wide, then narrowed down below.
The seagull went on, voice like whistling stone,
That skips across a lake, then sinks alone:

"I've tasted wind from every known domain,
From fields of wheat to narrow paths of pain.

I've seen a child asleep in mother's arm,
And murder done within a midnight farm.

I know the pulse of peace before the rain,
The hush of earth, the promise in the grain."
The hound lay down, his chin upon his paw,
His soul afloat inside the seagull's law.

The bird now turned and pointed to his wing,
"A map," he said, "of every living thing.
Where you have paws that press on heat and clay,
I have the gift to rise and drift away.

Where you have fur that dreams in warm delight,
I bear the memory of shattered night."
And now the world began to shift and blur,
The hound was falling deep inside that stir.

The words became a vision, high and vast,
Of skies and empires, present, future, past.
He saw a windmill bend to greet the sun,
A city burn, a mother clutch her son.

He saw the first and final cry of man,
And knew, at last, the sky's immortal span.
And then, he woke. The terrace shone once more,
The sun still danced across the marble floor.
The sofa breathed beneath his settled frame,
Yet all around him, nothing was the same.

The seagull gone, the parapet was bare,
But high above, in blinding blue and air,
A flock wheeled wide in freedom, fierce and high,
And one among them sang a farewell cry.

Part II

The days went on. The terrace breathed and shone,
Yet something in the hound had changed and grown.
Though birds still wheeled and winds still sought the shore,
He waited, ears half-pricked, beside the door.

He dreamed in silence, no more bound by bone,
He heard the sky now murmur like a tone.
And in his sleep, with paws upon the tile,
He traveled far and wide in seabird style.

The gull returned upon the seventh morn,
With wings outstretched and feathers slightly worn.
He landed light, the parapet his throne,
And gave a cry that sang like ancient stone.

The hound looked up, his gaze both calm and clear,
"I knew you'd come," he said, "I felt you near."
The gull bowed low, a smile within his eye,
"You listened once. So now, I've come to try,

To give you more than bones and fleeting light,
To show you how to dream with inner sight.
The body hunts. The soul must learn to see.
And seeing, learn the art of letting be."

"Then speak," the hound replied. "Unfold the wind.
My ears are tuned, my growl no longer sinned."
The gull stepped close, then tapped his breast once more,
"This cage of bone holds echoes from before.

The flesh you see has weathered storm and flame;
The wind has carved my wings and named my name.
But I am not this form, this heat, this shell,
I am a story, told by tide and swell."

He turned and flared a single speckled wing,
And all the sky bent low to hear him sing.
He told of winds that swept through Saxon stone,
Of Pharaohs' tombs where seagulls flew alone.

He spoke of ships that vanished in the mist,
Of prophets, madmen, kings who once were kissed
By gulls in flight, before their end began,
As if the sky had mourned the fall of man.

And then he spoke of love, a seagull's view:
A girl who wept, a boy who never knew.
A widow dancing barefoot in the rain,
A soldier's coat left hanging on a train.

He told of peace not made by law or sword,
But in the quiet look, the second word.
Of moments shared on rooftops drenched with tea,
Of silences as wide as any sea.

The hound lay still, his breath a tempered sound,
As if the very sky had touched the ground.
He felt his fur dissolve into the air,
His heartbeat slow, his mind laid soft and bare.

He dreamed of flight, of curling through the blue,
Of seeing all, yet holding nothing true.
The gull stood near, his voice now soft and kind,
"A soul is not a cage, but sky in mind."

And with that word, the gull began to rise,
His wings a sail, his body cut from skies.
The hound watched close, his eyes no longer sore,
But full of things he'd never seen before.

He did not chase. He only watched him climb,
Then turned and drank the stillness made by time.
The sun fell low, the terrace dimmed to rust,
The air held weightless hope without a must.

At dusk, the hound lay down beside the door,
And knew the seagull's tale was something more.
Not just a bird, nor beast to chase and rend,
But messenger of means beyond the end.

And as he slept, the terrace breathed once more,
The stars leaned in, the sky became a shore.
And all above, in flocks both fierce and high,
The seagulls carved a script across the sky.

Part III

That night, the hound began to stir in dream,
But not to chase, nor howl, nor fight, nor scheme.
He dreamt of voice, not bark, but something deep,
A song he'd buried long beneath his sleep.

He saw the gull again upon the wall,
As still as thought, as vast as any call.
And from his chest, the hound released a sound,
That traveled up through sky, yet touched the ground.

"I've heard your heights," he said. "Now hear my low.
I'll teach you what the feathered cannot know.
You soar through air that never holds its place,
But I have felt the earth's enduring face.

I know the press of stone, the scent of rain,
The smell of blood that speaks of joy and pain.
I've licked the wounds of those who could not rise,
And waited, sleepless, under dying skies."

He raised his head, the stars around him curled,
"I've walked the borders of the buried world.
My nose has found where bones forget their names,
Where ash still sings in silence after flames.

I've howled at moons too pale to give us light,
And stood between the hunters and the night.
You have the sky—but I have roots and clay,
And know the weight of what won't fly away."

The gull was still. A breath had stopped the air,
As if the cosmos paused to wonder where
Such truth had hid inside a creature mute,
With nothing more than fur and sleep and brute.

The bird drew close and perched beside the hound,
Their shadows met upon the heated ground.
"Then we are mirrors," said the gull at last,
"One made for future, one composed of past."

"I see in you," the hound replied, "a dream,
Of flight, of storm, of heights beyond the stream.
But I am made of hearth and rooted scent,
Of dens and dirt, of instincts never bent.

Together, we might map a fuller way,
The sky, the soil, the wind, the stone, the day."
The terrace stilled. The sun began to rise.
The gull took off, no farewell in his cries.

Yet in his arc, a feather loose did fall,
And drifted down along the hound's stone wall.
He watched it land and pressed it with his paw,
As if to write a truth the world once saw.

He closed his eyes, the feather in his hold,
And dreamed of tales both grounded and yet bold.
When next he woke, the sky was clean and vast,
The morning still, the winds not rising fast.

The feather gone. The dream had fled the stone.
Yet something in the world had overgrown.
He saw the birds above in widening rings,
And in his breast he felt the weight of wings.

The Noisy Silence

I sat within the crowd and heard the hush,
Not one of peace, but silence edged with steel,
Where voices flared like matches, then were crushed,
And laughter seemed too distant to be real.

A hundred steps rang out across the square,
But none belonged to anyone I knew.
The noise, a storm of sound, hung in the air,
Yet underneath it, silence pierced me through.

A silent room can scream in softer ways,
The groan of floorboards aching to be heard,
The whisper of the dust in lamplight's haze,
The echo of a long-forgotten word.

The chairs remember bodies once held warm,
The curtains shift as if from phantom breeze.
The silence sings in forms that twist and swarm,
It drags the mind through long-forgotten seas.

At times, I walk through forests dark and dead
Where even birds fall silent at my tread.
The hush is not a gift, but grief unsaid,
A pause that holds the weight of all things fled.

And in the heart, where silence might bring peace,
It sometimes shouts in thoughts we dare not name.
Regret, like thunder clothed in soft decease,
Will howl within the stillness just the same.

Yet stranger still: the silence up above,
Where planets spin in orbits cold and vast.
No voice, no breath, no human touch or love,
Yet motion sings, and nothing ever passed.

Their silence roars with heat and endless spin,
A noise that does not reach the human ear.
It speaks in fire and ice, without, within,
In time too vast for any soul to hear.

And so I stand, both deafened and alone,
Within a world that echoes what I lack.
The silence is not absence, but a tone,
A choir of ghosts that never answer back.

A tear, though soft, may strike like shattered glass
When falling in a place too still for sound.
The silence laughs in mirrors as you pass,
And mocks you with the things that can't be found.

There is no silence truly free from noise,
No calm untouched by grief or memory.
It shapes its voice in all we once enjoyed,
Then leaves us with a quiet agony.

The Petal and the Wind

A petal fell, released from bloom's embrace,
Its silken edge still kissed by morning's grace.
It spun through air like thought from weary mind,
Unfastened from the stem it left behind.

No trumpet marked the moment it withdrew,
No shadow cried, no voice of sorrow knew.
It drifted like a dream in daylight lost,
Unharmed by fate, unmeasured by the cost.

The wind approached, a quiet, watchful guest,
Who'd wandered far and never come to rest.
He caught the petal's curve within his palm
And bore it on, a murmur wrapped in calm.

They danced together, neither one in lead,
No destination named, no pressing need.
The petal knew the bloom could not endure,
The wind, that all he held would not be sure.

He twirled her high, then let her dip and glide,
A whisper in the turning of the tide.
She bent to him with elegance and ease,
As light as ash, as fleeting as the breeze.

They waltzed through orchards shedding all their gold,
Past fields where dusk had deepened into cold,
And through the hush of woods where branches sighed,
No eye to see, no judgment to decide.

The wind grew bold and tossed her higher still,
A reckless joy awakened by his will.
She curved, she spun, a syllable in flight,
Unwritten on the parchment of the night.

Then sudden stillness caught them in the hill,
Where stars grew sharp and every breath was still.
He held her close, not as a keeper might,
But like a flame that cannot hold the light.

He whispered, "You were never mine to keep,
But I have learned the ways that petals sleep.
They do not mourn the stem from which they part,
They float because they know the garden's heart."

She answered not, for petals do not speak,
Their language lies in softness and in streak.
Yet in her fall, she left a trace behind,
A silence that could soothe a restless mind.

They parted gently, neither torn nor worn,
Not bitter, not betrayed, not quite forlorn.
She settled where the wind could no more go,
Upon a stone, beside a drift of snow.

And he moved on, still whispering through the pine,
Still seeking out what cannot be made mine.
Yet in his flight, he sometimes thinks again
Of how they danced beyond the reach of men.

So let them say that beauty cannot stay,
It falls, it fades, it must be swept away.
But wind remembers, when the skies are dim,
How once a petal dared to dance with him.

To Walk the Floor in Rain

I stand above the hush the morning spills,
Where treetops breathe beneath a silver sky.
The air is soaked, the river slowly fills
With dreams the wind has carried drifting by.

No echo calls from rooms I used to roam,
No voice repeats the weight of what I said.
The walls have lost the shape that once was home,
And all that clung to me is soft and shed.

The floor is wet. I step with naked feet,
Each toe a note upon the quiet ground.
The chill, electric, rises through the heat
Of thoughts once loud, now smothered by the sound.

Of rainfall drumming faintly on the steel,
And leaves that shiver in their secret speech.
Each drop a truth I never thought I'd feel,
Now clear beneath the things I cannot reach.

The echoes once would greet me as I passed,
Reflections thrown against the brittle wall,
But none remain. Their hold has slipped at last,
Dissolved beneath the rain's unhurried fall.

My heels are black with dust the storm has stirred,
My arches ache from walking through the night.
But still I go, though no command is heard,
The floor ahead is neither dark nor bright.

It shines, untroubled, polished into glass,
A mirror not of self, but of the sky,
Where clouds in torn procession slowly pass,
And crows in hunger trace their question: why?

No slipper guards me now, no rule remains,
No polished path to tell me what is right.
The cold between my toes, the sharp, wet grains,
They mark the cost of choosing not to fight.

For I have fought the echo's every word,
And lost myself in battles with my name.
The silence now is neither just nor heard,
But it is mine. And it is not the same.

A blade of grass lies clinging to my sole,
A tiny world that traveled where I tread.
The river curves, as if it, too, is whole,
Yet shaped by all the fragments it has shed.

Let no one dry the path or light the way,
The rain is not a trial, but release.
To walk the floor in bare resolve, and stay
Within the storm, is not to seek for peace,

But something else: a voice without a sound,
A step that does not echo as it lands,
A knowing felt not high, but underground,
Where every drop redeems what life demands.

So let me walk this floor with naked grace,
And leave no mark upon its gleaming skin.
I do not seek a goal, or claim a place,
Only the truth of where I now begin.

Now here I stand, the wet floor under me,
My feet like roots, the rain a kindred skin.
The trees breathe out; I breathe in quietly,
No edge between the world and what's within.

The First Rain of Summer

The heat had hushed the forest into stone,
Each branch held breath, each root withdrew its thirst.
The leaves hung still, their green reduced to bone,
And even birds grew silent, as if cursed.

A ribbon of faint water barely moved,
A stream once bright, now dulled to whispered glass.
Its shallows bared the pebbles it once smoothed,
Now cracked with thirst, unmoving in the grass.

The ferns were curled, their fronds too tired to dream,
The moss had grayed beneath the stubborn sun.
No scent arose but bark and broken steam,
The forest seemed abandoned, every one.

But then, a shift, too soft to name at first,
A stirring in the canopy, so slight.
The light grew dimmer, not with dusk, but burst
Of breathless dark drawn sudden from the height.

And then, the air grew ripe with coming rain:
The musk of earth, like skin before a kiss,
The sharp green breath of bruised and waiting grain,
The root-deep spice that slept beneath the hiss.

A scent of moss awoke, of sap and pine,
Of petals damp with rot and slow decay.
It rose like memory, or blood in brine,
And swelled through bark and stone to meet the day.

The first drop fell, a whisper on the bark,
Another struck a fern with ticking sound.
Then rain, like sudden language in the dark,
Fell fast and fierce upon the waiting ground.

It hit the leaves with cymbals made of green,
It drummed the stream to laughter from its rest.
The water woke, and danced again between
The roots that reached like fingers for its chest.

The trees let go. Their silence split apart,
Each trunk resounded hollow, deep, and wet.
The forest breathed, it shook its rigid heart,
And took the rain like something long regret.

The soil sang perfume, cedar, rot, and rose,
A symphony of death and life combined.
The musk of beasts, of crushed and opened toes
Of bulbs that burst with secrets they had mined.

The rain brought breath from stones that once were still,
From nests long dry, from under every leaf.
It smelled like joy too wild for human will,
It smelled like sleep beneath the throat of grief.

I stood amid the storm, beneath the pines,
My arms slack-limbed, my heartbeat slow but sure.
The rain ran through me, tracing secret lines,
And named what even I could not endure.

It was not peace, it did not come to heal.
It came to wake, to startle, to unbind.
It touched the part of me I would not feel,
And left no word, no answer, and no sign.

But something opened, something shed its skin,
Some burden loosed its fingers from my frame.
The rain fell hard, and though I let it in,
I knew I'd not return quite as I came.

The forest roared in joy, or grief, or both,
The stream sang louder than I thought it could.
And I, remade beneath that summer's oath,
Was part of rain, and perfume, root, and wood.

DIRT

I. *The Sacrament*

The dirt is more than waste or weight or dust,
It is the sacred veil on which we tread.
It keeps the covenant with time and rust,
It sleeps beneath the altars of the dead.

The priests have knelt upon it in their robes,
And whispered names no longer heard aloud.
They spread it on the foreheads of the globe,
And praised the grave more softly than the crowd.

It drinks the blood of sacrifice and sin,
And cradles seeds with equal, solemn care.
It marks the place where endings dare begin,
Where silence fills the marrow of the air.

II. The Flesh and Weight of It

It cakes the heel, it stains the human palm,
It gathers under nails like buried guilt.
It clogs the throat of springs and smothers calm,
And builds the tombs our cities blindly built.

It crowds the cracks in every man-made wall,
It waits in boots and barns, in beds and rain.
It turns to stone or soup or sudden fall,
And laughs beneath a field of golden grain.

Beneath our floors, beneath our thoughts, it lies,
The unwashed handprint time will not erase.
We taste it in the storm, in fruit, in flies,
It smirks beneath the polish and the lace.

III. The Myth and Shadow

Some say the first of us were shaped from clay,
With dirt for lungs and starlight for a spine.
They claim we walked from loam into the day
And named the sky with mouths of ancient wine.

A serpent once was whispered in the dust,
And Eden fell with footprints in the mud.
The sacred ground was stripped of sacred trust,
The rose was drowned beneath a sea of blood.

Still, mystics write of soil in sacred terms,
As though it knew the names of unborn kings,
They say it hums with knowledge fed by worms,
And hears the death of all material things.

IV. The Filth and Fraud

But let us not romanticise its stink.
It chokes the lungs, it fouls the teeth and eyes.
It clogs the drains with rot, the pipes with drink,
It gathers where the rat and maggot rise.

It marks the poor more harshly than the thief—
The clean escape, the dirty take the blame.
It soils the face of joy, the hem of grief,
It mocks our hymns and sanitises shame.

What honour lives in earth that traps the meek?
What justice waits inside a crust of waste?
We wash and bleach, but still it climbs our cheek,
A slow, relentless god of scent and taste.

V. The Lover's Ground

But dirt can be the skin beneath the skin,
The raw, warm bed where love's first hunger grows.
Two bodies pressed on ground, and breath drawn in,
And dirt that clings like shadows to their clothes.

The sweat, the moan, the grass-stained trembling thigh,
The back against the bark, the soil's cold kiss.
The earth is not ashamed to hear a cry,
It holds the roots of every human bliss.

There's dirt beneath the sheets we fail to shake.
There's dirt in every gasp we try to hide.
It waits beside us, even when we wake.
A memory of bodies unified.

VI. The Artist's Medium

The potter loves the pliant, groaning clay,
And shapes from filth a cup, a bowl, a song.
A smear becomes a line, the line a way,
And what was crude becomes what might belong.

The painter smudges dust with oil and ash,
The sculptor cuts from soil a burning form.
Each smudge becomes a whisper, each a lash,
Each shadow turns abstraction into storm.

Is this not dirt: a chaos turned to grace?
A grave reshaped into a face, a vase?
A mess of minerals that dreams of space,
And learns to wear a robe, to bear a gaze?

VII. *The Industry of Soil*

It grinds beneath the wheels of every truck,
It coats the drills and gears with stubborn rage.
It clogs the lungs of miners till they're struck
By coughs that end their breath before old age.

It swallows wires and tracks and tanks and roads,
It eats the bridges, towers, pipes, and steel.
It shifts and groans beneath our concrete loads,
And proves that nothing man has built can feel.

We think we rule the world with glass and stone,
But every wall we raise, the earth will take.
The dirt will drag it down, reclaim its own,
And whisper, "You are dust, and dust must break."

VIII. The Ecology and Root

It breathes in cycles deeper than our clocks,
And speaks in scents of mushrooms, mulch, and rain.
It houses eggs in hidden, fragrant stocks,
And grows the bark that splits to birth a grain.

A million bodies rot to feed a leaf,
A single sprout drinks centuries of tears.
The dirt is not a bed for sleep or grief,
It is a mouth that eats and gives for years.

The ant, the mole, the root, the rotting lung,
They share the underground as one vast choir.
No word is louder than the worms among
The roots that climb toward light with green desire.

IX. The End and Start of All

The end of man is dirt. The final kiss
Is not a fire, nor wind, nor cruel regret.
It is the soil, and only this and this,
The damp, the dark, the weight we can't forget.

Yet in that dirt, the stars have dropped their gold,
The atoms of the galaxies are sown.
Our flesh is not condemned, but merely old,
The dirt was once the dust of what has shone.

So bend, and take it gently in your hand,
This loam, this ash, this unremarked abyss.
It is not death. It will not understand.
It simply *is*. And *you* are part of *this*.

X. *The Politics of Soil*

They fight for land with ink and blood and lies,
For borders drawn in sand, for claims of birth.
They plant their flags beneath indifferent skies,
And die for little more than chunks of earth.

The dirt is bribed by law, then soaked in war,
Its value weighed in oil, in gold, in grain.
Yet never once it asked what men are for,
It only holds their bootprints and their pain.

The tyrant feeds it bodies; then he weeps.
The peasant tills it once, then disappears.
The soil does not remember who it keeps,
It only drinks, and deepens with the years.

XI. The Play of Childhood

A child will kneel and draw a sun in sand,
Or dig for worms as if they were old friends.
He'll build a fort of mud with filthy hands,
And never dream how soon that freedom ends.

He tastes the dirt without a thought of shame,
He throws it skyward just to watch it fall.
He knows the earth is part of every game,
And sees no throne too proud, no path too small.

What we call filth, he calls a place to dream.
What we discard, he gathers like a prize.
And maybe, in his laughter, there's a gleam
Of how the dirt first saw us with its eyes.

XII. The Taste of It

The mushroom rises warm from loamy black,
The beet, the truffle, tuber, root, and rind.
We eat what crawls or grows along the track
Where mold and mulch and mildew intertwine.

The chef may lift a spoon with practiced grace,
And call it "earthy," "deep," or "mineral."
But what he serves has crawled through time and place,
It's memory with salt and heat and smell.

We eat the dirt in wine, in bread, in beans,
In what we call cuisine, in what we crave.
It seasons both our hunger and our genes,
We dine, and never see the waiting grave.

XIII. The Future's View

When towers rust and satellites decay,
When windmills grind to dust and drones grow still,
The dirt will hold the remnants of our day,
The plastic bone, the wire, the iron will.

What we have buried deep will not forget,
The circuits, shells, and scraps of fallen skies.
It holds our songs as rust, our wars as debt,
Our dreams as poison wrapped in alibis.

And maybe in a thousand years or ten,
Some creature not yet born will dig and ask,
"What were these things once called?" and once again
The dirt will hide its silence like a mask.

XIV. The Final Reflection

So here we are, with dirt beneath our feet,
And dirt behind our teeth, and in our names.
It is the hourglass by which we meet,
It is the smoke behind our altar flames.

It does not ask to be beloved or known.
It is not clean, or fair, or kind, or cursed.
It is the bed of every root and bone.
It is the last, and it was always first.

Let every part of us return at last,
The skin, the voice, the tears, the hope, the hurt.
And may we never look too high or fast
To miss the wisdom rising from the dirt.

Glasgow Poems

Flow Gently, Swift Clyde

Flow gently, swift Clyde, through stone and timeworn quay,
Where morning's hush still stains the sky with grey.
You carry years no map or chart could hold,
Yet never pause to mark the young from old.

The city leans upon your moving grace,
Its pulse half-hidden in your mirrored face.
Beneath the towers, glass, and iron lines,
You wear the past like silt between the pines.

No shepherd's song, no field of painted bloom,
But docks and cranes and barges lost to gloom.
Their hulls still glide within your deeper stream,
Like thoughts that drift between the real and dream.

The ghosts of trade still haunt your shifting tide,
Great boats once laden, creaking side to side.
They brought the world in barrels, bolts, and coal,
Then vanished, slow, into the fog's control.

You bore the weight of nations in your flow,
And still you move where silent echoes go.
Each ripple tells of salt and rusted chain,
Of hands long gone, of toil, of loss, of gain.

They say the canal hums at close of day,
A path through trees where shadows softly sway.
The barges pass, no steersman now in sight,
Just memory moving through the edge of night.

Flow gently, Clyde, through moss and iron rail,
Through rain-soaked towns and every weathered tale.
You are not sweet, you're sterner, slow, and wide.
You are the truth that no one else can guide.

So let the poets sing of bonnie streams;
I'll walk your banks and speak in darker dreams.
You teach me still, though cold and dimly lit,
That time goes on, and we must follow it.

The Duke of Wellington

He stands above the square with iron will,
A sentinel who watches, proud and still.

Upon his steed, he rides though never moves,
A soldier cast in bronze, yet still he proves
That time won't dim the bearing of the brave,
He guards the Merchant City like a grave.

His eyes are set in deep, unyielding gaze,
As if he scans the dawn through battle haze.
No jest can break the steel within his stare,
It pierces through the laughter in the air.

Though made of metal, still his look commands,
As though he's weighing fate in silent hands.
His coat is buttoned tight with sharp decor,
Each fold and stitch a tale of days of war.

Epaulettes gleam with honour's quiet thread,
And medals near his chest shine for the dead.
A sash across his form, a saber near,
He wears the calm of those who've known no fear.

His horse beneath him rears with bridled might,
One leg in air, its muscles bound in flight.
The veins are caught in tension through the flank,
The nostrils flared, the neck both taut and rank.

Its tail is swept behind in sculpted wind,
As though it feels the charge it holds within.
And yet, upon his head, a traffic cone,
Set there by hands that laugh and call it home.

A jest, they say, a Glaswegian delight,
But look again, it crowns him in the night.
For what is rule without the people's cheer?
Their mock becomes a homage, bold and clear.

No golden band, no laurel-wreathed design
Could better show the love that makes him shine.
O Glasgow, fierce with humour, grit, and heart,
The Duke reflects your most defiant part.

He stands where once the merchants built their reign,
In streets that hum with both delight and strain.
Their wealth, their ships, their fortunes' swelling tide,
Now echo in the steps that tourists bide.

But he, the Duke, remains through dusk and dawn,
Your city's crest, your jest, your mast, your brawn.

Lochburn mist

The sun begins to breathe behind the veil,
A tender glow within the heavy grey.
It does not force, nor yet attempt to scale
The walls the morning builds to stall the day.

The mist lies thick across the Clyde Canal,
As if the sky forgot to draw its line.
No wind, no bird, no echo, none at all,
Just breath held tight, and time not yet inclined.

I watch from where the terrace meets the air,
Above Lochburn, where silence softly clings.
The world below is paused in perfect care,
Suspended in the hush that waiting brings.

This is the hour the future hides its face,
And offers us a moment full of grace.
The water does not ripple, does not race,
A silver skin untouched by time or place.

The trees stand still, their green a deep, held breath.
No leaf betrays a breeze, no branch a sound.
As though the whole canal were touched by death,
Yet life unseen still murmurs underground.

A car moves slow, its presence barely known,
Its hum absorbed beneath the sky's pale shroud.
The rooftops keep their secrets, stone on stone,
While chimneys lift their necks, discreet and proud.

And I, a witness here above the street,
Feel smaller than the morning's quiet vow.
I do not speak. I do not shift my seat.
I only watch what's held between the now.

For mist is not mere weather come and gone
It is the mind of morning, soft and strange.
It shields the shape of things we look upon,
And grants the gift of pause before the change.

What waits beyond this gauze I cannot say.
The sun may break, or rain may take its claim.
But in this breath before the birth of day,
There lives a peace that has no cause or name.

The still canal, the trees, the quiet sun
They do not rush, and neither shall I run.
But gently now, the veil begins to thin,
A soft retreat across the waking land.

Light reaches out, and morning enters in,
With gold dust laid by some celestial hand.
The rooftops bloom in ochres, browns, and red,
Each window catches fire from the sky.

The trees, once ghostly, lift their leafy head,
And every branch is drawn in bold reply.
The water stirs, a shimmer on its face,
No longer steel, but copper touched with blue.

The path beside it finds a clearer place,
As blades of grass show every shape and hue.
The mist unknots from chimney, field, and rail,
Its silence breaking into birdsong thin.

The colours rise. The day begins to sail,
And Scotland, slow, remembers where it's been.
The hills reveal their backs, the stones their names,
The tenements their rhythm, old and wise.

And in the warming light, the city frames
Her story in the contours of the skies.

Glasgow journey

The city wakes with steam upon its skin,
As morning breathes through concrete, glass, and stone.
I step from George Square, feel the current spin,
A heartbeat made of voices not my own.

The statues stand like ghosts of borrowed time,
Their bronze gone green with pigeon-shite and rain.
They watch in silence, dignified, sublime,
While buses snarl and taxis swear again.

Queen Street unfolds, a river made of folk,
Wi flurries o' "awright?" and boots that slap.
A jakey lights a rollie through the smoke,
And school-kids fight in Nikes, yap for yap.

A woman, late, is clatterin her heels,
She skelps her wean for spillin juice too fast.
A lad screams "see you, ya fuckin cow!"—it feels
Like every hour o' Glesga's rushin past.

I turn to Ingram, where the city tilts,
Where neon blinks against designer glass.
At Mediterraneo, the guilt's
All buried deep in pasta, wine, and sass.

The crowd's dressed up, they're dressed to make a show,
Lips lined to heaven, hair scraped tight and high.
You smell the Polo queue before you know
They're clubbin—heels, fake lashes, glittered eye.

They shout "youse comin or no?" through the smoke,
While taxis crawl like tired, impatient beasts.
Each face a flawless mask that willnae choke,
Each weekend rise a battlefield of feasts.

Argyle Street hums loud wi traffic's roar,
The Primark doors a floodgate ope and wide.
A lassie shouts, "Ma phone! Ma phone!" once more,
While sales and bags form rivers deep and tied.

The buskers sing on corners, guitars worn,
Their melodies rough-hewn, sometimes sweet,
A man with pipes plays tunes like he's reborn,
His breath like wind that cuts the city's heat.

The crowds drift past, some drop a coin or two,
Some pause, then rush on in their daily race.
Their faces etched wi stories no one knew,
Each step a part of Glasgow's restless pace.

Buchanan's stone is slick with footsteps worn,
The fake tans glowing 'gainst the winter's bite.
Black leggings, cropped tops, the same hair worn,
A thousand faces glowing under light.

The Duke still stands, wi cone upon his crown,
A statue jest that's lasted many years.
He keeps his watch o'er all this bustling town,
A king who knows the laughter, sweat, and tears.

Beneath the GoMA's glass, the people rest,
A smoke, a chat, a moment from the storm.
They find in silence what they need the best,
A city's heart that keeps them safe and warm.

Past Merchant City, where old bricks hold fast,
The pubs spill stories thick wi ales and song.
The night grows loud, the hours never last,
But here the city's soul still hums along.

The early morning holds a softer breath,
The streets are empty, wet wi fading rain.
A dog barks once, then quiet falls like death,
The cobbles gleam beneath the lamplight's chain.

The city sleeps but dreams of noisy days,
Of lovers lost and found, of fights and friends.
The fog rolls in like ghosts in blurred malaise,
Yet life is ready for the day's loose ends.

Late taxis creep like shadows in the dark,
Their headlights cutting lanes through empty streets.
The drivers curse, still hunched above their mark,
While tired voices echo late night beats.

At Sauchiehall, the revellers spill out,
Wi laughter loud and heels that click and clack.
The clubs erupt in bass and shouted shout,
The night's a dance, and no one's turnin back.

The cheap perfume, the smoke, the sweat, the tears,
The stolen kisses 'neath the flickered lights.
The music pounds and covers all our fears,
The city breathes in those electric nights.

Some corner shop sells pies that smell like home,
The baker waves as I pass by again.
The neon signs proclaim the night to roam,
And promise warmth beyond the cold and rain.

The junkies drift, their world a faded script,
Their eyes glazed o'er with dreams and poison's grip.
Yet in their silence, stories tightly lipped,
A city's shadow, walking, torn and ripped.

And walking home through puddles dark and deep,
I feel the city's pulse beneath my soul.
The madness, kindness, laughter that we keep,
The heart that beats beyond the broken whole.

It's beauty wrapped in grit and faded jeans,
In voices shouting "We're alive, we know!"
A city born of dreams and battered scenes,
Glasgow calls loud: "Here we fuckin go."

Summer at Clyde Canal

The sun leans in through panes with steady grace,
Its warmth now pools across the wooden floor.
The afternoon has stilled the air outside,
The trees stand watchful by the Clyde canal.

No breeze arrives to stir their folded leaves,
No rustle breaks the hush that holds the day.
The birds call out, but even they seem slow,
As if the heat has lulled their song to stay.

Above, the sky is stretched in endless blue,
A polished dome with not a cloud in sight.
It bears the sun like something sacred, still,
And casts the world in calm, unwavering light.

The Clyde lies dark and quiet as a thought,
Its mirrored surface smooth as beaten glass.
It holds the weight of sky and branch and time,
And lets the slow hours of summer pass.

The water holds a quiet kind of grace,
It slides beneath the trees in muted light.
From Lochburn's height, I watch the soft green world,
And wish my love were near to share this sight.

One part of me would walk its edge and dream,
To feel the sun upon my idle skin,
To wander where the water bends and gleams,
And let the hum of summer draw me in.

Yet here I sit in Lochburn's shaded peace,
Where ivy climbs and gardens hold their breath.
The kettle cools; the room is sweet and still,
As if the world has paused to rest from death.

This day, untouched by rush or voice or need,
Unfolds in golden silence, soft and deep.
I lean into the hush, and let it hold,
And give myself, this once, to summer sleep.

Cadder woods

At dawn I walk where Cadder's silence sings,
With Lola trotting close on eager feet.
The dew still clings to leaves like silver rings,
And every breath of breeze is soft and sweet.

The canopy is laced with waking light,
A hush of green where whispered lives arise.
Each step is met with birdsong taking flight,
A music spun beneath the waking skies.

The blackbird's call is low and rich with praise,
The robin's note, a ribbon through the air.
Soft coos of pigeons blend with rustling days,
And squirrels dance like shadows unaware.

Beyond the trees, the Clyde Canal runs wide,
And from its edge the ducks begin to play.
Their calls roll out in laughter, echoed, tied
To morning's peace in ripples thrown away.

Far off, the workers pedal through the grey,
Their bikes hum faintly on the distant trail.
The city stirs, but here the woods delay
The world's fast march, its rush, its cold detail.

Deer hide in ditches, quiet, barely seen,
Their eyes like glass between the trunks and fern.
The squirrels pause mid-leap in flashes keen,
And all is dusk and dawn in trembling turn.

The colours blaze in gentle, living fire,
Bright buds of yellow, violet, and rose,
Fresh leaves in emerald, and fields entire
Aglow in bluebells leaning as they doze.

Each petal sings, each blade of grass refrains,
A painter's dream beneath the morning rains.
May crowns the wood with blossoms newly spread,
The trees breathe out their green in wild relief.

A lilac breeze comes dancing from ahead,
It chills the skin, but warms the heart beneath.

And I, a witness to this grace so still,
Walk soft beside my dog, and feel the soul
Unfurl like petals on the woodland hill,
Made whole again, in nature's quiet role.

A paradox, this place so near the roar
Of Glasgow's streets and city's iron heart.
And yet within these woods, one finds much more—
A world apart, a spell, a sacred art.

So close to stone, yet singing like a stream,
A breath held just beyond the city's dream.
For here, alone, I feel the world's great spin,
And yet, within it, held as something true.

So small beneath the trees, and yet within
Their arms, I am the centre of the view.
How marvellous this truth the woods impart:
That we are vast when still, and seen by heart.

For in these steps through Cadder's blessed maze,
Where every leaf is lit and shadows fall,
I find the peace that sings through morning's haze.
How wonderful, how simple, and how small.

The Tree and the Cat

Part I

The barge moves slowly through the morning grey.
The Clyde reflects the shifting skin of sky.
The wind is low, the herons watch in stills,
And reeds bend back to whisper what they know.
Beside this mirror, rooted in the silt,
A tree has stood for longer than it tells.

Its bark is thick with weather, time, and ash.
Its crown has held both nests and plastic bags.
It knows the soot that drifts from factory roofs,
The starlings' songs, the silence after frost.
It was not planted, blessed, or shaped by hand—
It simply grew, and grew because it could.

It has no name, for names are human tricks,
A net to catch a thing before it moves.
But still, it learned to read the world by weight:
The tug of rain, the crack of snow at night,
The thawing step of foxes through the brush,
The heavy sigh of summers filled with dust.

It thought in rings, and not in syllables.
It did not crave, but knew the taste of need.
Its knowledge was not forged by counting hours,
But by the length of roots through stone and sand.
It never prayed, but sometimes felt a pull—
A bending toward the light that wasn't seen.

Then one grey spring, a whisper split the reeds.
A body soft and sharp emerged from shade—
A Russian Blue, her fur the colour grief
Might take if grief were lit from deep inside.
She had the eyes of creatures who don't ask,
But know that everything will end in dusk.

She leapt into the tree without a pause.
Her claws did not disturb the sleeping moss.
She stretched along a branch, then turned and spoke,
"My name is Rosie. I am here to think."
The tree said nothing, for it always heard,
And silence was the closest thing to speech.

"I've watched this river daily, step by step,"
She said. "Its movements never seem to end.
Yet nothing that it holds can hold itself—
It gives, and all it gives becomes undone."
The tree responded, slow as changing leaves:
"The river's task is not to keep, but pass."

She curled her tail and met the morning sun.
"I'm told I'm fading, though I feel quite whole.
My legs still leap, my thoughts still chase the birds—
Yet something low is curling in my chest."
The tree said, "Fading is not always end.
A leaf must fall for buds to find the light."

"But will I be?" said Rosie, "Will I be?
Or will I be a thought the roots forget?"
The tree considered. "What you call your 'self'
Is only what your body dreams it is.
That self will shift. But what you are—will feed.
And what you feed may one day speak again."

"That's not enough," she said, and licked her paw.
"I want to know that I will still be me—
That something thinks, or purrs, or knows my name."
The tree replied, "Then you must choose what 'me'
You wish to keep: the shadow, or the claw?
The breath, or just the idea of being warm?"

The cat grew quiet. "I don't know what I want.
Perhaps to leap forever through the dusk.
Or curl upon a branch that does not fall,
And sleep through every ending still to come."
The tree said, "That is not a cruel desire—
But nothing leaps forever in the dusk."

Below, the canal rippled at a breeze.
A gull flew low and called without reply.
And Rosie watched the sky between the boughs,
And felt the hush that only trees can keep.
"You do not fear," she said. "But is it peace?
Or is it just you've never had a choice?"

"I've had no name, but I have had to grow,"
The tree replied. "And growing is a choice.
Each year I must decide: withdraw, extend?
Retreat to bark, or gamble for the sun?
What seems like stillness is a civil war—
Between the wish to thrive, and not to break."

"You're wise," said Rosie. "Wiser than my kind."
"I've had more time," the patient tree replied.
"But you've had movement, which I cannot claim.
I learn from those who pass across my shade.
Each child who climbs, each lover who carves names—
They leave behind a question I must keep."

A pause. The air grew gold with thinning light.
The water mirrored clouds that did not stay.
"And what of pain?" the cat asked. "What of loss?
What of the hands that never came again?"
"I do not grieve," the quiet tree began,
"But I remember. And remembering is pain."

That night, the stars like lanterns blinked above.
And Rosie nestled low along a limb.
The tree stayed watchful as the foxes called.
Its leaves grew still, and something deep within—
A knot long held in heartwood, hard and dry—
Began to soften just enough to bend.

Days passed. Then weeks. And seasons walked away.
The cat grew slower, as the roots grew long.
Her body shrank; her eyes began to close
More often than they opened to the light.
And in the crook between two gentle limbs,
She curled herself into a deeper night.

She dreamed of things no daylight could recall—
A bridge of breath, a meadow made of hush.
She dreamed the tree had walked across the sky
To gather stars and bring them to her feet.
The tree, though still, could feel her dream take root—
A pulse of rest that echoed through its shoot.

Each morning, she would stir, but not for long.
The wind would lift a whisker, then retreat.
The tree grew used to listening for her—
The slight repositioning of paws on bark,
The way she shifted slowly in her sleep—
A sound more known than even rain could keep.

It did not count the hours that she lay,
Nor wonder if the stillness meant a change.
The tree had learned from shadows and from light
That presence isn't always born in sound.
And Rosie, breathing slow beneath its limbs,
Was more than leaf or birdsong ever hymned.

One day she yawned and stayed a little still.
The wind passed by without a need to ask.
She blinked, then watched the leaves above her head,
As if the world were softer than before.
"I'm not a thing that answers anymore,"
She said. "I'm more a space that questions fill."

The tree, which never asked to be or seem,
Felt something in its sap begin to stir.
It did not shift its bark or drop a limb—
It simply leaned a silence toward her thought.
And Rosie knew, though nothing had been said,
The hush was how the rooted speak of thread.

A rain began, but light and shy of sound.
The moss grew rich beneath her resting side.
She stayed, and let the drops adorn her fur—
A constellation mapped without a name.
The tree drank in the rain without a thought,
But something in its core grew wide and caught.

She whispered, "I have never been the same.
Each nap I take, I wake in some new form.
Not all at once—but bits of me dissolve,
And others come to curl in where they left."
The tree said, "Change is not what we control.
It's what we serve, and slowly come to hold."

The sun returned, then bowed behind a hill.
The light turned lavender, then fell to grey.
And Rosie didn't move, but breathed so deep
It seemed her ribs had room for more than breath.
The tree held every second like a bell—
Rung not in sound, but how the shadow fell.

Another week, the sky turned blue, then green.
The Clyde rolled on with nothing new to show.
But Rosie, now a figure in the tree,
Had learned the art of motion made in thought.
She chased no longer what she could not catch,
And found in staying still a kind of stretch.

The bark grew marked with scratches faint and fine—
Not gouges, but the echoes of her leaps.
And in those lines, the tree began to feel
A texture that had not been there before.
No human carved, no lightning broke the grain—
Just claws that pressed the silence into name.

One morning, she arose before the light.
She walked the length of branch and sniffed the air.
Then turned and said, "This limb is now my path.
I do not own it—I remember it."
The tree replied, "And I remember you—
Not as a mark, but as a way I grew."

She purred again, but now the purr was low—
A hum beneath the belly of the dawn.
It wasn't meant for comfort or for peace,
But just to show the hush had found a tune.
The tree, which never hummed or spoke aloud,
Felt something bloom beneath its wooden shroud.

And now the world resumed its turning pace.
The barge returned, the birds resumed their song.
The wind came back with scent from further fields,
And Rosie turned to watch it pass once more.
She did not chase it—only let it brush
Her cheek as though it were a poem's hush.

One day she yawned and stayed a little still.
The wind passed by without a need to ask.
She blinked, then watched the leaves above her head,
As if the world were softer than before.
"I'm not a thing that answers anymore,"
She said. "I'm more a space that questions fill."

The tree, which never asked to be or seem,
Felt something in its sap begin to stir.
It did not shift its bark or drop a limb—
It simply leaned a silence toward her thought.
And Rosie knew, though nothing had been said,
The hush was how the rooted speak of thread.

A rain began, but light and shy of sound.
The moss grew rich beneath her resting side.
She stayed, and let the drops adorn her fur—
A constellation mapped without a name.
The tree drank in the rain without a thought,
But something in its core grew wide and caught.

She whispered, "I have never been the same.
Each nap I take, I wake in some new form.
Not all at once—but bits of me dissolve,
And others come to curl in where they left."
The tree said, "Change is not what we control.
It's what we serve, and slowly come to hold."

The sun returned, then bowed behind a hill.
The light turned lavender, then fell to grey.
And Rosie didn't move, but breathed so deep
It seemed her ribs had room for more than breath.
The tree held every second like a bell—
Rung not in sound, but how the shadow fell.

Another week, the sky turned blue, then green.
The Clyde rolled on with nothing new to show.
But Rosie, now a figure in the tree,
Had learned the art of motion made in thought.
She chased no longer what she could not catch,
And found in staying still a kind of stretch.

The bark grew marked with scratches faint and fine—
Not gouges, but the echoes of her leaps.
And in those lines, the tree began to feel
A texture that had not been there before.
No human carved, no lightning broke the grain—
Just claws that pressed the silence into name.

One morning, she arose before the light.
She walked the length of branch and sniffed the air.
Then turned and said, "This limb is now my path.
I do not own it—I remember it."
The tree replied, "And I remember you—
Not as a mark, but as a way I grew."

She purred again, but now the purr was low—
A hum beneath the belly of the dawn.
It wasn't meant for comfort or for peace,
But just to show the hush had found a tune.
The tree, which never hummed or spoke aloud,
Felt something bloom beneath its wooden shroud.

And now the world resumed its turning pace.
The barge returned, the birds resumed their song.
The wind came back with scent from further fields,
And Rosie turned to watch it pass once more.
She did not chase it—only let it brush
Her cheek as though it were a poem's hush.

She leapt down once, then paced a ring of roots.
The tree stood tall, but felt her thought descend.
She did not go—she only moved to feel
The soil beneath her soften to her step.
And in that tread, the bark was memory,
A woven mesh of being here and free.

The water rippled softly at the bend.
The sun was bright, but distant in its heat.
And Rosie found her shadow at the base—
A shape not quite her own, and yet still kin.
"I think," she said, "I've stretched beyond the frame.
But still I curl where something knows my name."

The tree, who'd never known the need for names,
Still felt her weight in more than just its bark.
A knowledge passed like sap between the cells—
A silent tale made visible by time.
And Rosie sat, then blinked against the sky,
As if to say, I've never said goodbye.

She found her perch again by noon that day.
The breeze was kind, the sun not yet too bold.
And from the branch, she stared across the Clyde,
Then closed her eyes and dreamed without a twitch.
The tree did not disturb a single leaf—
For dreams like this are not a thing to breach.

A blossom brushed her back and did not fall.
She wore it like a crown she hadn't asked.
And in that moment, something in the shade
Grew deeper than the roots had dared to press.
For in the hush between her breath and limb,
The world became more full, and less of whim.

She stirred by dusk, and stretched into a curl.
The branch grew warm beneath her measured weight.
And from that point, she watched the stars arrive,
But did not chase them, nor remark their place.
She only blinked, and blinked again, then still—
Her eyes now wide enough to hold the hill.

The Clyde grew dark, but kept its steady pace.
The reeds grew hush, the shadows changed their tone.
And Rosie, from her throne within the limbs,
Felt all the world grow quiet in her skin.
The tree, which knew no throne, no need to reign,
Still bowed inside its bark to share the gain.

She said, "I am not old, but I am slow.
I do not chase the same as once I did.
But what I catch now stays inside my chest—
It doesn't flee, or flinch, or twist away."
The tree replied, "Then let that stillness grow.
The slowest things are those the earth will show."

The stars grew sharp, then vanished with the fog.
The morning came, a blur of rose and slate.
And Rosie stretched before the mist had gone,
Then leapt once down to mark the moss again.
The tree stood tall, and held the place she left—
Not as a loss, but as a kind of depth.

And in the days that followed, she would come—
Then go, then come again, but always pause.
The tree no longer marked her time in rings,
But in the ways her absence shaped the air.
A root grew deeper every time she left—
As though her going fed its reaching breath.

She told no tale of where she went or why.
She told no tale of what she thought or saw.
But when she curled again within the bough,
The way she sighed made all the difference clear.
The tree had changed—not outwardly, but far
Beneath the grain, where time can feel like star.

She pressed her paw against the bark one dusk.
The touch was brief, but something seemed to spark.
And though she didn't speak, the tree could feel
A language pass that had no need for words.
It wasn't thanks, and wasn't meant as prayer—
It was a bridge between the branch and air.

And every time she climbed or crouched or leapt,
The bark remembered how her paws had danced.
It held her shape not only in the grain,
But in the way it waited for her weight.
The cat was not a guest, nor quite a ghost—
But something close to what the roots loved most.

She stayed one morning longer than before.
She did not stretch, nor blink, nor mark the dawn.
She only sat, and let the sky grow blue—
Her tail a stillness draped across the wood.
The tree stood tall, but softened in the breeze,
As if her stillness echoed through its knees.

The sun rose high, then slipped behind a cloud.
The day grew warm, then cool, then still again.
And Rosie stayed, as if to say, I know.
Not know a fact, but know a kind of way—
The way the bark remembers when it's climbed,
Or how a leaf will turn before its time.

A heron passed, but made no sudden cry.
Its wings were wide and soft against the air.
And Rosie followed it with steady eyes,
Then blinked once slowly, like a closing book.
The tree had seen the birds for many years—
But none had felt so silent in its gears.

A seed fell down, and Rosie tapped it twice.
She did not chase it, nor did she retreat.
She let it roll and watched the way it turned,
Then nodded once, as if to mark the spin.
The tree let go another just the same,
And Rosie smiled, though never said its name.

The dusk returned, and so did her repose.
The moss grew thick where she had often laid.
And though she'd never claimed a single inch,
The branch she chose had altered in its strength.
The tree had bent, not broken, in her care—
A shape that knew how long she had been there.

She purred once more—a pulse that reached the bark.
The tree received it like a sacred chord.
Not holy, but a hum that told the air
That something more than silence had been shared.
And Rosie, knowing that the tree had heard,
Stretched out and let the night absorb her word.

The wind returned, a whisper through the leaves.
The Clyde grew dim beneath the final light.
And Rosie closed her eyes, but not to dream—
She only wished to feel the tree again.
The tree, now filled with every breath she gave,
Stood rooted in the hush it could not save.

The tree stood still, yet every cell was flame—
Not fire that burns, but fire that understands.
For what had passed between the bark and fur
Was not a story written down in words.
It lived in weight, and silence, and return—
A bond that only time and trust can earn.

Rosie did not stir. The stars came out.
Their patterns traced the shape of things unsaid.
The sky was deep, but not beyond her gaze—
She seemed to hold the firmament in thought.
And in her breath, the tree could feel a note—
Not song, but something silence wants to quote.

She shifted once to find a warmer curl.
The moss beneath had learned her shape by heart.
No throne, no bed, no sacred chosen stone—
Just branch and fur, together in the dark.
And though the air grew colder with the hour,
She did not shiver, break, or ask for power.

The tree remembered winds from other years,
And droughts that pulled the green from every leaf.
But none had taught it more than Rosie's weight—
A presence made of questions held in peace.
And now, beneath the sky's wide glowing arc,
It kept her shape engraved into its bark.

She murmured, "I am not a tale to end.
I am a thread still weaving through the tree.
I do not need to close the book tonight—
I only need to breathe, and be, and see."
The tree replied, "Then let your breath be known.
This branch is not alone, nor are you gone."

A hush more rich than hushness ought to be
Settled between the stars and mossy limb.
The Clyde moved on, the reeds began to bow,
And Rosie did not move, nor need to speak.
For stillness now was not a waiting place—
It was a form, a dwelling, and a grace.

She blinked, then blinked again, then closed her eyes.
A single leaf slid off a higher bough.
It spun, then fell, and brushed against her ear,
Then vanished in the undergrowth below.
The tree did not remark, nor seek to see—
It knew the leaf would stay in memory.

The stars had multiplied, but none looked down.
They simply shone, and Rosie simply stayed.
The limb she'd chosen swayed beneath her calm,
But didn't drop, nor tremble, nor forget.
And she, the shape of thought made small and grey,
Was nothing less than what she chose to say.

She said no more. Her words had found their shell.
The tree, which needed none, had heard them all.
It carried each along the vascular strands—
A vessel for the meaning in her paws.
And deep below, where roots entwine like dreams,
It shaped her story into living seams.

The Clyde turned silver under rising moon.
The sky was rich with questions none could ask.
And Rosie now was only breath and shape—
A curve of warmth against the ancient limb.
The tree grew quiet not from lack or doubt,
But from the awe of knowing she was about.

A gust of wind came tumbling from the west.
It brushed the bark, then stroked along her spine.
She didn't flinch—she only took it in,
Then breathed it out as if it were a hymn.
And in that breath, the air itself grew kind—
As though it, too, had changed the shape of mind.

The moon grew pale. The water whispered slow.
The tree had learned the cat's specific weight.
It felt her there the way one feels a vow—
Unspoken, but impossible to break.
And though the morning hadn't yet begun,
The hush between them gleamed like something done.

No tale was told. No memory was made.
No record kept in bark or stone or sky.
And yet, a chapter turned inside the rings—
A growth that bore the texture of her name.
The tree, still silent, reached a little wide—
As if to keep her further in its stride.

She did not shift, though dreams now brushed her fur.
They came like fog and settled in her chest.
She dreamed, perhaps, of Clyde, or stars, or wings—
But none would know, and none would need to know.
The dream, like breath, was part of how she stayed—
A rhythm that the bark itself obeyed.

The darkness gathered, softer than before.
The shadows didn't hide, they only held.
And Rosie, curled and quiet as a tune,
Had grown into the branch as branches do.
The tree no longer knew where she began—
Only that now, its limbs had more to span.

The dawn came not with noise, but with a blush.
It painted sky and Clyde and sleeping fur.
And still she stayed, not waiting for a cue—
But only being, just as light must be.
The tree let shimmer pass across its bark,
Then listened for the morning in her spark.

She stirred at last, but only with a sigh.
Her breath was deep, and yet not filled with need.
She looked once at the sky, then shut her eyes—
Not tired, but full, as rivers are with tide.
The tree, who'd watched her wake from countless dreams,
Now watched her rest within the dawn's blue seams.

She twitched one ear, then let it fold in peace.
A single thought might still be on her tongue.
But nothing pushed it outward into sound—
It curled instead like paws beneath her chest.
And in that curl, the tree found something rare:
A shape of stillness breathing in the air.

She did not stay forever, nor did leave.
She simply was, and that was all to be.
The tree did not ask when she might return,
Nor count the days she lingered in its shade.
For what they shared was not a thing to hold—
But how the holding made them both more whole.

And so the tree stood still, but never same.
It bore the mark of paws upon its bark.
And every time a cat passed through its shade,
It stirred, and offered up a gentler limb.
For what we touch becomes what we remain,
And every root drinks memory, not just rain.

Part II

The morning came with fog that touched the leaves.
The air was pale, the sun not quite awake.
And Rosie climbed without her usual sound—
No purr, no word, no whispered leap of thought.
The tree stood still and felt the shift begin,
A silence like a seed beneath the skin.

She did not speak. She nestled on a branch.
Her tail curled round, her paws concealed her eyes.
The tree, accustomed now to daily speech,
Felt something hush within its ancient rings.
A quiet not of loss, but something new—
As if the day itself had paused to view.

The river passed without its usual song.
The reeds bent low, as if to better hear.
And overhead, a gull flew without cry—
Its wings alone the language of the sky.
The tree observed, and did not think it wrong
To call this quiet something more than long.

It thought: She listens now instead of speaks.
She listens not to me, but something else.
A knowing stretched between her breath and fur—
A sense too wide for syllables to hold.
The cat had found a space the tree had known—
A silence made of more than just alone.

No branch was moved. No wind disturbed the leaves.
The moss grew damp with waiting, but not pain.
The tree recalled a winter long ago
When frost had covered all, yet nothing broke.
That silence felt like Rosie curled in thought—
A pause that asked the world what time had brought.

The tree considered speaking once or twice,
But held its voice like root within the stone.
To interrupt the moment was to claim
A truth that wasn't ready to be known.
So it remained a vessel for the hush—
A page unturned, a path without a rush.

The hours passed like footsteps far away.
The tree began to hear things it had missed—
The distant ticking of a beetle's walk,
The gentle crack of lichen in the sun.
And Rosie, still, was shaped by every sound—
Though none escaped her lips, nor stirred the ground.

A breeze arrived, then left without a trace.
The shadow of a cloud slid down the trunk.
The cat did not respond, nor shift her weight.
She breathed with rhythm, but not with reply.
And in her stillness, something seemed to speak—
A voice not hers, but echoing through cheek.

The tree recalled: I too have had such days—
When no one carved their names, when no one came.
And in those hours, I learned what growth could be—
Not loud, not seen, but deeper in the grain.
Perhaps, it thought, this silence is her way
To stretch a kind of root through what won't stay.

A crow passed by, then did not call aloud.
It landed once, then quickly flew again.
And Rosie's ear did twitch, but nothing more—
No chase, no sound, no flicker of the claw.
The tree could feel her wakefulness intact—
But all of it withdrawn, and not detract.

The silence thickened—not in weight, but shape.
It formed a loop, a circle through the air.
The tree began to feel it like a gift—
A woven net that held the day with care.
And Rosie, still as root, remained within—
A cat composed of listening and skin.

The past was loud with things they'd said before.
Philosophies like birds had come and gone.
But now, the tree was learning once again
That presence need not come with argument.
A mind can speak without the need for sound—
And still leave rings that echo through the ground.

The tree then sent a single leaf adrift.
It spiralled down, then landed by her side.
She did not move, but one eye opened slow—
A golden sliver cupped in silver blue.
And though she blinked, she said no single word—
Yet all the world, it seemed, had clearly heard.

Another leaf, then two, began to fall.
Not wind, but invitation set them free.
And Rosie watched them drift like half-formed thoughts—
Too light to grip, too full to not be known.
She let them come, and still she did not move—
A statue carved of whisper and of groove.

The river glimmered silver without noise.
A fish broke surface, vanished with no splash.
The silence was not empty, but alive—
A silence made of moments not yet said.
And in it, Rosie breathed a deeper breath—
Not heavy, not afraid, but near to depth.

The tree grew stiller, though it could not move.
It deepened in a way beyond the root.
It felt the weight of questions not yet formed—
The quiet that precedes a change in truth.
And Rosie seemed the source of that descent—
A question born in pause, not argument.

How long they sat like that, no clock could mark.
The sun passed over slowly, then began
To tip its light along the western rim—
A glow that softened bark and paw alike.
And still she said no word, nor moved to go.
And still the tree stood listening to her soul.

She stretched at last, but not with aim or need.
Her limbs unfolded like a windless flag.
She turned her face toward sky, then toward the leaves—
And offered up a breath, but not a sound.
The tree responded not with leaf or voice,
But simply with the knowledge of her choice.

She placed her paw against the limb below—
A press, not strong, but gently firm and sure.
It was not meant to stir, but just to feel—
To let the silence end with simple touch.
And in that moment, silence said its part—
A speechless line impressed in bark and heart.

Then Rosie leapt—but not away from thought.
She landed light upon the lower bough.
She did not speak, but turned her eyes to his,
The tree who'd never asked, nor ever bowed.
And in her gaze, he saw the shape of peace—
Not final, but a moment held in ease.

The evening spread a hush across the sky.
Its colours spoke in tones too soft for names.
And Rosie paused upon a sturdy branch,
Her tail a question curling into dusk.
She blinked once slowly, not in thought or fear—
But simply in the rhythm silence wears.

The tree absorbed the moment like the dew.
No impulse stirred, no commentary bloomed.
Instead, it let her gaze dissolve the space—
Like light through glass that does not block but bend.
For sometimes, knowing comes when nothing seeks—
A wisdom made of quiet, not of speech.

She circled once, then lay across the limb.
Her belly met the bark as if they'd met
A thousand years ago, beneath this sky,
And only now recalled they had returned.
The silence thickened not with weight, but thread—
A weave of every word they'd never said.

And in that hush, the tree began to feel
The ways that presence shaped its inner form.
No storm had carved such patterns in its rings—
No frost had etched such whispers in its grain.
It understood that silence was a hand—
Not grasping, but inviting it to stand.

A squirrel passed by, then paused to view the pair.
It twitched its tail, then vanished in a flash.
But neither cat nor tree broke from their pose—
As if the world were paused just for their breath.
And breath it was, that held them in their place—
A pulse of stillness shaped in open space.

The silence did not offer simple peace.
It asked of both a patience hard to keep.
It asked the cat to hold what could not speak.
It asked the tree to feel without a frame.
And yet, they stayed—not out of bound or chain—
But through the trust that silence would remain.

Rosie's ear twitched once, then stilled again.
A leaf had landed lightly near her paw.
She did not move to swat or chase it off.
Instead, she let it sit, as if to say:
Not every contact calls for consequence—
Some things are meant to share a simple sense.

The tree recalled a time a child had climbed—
A voice had echoed laughter in its limbs.
That sound had passed, and yet its print remained,
A phantom press of footfall in the bark.
But Rosie left no sound and made no claim—
Her silence carved a presence just the same.

The river, in its mirror-self, looked up.
It held the tree and cat within its glass.
And in reflection, silence found a form—
Not bound by edge or colour, just by gaze.
She saw herself, but did not flinch away—
For silence had become her shape today.

The stars began to blink in growing dark.
The world gave up its chatter bit by bit.
And Rosie breathed a sigh that made no sound—
A gesture, not a grief, not quite a thought.
The tree replied with nothing, yet it knew—
That silence had become a kind of you.

One branch above her shifted in the breeze.
The motion spoke of years the cat had not.
The tree, with leaves like eyelids over thought,
Felt all the space between them come alive.
She looked above, and did not speak or blink—
As if to say, This too is how we think.

No meaning clung to silence like a word.
It did not ask to be defined or held.
It moved between them like a breath of dusk—
A presence made of listening alone.
And Rosie knew, though not in human terms,
That stillness was not void, but what affirms.

Her fur caught starlight like a woven net.
Each hair held night, but also something more.
The tree could feel the light upon her back
Before the light had even touched its bark.
For silence sometimes speaks through other skin—
And lets one being feel where one has been.

She stood again, but did not stretch or pace.
She walked the branch with balance born of thought.
And every step she took was soft, precise—
As if the limb might hum beneath her weight.
The tree did not adjust, nor need to shift—
It held her with a silence made of gift.

Then, near the base, she found her mossy nook—
A space she'd shaped across a dozen days.
She did not curl within it yet, but stared
At where it lay, as if it held a sign.
The tree, observing close, could nearly tell
She'd asked a question deeper than a spell.

She placed one paw upon the moss, then paused.
She breathed, then pulled it back without a sound.
The act was simple, small, and brief to see—
But something in it rang like distant bells.
The tree received it not as gesture made,
But as a kind of silence now conveyed.

The moon had risen, polished by the mist.
Its face looked down, but offered no command.
And Rosie turned her eyes toward it slow,
As though it might reflect a thought she knew.
The tree looked too, though not with eye or sight—
It simply felt the moon across its height.

Another breeze, but gentler than the last.
It passed through fur and leaf with equal care.
It stirred the hush but never broke its thread—
A whisper that had learned the ways of cloth.
And Rosie blinked again, her thoughts unread—
But full of meaning silence only brought.

And now the stars grew brighter, one by one.
The tree stood tall. The cat lay low and calm.
Together they composed an unseen hymn—
A song not sung, but present in the still.
The hush became a mirror, wide and deep—
And both of them were what the mirror keeps.

She closed her eyes, but not to leave the day.
The tree, in turn, leaned inward with its rings.
No part of them was separate or alone—
For silence is a way to hold what sings.
And in that hush, too large to be defined,
They spoke in what connects the root and mind.

The wind lay low, as if it too had heard
A lullaby not made of tone or tune.
And Rosie, half-asleep but fully there,
Lay like a thought that no one dares disturb.
The tree looked inward, toward the sap and rings—
And found her there, as part of how it thinks.

No sound escaped the grove, and yet it moved—
In rustling not of leaves, but something else.
The silence had become a living thing,
A thread that linked each breath without a knot.
And in that thread, the cat and tree were twined—
Not owned, not bound, but closely yet aligned.

A fox passed by, its footfalls soft as smoke.
It did not stop. It felt the silence too.
The grove had drawn a border none could cross—
Not from command, but reverence of space.
And Rosie, still within her mossy bed,
Remained a thought too quiet to be said.

The stars, now legion, shimmered without rush.
The sky held stories it would never speak.
And Rosie turned, not up toward distant fire,
But toward the bark that framed her sleeping place.
She placed her head where roots began their stretch—
A silent bow that words could never catch.

The tree, in turn, allowed its weight to shift—
Not movement, but a yielding deep inside.
A knot relaxed that had not known its name.
A pressure eased where memory had held.
For silence, when respected without fear,
Can soften what has stiffened through the years.

No sudden thought, no metaphor appeared.
No grand epiphany disturbed the night.
But in the gap where noise had once been king,
A truer knowing formed without a shape.
Not fact, nor faith, nor vision from above—
But presence filled with recognition's love.

She breathed. He listened. Time became a pool.
Its surface stilled, its depths too wide to chart.
And though no word had passed between them yet,
They'd said far more than many who had tried.
For some exchanges bloom without a sound—
A dialogue where thought and soul are bound.

And Rosie shifted slightly in her sleep.
A paw unfurled, a whisker twitched with thought.
She dreamed, perhaps, though neither truly knew—
For dreams can pass through bark as well as bone.
The tree received the tremor of her rest
Like roots receive the rain through quiet stone.

A branch above her dipped beneath the moon.
Its leaves moved slow, like pages turning back.
The tree recalled a breeze from long ago—
A spring before it knew the taste of moss.
But Rosie, now within its closest shade,
Had joined that memory without a cost.

She murmured once, a sound not meant to last—
A sigh of sleep, or maybe something more.
It held no word, but something deep and warm—
A centre made of nothing but the whole.
And in that sound, the silence took a breath—
A proof of life that did not challenge death.

The bark beneath her formed a gentle cup.
The moss had learned the way her weight would fall.
And even now, the shape she made remained—
A hollow shaped by habit, not by law.
The tree felt pride, though not the kind that shouts—
But pride in having held a life that doubts.

No lesson closed the hush with final thought.
No theorem cracked the riddle of the day.
Instead, the silence swelled to something wide—
A space where every paradox could stay.
And Rosie, twitching once, resumed her rest—
As if to say, This moment is the best.

The moon began its slow descent through sky.
Its light now paler, slanting through the green.
And Rosie's fur, once silvered, dimmed to grey—
Yet not with loss, but with a softer gleam.
The tree looked on, and felt without regret
The quiet growing where their minds had met.

A single cloud slid past like folded time.
It did not speak, but altered what it touched.
The silence bent around it, not to break,
But to include its drift within the peace.
For not all change must come with noise or fear—
Some shifts arrive to say: You still are here.

The river whispered something to the stones.
A reed let fall a drop from leaf to root.
And Rosie, now half-dreaming, half-aware,
Seemed not to move but more to *let* things move.
The tree, attuned to subtler forms of call,
Knew this was language deeper than them all.

The silence now had edges like a bowl.
It held them both, yet did not hem them in.
It shimmered with the breath they did not share—
For silence often links by what is spared.
And Rosie, sensing morning on the rise,
Did not yet stir, but blinked with waking eyes.

She yawned without a sound, her mouth a wave.
Then slowly stood, as if rehearsing thought.
Each motion small, deliberate, and sure—
A choreography not learned, but known.
The tree, in awe, received her weight once more—
And knew the silence taught more than before.

She did not speak. The hush had not yet passed.
It lingered still, though morning's hand drew near.
And in its glow, they welcomed what they'd grown—
A field of shared awareness deep and vast.
For even now, with sounds about to start,
The silence stayed within the roots of heart.

The sky turned pale, then blushed a peach-toned blue.
A thrush began to trill beyond the reeds.
Yet Rosie only watched, and did not sing.
Her silence was too full for smaller songs.
And though the world resumed its daily play,
The cat and tree had learned a different way.

And in that final hush before the noise—
The footfalls, wings, and laughter from the shore—
The tree and cat remained inside a truth:
That presence does not need a voice to grow.
And in their shared, unspoken reverie,
They found the shape of what it means to be.

She circled once upon the mossy bed,
Then stopped, not out of need but simple thought.
Her gaze was fixed on nothing in the world—
Yet everything was caught within her glance.
The tree stood still and mirrored back her gaze,
And found in it the shape of inner space.

The silence now was neither deep nor wide—
It had no shape the mind could draw or keep.
It hovered like the moment just before
A drop of rain detaches from the sky.
And in that poised, unwritten atmosphere,
The cat and tree became what they revere.

She pressed her paw against the bark once more.
The press was small, but all the meaning stayed.
And though no sound emerged from limb or mouth,
The tree replied in pressure, curve, and grain.
For when the world grows quiet to its core,
A single touch can open every door.

The dawn had broken, though it made no call.
The mist withdrew, revealing streets and stone.
But Rosie turned away from all of that—
Her place was not in rush or clamour's cry.
She blinked, then let her breathing guide her shape,
And settled once again without escape.

The tree had learned from storms and growing things,
From birds who stayed and birds who moved along.
But never had it learned from silence so—
A quiet not of lack, but full design.
What Rosie brought was not a day of sleep,
But rather, rest so loud it seemed to speak.

A leaf fell down, though not from sudden gust.
It tumbled gently, like a held release.
It brushed against her fur and did not wake—
For silence has no need for sharp goodbyes.
The tree, in feeling where the leaf had lain,
Felt part of her in every brushed refrain.

A thrush flew close, then changed its path mid-air.
It saw the cat, the stillness in the tree,
And seemed to understand that flight could wait—
That something here was larger than its song.
So even those with wings and noise to give
Paused briefly just to watch the silence live.

She shifted slightly, not to rise or flee,
But just to feel the branch beneath her spine.
And in that shift, the hush became a hum—
A warmth not made by sound, but sensed by all.
The tree received her weight as it had grown:
A blessing shaped by fur and thought alone.

The river found its voice again by noon.
A distant bark, a distant wheel, a shout.
But none of it broke through the tree or cat—
Their silence had not faded, only moved.
It lived beneath the sound as strong as root—
A song beneath the song, a second truth.

She leapt down low, then landed near the trunk.
She did not stretch or race into the field.
Instead, she pressed her cheek against the base—
A greeting made of memory and now.
The tree absorbed her touch with grateful grace,
And let its bark reply in slow embrace.

No ritual, no formal end was planned.
The day moved on, but they did not depart.
For what they'd made was neither done nor lost—
It was a room that followed where they went.
A hush that stayed inside, beneath, between—
Where everything is felt but rarely seen.

She trotted once along the winding root.
Then paused, her tail flicked once, and paused again.
She seemed to ask if silence would remain—
If absence would not turn the peace to ache.
The tree responded not with word or sign,
But by not bending when she crossed its line.

She climbed again, but not to reach a height.
She only moved to find the air she knew—
A certain branch, a certain stripe of light,
A place where paws and shadows often met.
And though the silence hummed with things to say,
They let it be, and kept their words at bay.

A dandelion seed spun through the air.
It hovered near, then caught a rising breeze.
Rosie, unblinking, watched it wheel and fall.
The tree watched her, and through her saw it too.
In silence, they had both become the seed—
Not blown away, but carried by their need.

And though the world returned to noise and role,
They carried with them something never named.
A pocket in the cloth of all that is—
A crease where something different could remain.
And Rosie knew, and so did trunk and bough,
That silence had become a kind of vow.

Not promise made of future, past, or pact—
But one of presence, strong as curling bark.
It did not ask them to remain the same,
But only to return when time allowed.
And both of them, in knowing what was kept,
Had nothing more to say, and so they slept.

That sleep was not escape, nor was it end.
It was the silence folded back on self.
It hummed like roots through soil never claimed,
It stirred like fur beneath a steady breath.
The cat, the tree, the hush that held them fast—
Were more than moment: they were what would last.

A bud began to swell along a twig.
A blade of grass leaned slightly toward the sun.
A moth passed by, too soft for cat to chase.
Yet still, she watched—her stillness not undone.
And through her gaze, the world was made anew—
A silence wide enough to hold the true.

The tree did not reflect upon the day.
It simply lived the echo she had left.
And Rosie, though she blinked and stretched once more,
Still bore the hush like fragrance in her fur.
No closing act, no final line was drawn—
The silence stayed, long after words were gone.

And so the cat and tree, by branch and root,
Remained entwined in quiet's pure design.
No phrase could match the stillness they had found,
No metaphor could frame the form they made.
But in the hush, a life began to grow—
Where being spoke, and words were not the way.

Part III

A cloudless night arrived without a sound.
The stars were sharp, the moon a polished mask.
And Rosie, restless on her usual perch,
Stared upward with a squint of sleepless thought.
"I think," she said, "tonight I won't pretend.
The sky's too loud for dreams that never bend."

The tree stood quiet, sensing what would come—
A wakeful kind of dream, not born of sleep.
For sometimes thought will climb beyond the root,
And wander through the branches like a wind.
And Rosie's voice had taken on that tone—
Of questions pressed through silence into bone.

"I dreamed," she said, "that I was made of mist.
My tail was smoke, my whiskers were the breeze.
I passed through doors and never left a trace.
I moved through fields that whispered what I was.
But every time I tried to call my name,
The sound would break, as if it feared the game."

The tree did not reply with leaf or bark.
It let the echo settle through its rings.
It knew that dreams were not for answers first,
But for the shaping of a yet-formed shape.
And Rosie, swaying with the darkened limb,
continued on with eyes no longer dim.

"In one strange part, I floated through a house
That had no walls, but still it held a floor.
I climbed a stair that led to falling skies,
And every room remembered I had been.
But when I asked the ceiling who I was,
The beams just laughed and left me with applause."

The tree considered what a dream might mean
To one who sleeps upon its shifting frame.
It thought of birds who sang while half-asleep,
Of roots that twitch with echoes underground.
Perhaps, it thought, a dream is not escape—
But what the waking world cannot reshape.

"I met a second me," the cat confessed.
"She wore my fur but walked with different thought.
She asked me why I bothered being real,
When dreams could make a world that had no weight.
And when I answered, I forgot the sound—
My words dissolved before they touched the ground."

The tree recalled how rain will sometimes fall
So soft, it's lost before it hits the leaf.
It nodded inward, though it made no move—
For dreams, like rainfall, often slip through thought.
And yet they carve, not deep like roots or blade,
But with a touch that asks to not be weighed.

Rosie uncurled, then stretched across the bough.
Her spine a bow drawn tight with restless thought.
"I think I dream because I need to break—
To bend the lines that day too firmly draws.
I do not wish to leave, or run, or fly—
But only ask if form must always lie."

The tree responded slowly, through its grain—
A hum that lived in bark and leaf and time.
"Your form is not a lie, but not a law.
The shape you take is only one of many.
A tree may grow, and still remain a tree—
But dream of wind, and know what flight might be."

She blinked, and in the blink the stars grew close.
"I dream the sky is something I could touch—
A surface made of breath and woven light,
A mirror for the things I haven't said.
But when I leap, I never cross the veil—
The sky remains a whisper I can't trail."

The tree, who never dreamed in human ways,
Had felt the sky press down in storms and snow.
And once, when lightning split a higher limb,
It tasted light like sorrow without shape.
It did not say if sky could be embraced—
But offered bark, where stars were once encased.

Rosie leapt down, then back again in thought.
Her body moved like lines across a page.
"I dreamed that you were walking like a cat.
You crossed the water, trailing moss and flame.
And when I asked if trees could choose to move,
You only said, 'We've never asked to prove.'"

The tree imagined roots that slipped their bounds—
That danced along the stones and felt the grass.
It pondered what it meant to not remain,
To stretch in more than limb or ring or span.
And in that thought, it let a small leaf fall—
Not as an end, but sign that change can call.

The cat spun twice, then sat with solemn poise.
"In dreams I meet the things that wear my face,
But speak in riddles made of smoke and thread.
They ask me questions I have asked before—
But turn them backward, so they never land.
I wake, unsure of what they hoped I'd understand."

The tree had held the echoes of such loops—
The child who carved a name and came no more,
The wind that murmured languages of dust,
The years that passed without a single ring.
And so it said, "Not every thought must hold.
Some truths are only shaped enough to fold."

"I dream of clocks that melt, of doors that breathe,
Of hands that hold but cannot feel the weight.
And every time I try to reach the source,
It splits into a thousand mirrored thoughts.
Perhaps," she said, "the self I am in sleep
Is truer than the self I try to keep."

The tree absorbed her words like morning dew.
It did not fear the shift of solid ground.
For even bark, when aged and worn by time,
Can bear the image of what passed unseen.
"Perhaps," it said, "your self is not a line—
But like a flame: a shape that's never mine."

She yawned, and yet her eyes stayed sharp and clear.
"I dreamed the wind spoke back, but not with voice—
It answered by becoming what I meant,
And told me I had never asked for much.
It said that dreaming wasn't just a flight,
But how we pull the stars into the night."

The tree reflected on its dreaming cat—
A creature made of night and ear and spark.
It felt the dream pass through its quiet rings,
And welcomed it like rainfall through the shade.
For though it could not dream the way she did,
It felt her thoughts take root beneath its lid.

"I've flown," she said, "through windows shaped by sound,
And landed on a bridge that sang my name.
The stones were words I hadn't used in years—
But knew again as soon as I stepped through.
And in that place, the wind was made of light,
And memory was not a thing of sight."

The tree recalled a single gust last spring—
So warm, it woke the buds before their time.
The branch that bore the earliest leaf still bent—
A scar of dream made manifest in form.
It understood: the dream is not escape,
But what persuades the world to let us shape.

Rosie began to pace along the bark.
Her tail described a question in the air.
"I sometimes wonder if I dream *too* much.
If all these worlds distract me from the ground.
But every time I try to not return,
I miss the place where all my leaping burns."

"You balance," said the tree, "between the planes—
You walk where wakefulness begins to bow.
And in your steps, I see the path I lack—
The route where fur and thought and vision grow.
Your dreaming isn't distance, but a bridge—
A limb that stretches past the outer ridge."

She purred, but not for comfort or for ease.
It vibrated like thought within the wood.
A song not made of joy or common sense,
But resonance—the kind that trees can hear.
And through the bark, the purring found its thread—
A hum that stitched the dreaming to the stead.

"I've built a house in dreams," she said at last,
"A spiral tower balanced on a root.
It shifts each time I climb it, room to room—
But somehow leads me always to the tree.
Not you, perhaps, but something shaped the same—
A figure grown from quiet, light, and name."

The tree stood still, but something deep within—
A knot of rings grown tighter through the years—
Began to loosen, not in fear or doubt,
But recognition of another mind.
For in her dream, it saw itself anew—
Not bark and root, but thought in spiral view.

And Rosie blinked, as if to close a door—
Not lock it, but to keep the dream inside.
"The dream is done," she said, "but not complete.
It lingers like a scent across the day.
And I must think about the parts I kept—
The ones I held, the ones I let be swept."

The tree said nothing, but the branch she knew
Bent ever so, as if to catch her breath.
For dreams are not for answers carved in stone—
But for the shaping of a deeper path.
And Rosie, resting now against the limb,
Carried the dream not on, but into him.

They watched the moon complete its slow descent.
The stars grew pale and vanished into air.
And morning, soft as thought before it speaks,
Unfurled its gold across the patient Clyde.
But though the night had passed without a cry,
The dream remained beneath the open sky.

She placed her paw upon a woven sprout.
It bent, then straightened, nodding in return.
"A dream," she said, "is neither fake nor true.
It's made of something thinner than a thought—
But when it's gone, the body knows the loss,
The soul still shaped by what it could not cross."

The tree agreed, not with a word or sound,
But with a stillness deeper than before.
It let the bark remember what she said,
And held it close in silence long and sure.
For dreams, it knew, are carried not by sleep—
But by the way the waking starts to keep.

Rosie reclined, her breath a gentle tide.
Her whiskers trembled once, then stilled again.
"I'll dream again," she said, "but not too soon.
Some dreams require waiting to return.
For if they come too often, they grow thin—
And wear away the world we're living in."

The tree respected that—this space, this law.
A rhythm formed between the leap and rest.
It sensed her thought, the edge of deeper sleep,
But knew the dream had paused, not yet replaced.
And in the hush that followed, morning stayed,
As if the world itself were still afraid.

And so the cat and tree remained once more—
Two figures shaped by questions, breath, and bark.
No dreams were told, but still the air was full
Of what the night had etched across their gaze.
They'd walked a thread between the known and vast—
And left a trace no waking thought could grasp.

She stretched and yawned, her spine a question mark.
The morning wind arrived with scent of stone.
And Rosie sniffed, then laughed without a sound—
A ripple that the tree could nearly feel.
"I think," she said, "my dreams have gone to play.
They're hiding in the corners of the day."

The tree had never chased a dream through light—
Its thoughts did not divide in sleep and sun.
Yet something in the rhythm of her tone
Made even rooted rings begin to shift.
For dreams, when spoken by the ones we trust,
Can echo in the chambers of the just.

"I've dreamed of tunnels filled with coloured fire,
Of cats with wings who flew but would not land.
Of mirrors shaped like questions left unread,
And stairways made of fur that led to sky."
She paused, then added, "None of them were real—
And yet they left a scent I still can feel."

The tree recalled the phantom scents of spring,
When buds would form before the snow had fled.
It had no nose, but still it knew the time—
The rhythm of what almost came too soon.
So dreams, it guessed, were something close to that—
A bloom the world imagines, soft and flat.

"I do not mind," she said, "if dreams confuse.
Confusion makes the line between things wide.
I like to walk where one thing turns to two,
Or maybe none, or maybe back again."
The tree admired how she held her doubt—
As if it were a thread she'd never route.

A bee went past, too fast to draw her eye.
A drop of dew slipped off a curling blade.
And Rosie blinked, then turned her head just so—
A movement small enough to hold a thought.
The tree could feel the tension in the air,
Like breath held back before it turns to prayer.

She whispered low, "Do you believe in forms?
That anything is truly what it shows?
Or is each thing a mask worn for the hour—
A dream we wear because we've been assigned?"
The tree, uncertain, did not rush reply—
It knew some thoughts grow best beneath the sky.

"I've seen a shadow cast without a cause.
I've watched a cloud dissolve before it wept.
And once I chased a shape across the grass
That vanished just before I learned its name."
She twitched her ear and added, "Dreams or real—
Sometimes I think the line itself can feel."

The tree, though firmly rooted in the world,
Had watched illusions come and pass through years.
It knew that even stone will shift with time,
And even names will rot within the bark.
It answered slow, "The form may fade or lie—
But still it shapes the way the winds go by."

She nodded once, then jumped to lower limb.
Her paws pressed soft, like syllables in sand.
And there she lay, her body stretched and loose—
The very pose of one between all things.
A cat who'd dreamed herself beyond the edge,
Yet woke without the need to chase or pledge.

"I dreamed you were a harp," she murmured low.
"Each branch a string, each leaf a trembling chord.
I walked beneath, and every step I took
Played out a song I'd never heard before.
The tune was strange, and yet it knew my name—
It called me not to come, but just to *stay*."

The tree remembered wind that sang that way.
A storm that passed and left the bark in hum.
It had no voice, but when the cat had purred,
It felt what music meant without a tone.
So maybe she had dreamed not far from true—
A tree that sang a name it never knew.

"I build my dreams from scraps I find in life—
A whistle, cloud, a ripple on the stone.
I carry them like pebbles in my mind,
And when I sleep, I scatter them again."
She turned her gaze and added with a smile,
"They always land in some new kind of style."

The tree admired how her mind could weave—
How pieces taken in would later bloom.
It thought of leaves that gathered light and dust,
Then dropped them in the autumn with a sigh.
Perhaps, it mused, the dream is like a leaf—
That falls but marks the soil with quiet grief.

She stood and walked in spirals round the limb.
Each step a circle larger than the last.
"I think," she said, "that dreams don't want to end—
They only change their clothing for the day."
The tree let fall a seed it had not planned,
As if to echo what she'd just made grand.

The Clyde moved on, indifferent in its flow.
A heron stood in pose too still to name.
And Rosie watched, but did not interrupt—
Her silence now the silence of the stream.
She knew the dream had closed, or maybe paused—
But what remained would not be known as lost.

She yawned again, but this time like a stretch—
A way to let the waking world return.
And as she leapt down gently from her perch,
She looked once back, then pressed her paw to trunk.
"I dreamed of you," she said. "You were the gate—
The part of me that knew how much to wait."

The tree accepted what her paw had meant—
Not weight, not need, but recognition's shape.
And in its rings, a tremble ran like thought—
Too faint for sound, too deep for bark to show.
For now it knew: a dream is not a flight—
It is the branch that learns to hold the night.

The wind returned, but softer than before.
It carried with it petals from a hedge.
And Rosie watched them dance and fall and pass—
Then leapt through one, as if to test its dream.
She did not catch it, but she caught the feel
Of what it meant to move without a wheel.

The grass was wet beneath her careful steps.
She padded back and forth, then paused again.
"I dreamed of silence once, but not like this—
It echoed like a bell that had no rim.
The silence woke me with its empty hand,
And told me everything I'd built would stand."

The tree had known that silence, long and low.
The winter hush when all the sap recedes.
The moment just before the frost lets go—
When nothing speaks, yet all is held and freed.
It bowed, but only in its inward sense—
Acknowledging her dream's deep evidence.

She climbed once more, but not to chase or flee.
She simply sat, and let the morning come.
And in her eyes, the dream was not yet gone—
It shimmered still, like light upon the limb.
The tree could feel it flicker in the grain—
A promise made in sleep that still remained.

"I dream to stretch," she said, "not to escape.
To press my thoughts into another skin.
The world is wide, but sometimes much too loud—
So dreams are how I breathe beneath the din."
The tree replied, "Then dream and still be near.
I'll hold the hush that makes your dreaming clear."

They sat like that until the sun grew high.
The day resumed its rhythm, step by step.
But neither one had left the space they made—
A pause that grew a path beneath their words.
And every breath they shared became a thread
In tapestries the waking world would shed.

And as she blinked, the morning turned to song.
A bird began to call, then two, then three.
But still, the dream remained like scent in fur—
Too faint to name, too near to be denied.
And Rosie curled herself upon the bough,
Still dreaming wide, though fully here and now.

The sun rose high, but shadows stayed the same.
The branch still held the weight of thoughtful pause.
And Rosie lay not still from sleep or rest—
But from the dream that hadn't quite let go.
She blinked, then whispered, "Dreams are not a trick.
They are the mirror turned until we stick."

The tree considered every word she spoke—
And how her thoughts would twine through bark and ring.
It did not dream, and yet it understood
The pull to shape what hasn't come to be.
In Rosie's voice, it heard the world expand—
A stretch that left the air itself unmanned.

"I dreamed the sky had stairs," she said at last,
"And each one hummed a note too low to hear.
But as I climbed, the tune began to build—
And when I reached the top, I sang it whole.
I did not know the words, yet still I knew
That what I sang was made of something true."

The tree recalled a night of sudden wind
That played its limbs like strings upon a harp.
It did not make a melody of thought,
But still the wind had told it something deep.
And so it bowed a branch above her frame—
A gesture not of music, but the same.

She smiled, then closed her eyes, but not to sleep.
Instead, she seemed to drift in waking calm.
The tree felt time begin to lose its thread—
The now and then becoming like a braid.
And in that knot, their two minds quietly met—
Where fur and bark share something like regret.

"I've never dreamed I'm someone else," she said.
"I always look the same, but act with doubt.
It's not that I forget my claws or name—
It's more I feel I've stepped beyond a shape.
And when I wake, I know I'm still the same,
But something shifts that I cannot reclaim."

The tree had never lost itself in dream,
But it had watched the shape of shade evolve.
What once was dark grew softer through the years,
And not because the sun had moved its place.
Some shifts, it knew, occur without a plan—
Like thoughts that tilt the moment in a hand.

She rolled onto her back and watched the sky.
A single leaf detached and drifted near.
She let it fall and land between her paws,
Then stared at it as if it were a sign.
"This leaf," she said, "is all the dreams I keep—
They fall from heights I never meant to reach."

The tree accepted that without reply.
The falling leaf had not disturbed its calm.
For leaves will fall, and dreams will lift and fade—
But still their passage marks a living thread.
And Rosie, seeing how the leaf was curled,
Felt suddenly as old as all the world.

She stood, and though the motion broke the pose,
The silence that had held them did not end.
Instead, it spread—like rings from water's pulse—
A quiet echo not in sound, but sense.
And Rosie knew, though nothing had been said,
That dreams remain where presence lays its head.

"I do not dream for prophecy or plan,"
She said. "I do not seek a hidden law.
I only want to know that when I leap,
The ground or sky will answer back in kind."
The tree said, "Leaping is its own reply—
A question made of muscle, not of why."

She flicked her tail and leapt onto a stone.
The Clyde looked wide and loud but slow today.
And Rosie stared into its curling skin,
Then looked once back to see if she was seen.
The tree stood tall, unmoving, but aware—
It saw her, not by sight, but how it *shared*.

"I dreamed I was a thought no one could keep,"
She said, her voice a ripple through the grass.
"I slipped between the fingers of a god,
And landed in a place without a time.
It wasn't frightening—it just was wide—
Like wind that couldn't pick a single side."

The tree had known the wind that had no course—
The wind that spun the leaves without intent.
It let her dream replant itself below—
Not lost, but folded deep into the core.
For even drifting has a part to play,
When roots are strong enough to hold the sway.

The sky was clear, and yet a shadow passed—
A cloudless shade that did not block the sun.
And Rosie froze, then turned and gave a smile.
"That," she said soft, "was something I don't know."
The tree agreed. Not every dream is known—
Some pass like guests who leave us more alone.

She climbed again, this time without a goal.
Each pawstep light, each branch a whispered note.
And when she reached the crook she called her own,
She didn't curl, but sat and faced the wind.
"Today," she said, "I'm not the one who asks.
Today, I let the world compose the mask."

The tree let fall a blossom near her ear.
It did not touch, but drifted in her field.
And Rosie watched it spin and twist and sway—
A dream in air that never met the ground.
"I think," she said, "I'll never need to know.
The dream was not a where but how to *go*."

The wind grew thick with sun and scent and spring.
The branches swayed in rhythm soft and round.
And Rosie closed her eyes, not out of need,
But as a way to make the silence bloom.
She dreamed again, though this time while awake—
A dream that did not ask the world to break.

The tree, though still, had shifted in its rings.
A new alignment formed from all she gave.
And every word she'd spilled upon the bark
Had grown into a silence shaped like thought.
They did not end the dream or speak it through—
They simply let it pass and become true.

And so the tree and cat endured the day—
Not changed by dream, but opened by its reach.
For dreams are not escape or cryptic sign—
They are the way we ask without a speech.
And in the hush that followed light and theme,
The world itself became a kind of dream.

Part IV

The morning came with something strange and still.
The breeze arrived but didn't touch the grass.
The sky was pale, the clouds were slow to form,
And birds forgot to speak until they flew.
The tree, though rooted deep in ancient ground,
Felt something stir that hadn't been around.

Its limbs were bare of cat, its shade was wide.
No paw had pressed the bark since yesterday.
And though the trunk was firm and full of breath,
A silence grew that didn't quite belong.
It wasn't loss, nor waiting tinged with fear—
But something near the shape of not yet here.

The river moved, but lacked its mirrored weight.
The reeds stood tall, but bent with no command.
The wind arrived in halves, then left again—
As if it sought a rhythm it had lost.
And through it all, the tree began to bend,
Not from the air, but from the thought of friend.

Then in the brush, a flicker brushed the light.
A tail like ink, a step without a sound.
And Rosie came, unhurried as the tide—
As if the world had never marked her gone.
The tree grew still, then stilled itself again,
And knew that time had folded back to when.

She did not leap at first or speak her name.
She walked the path she always walked before.
But something in her pace was wrapped in pause—
A measure not of doubt, but of return.
As though she knew the moment she arrived
Would not be marked by how she was described.

The tree let down a branch she used to climb.
It curved with ease, like memory in bark.
And Rosie saw, and leapt without a thought—
But halfway up, she stopped and closed her eyes.
She breathed as though the moment had to hold
A silence shaped by all she hadn't told.

Then up again, her body light with poise,
She landed in the crook that knew her best.
She turned around, then curled into herself—
But didn't sleep, and didn't start to speak.
The tree felt something ripple through its rings—
A hush that bore the weight of traveling things.

"I went," she said, "not far, but far enough.
Not wide in miles, but deep in what I mean.
I didn't leave because I couldn't stay—
I left because the staying had grown still."
The tree replied, "And stillness needs to grow—
By learning how to bend and not to know."

She purred, but not the kind that comes with ease.
It rumbled like a voice behind a thought.
"I thought I might return and feel the same.
But now I see, returning means I've changed.
I am the cat you knew and did not know—
The one who left to let the self regrow."

The tree did not respond with limb or leaf.
It did not need to name what it could feel.
For Rosie's presence carried all the proof—
A different silence gathered at her side.
And in that hush, the bark began to shift—
As if the time away had been a gift.

She stretched along the branch she once called home.
The bark was rougher now, but held her well.
"I didn't dream," she said, "not like before—
At least not dreams that change or try to stay.
I only watched the world behind its veil,
And let it move without the need to trail."

The tree could feel the rhythm of her breath—
Not hurried, not at peace, but full of thought.
It did not press for answers or for cause;
It simply held the space her pause had brought.
For not all questions come in word or claw—
Some leave behind the shape of silent awe.

She looked down through the boughs and past the grass.
The Clyde moved on, as steady as before.
"It's strange," she said, "how nothing seems to shift,
Yet every blade has changed its place with time."
The tree replied, "The world returns in loops.
It doesn't wait—but everything still groups."

She flicked her tail and tapped a higher limb.
"Did you," she asked, "imagine I was lost?"
The tree stood firm and did not turn or lean,
But let its silence answer through the grain.
"I do not call what's far from me away—
I only wait to see if it will stay."

She nodded, though no one could see the sign.
"I walked through fields that looked like folded thought.
The wind there didn't move—it only leaned.
The sun arrived but never chose to shine."
The tree imagined wind without a chase,
And knew she'd wandered through a changeless place.

"And still," she said, "I never felt alone.
The path I walked had something near my side.
Not voice, not touch—but maybe just the sense
That every place still bore a thread of here.
And now I know: returning is a fold—
A corner where the past and present hold."

The tree received her words like water does—
Not rushed, not spilled, but carried to the root.
And something in its inner rings began
To turn, not quick, but just enough to stretch.
For what returns is never what once went—
It carries light the branches never lent.

She settled in the crook and closed one eye.
Her breathing slow, but wakeful in its pace.
"I watched the moon forget to leave the sky.
I watched a shadow pause and turn to glass.
And nothing told me what to think or say—
So I became the silence of the day."

The tree, who knew the silence she had shaped,
Now found it changed, as though it had been aged.
It still was calm, but held a second tone—
A chord that hadn't been there once before.
The hush she brought was not the hush she left—
It bore the signs of something softly cleft.

She placed her paw against the limb once more.
The groove she found had deepened just a touch.
"I left," she said, "to see if I would miss—
But missing isn't quite the way it works.
It's not a pull, it's more a widening—
A way the world begins remembering."

The tree let fall a blossom down the path.
It twirled in air, then came to rest in moss.
And Rosie watched it land, then said at last,
"That's what I was. A drift. A turning bit."
The tree said, "Even drift returns to root—
It only needed time before its route."

She licked her paw and cleaned her thoughtful brow.
Then looked beyond the boughs toward rising light.
"The world feels smaller now, but not unkind.
I used to chase the edges, now I wait.
I do not need to grasp what moves too fast—
I only need to notice what will last."

The tree admired that her breath was slow.
The tempo of her thought no longer raced.
She once had asked what form or self could be—
Now she inquired through the space she gave.
And every pause she shaped became a stem—
A quiet root that reached and held the limb.

"I once believed return meant something failed.
A loop, a back-step, something left undone.
But now I see return's another form—
Not of retreat, but spiralling into one."
The tree, long fond of rings that loop and grow,
Felt something stir where it had long been slow.

A single breeze began to stroke the leaves.
It didn't push—it only passed and saw.
And Rosie blinked, then turned her ear to it,
As though it bore a story not yet told.
"The wind," she said, "remembers how I sound.
It plays the tune of where I once was found."

She climbed once more, but not with urgency.
Her movements now were settled, yet alive.
Each step she took returned what she had learned—
Not spoken, but in muscle, breath, and line.
The tree did not applaud or interject—
It only bent to where her thoughts reflect.

She stared out at the water for a while.
The ripples seemed to echo what she'd been.
"I see myself," she said, "in things that move—
Not for escape, but just to feel the sway.
The self I am today is not a break—
But what the last one made when wide awake."

The tree remembered seasons long ago—
When limbs were small, and roots still searched for stone.
It did not mourn the bark it used to wear,
Nor grieve the leaves it dropped upon the ground.
Instead, it saw in Rosie now the truth:
That change is not a leaving, but a proof.

She curled again, but not to close or hide.
She curled to keep the shape of what she'd grown.
A circle made of breath and day and thought—
A form that didn't end, but simply held.
The tree leaned just enough to touch her fur,
And knew her quiet had begun to purr.

The Clyde continued, constant in its drift.
The reeds had long resumed their gentle talk.
But here, within the shade of leaf and cat,
A silence softer than the wind took hold.
And in that hush, they met for something true—
Not something new, but something seen anew.

She blinked again, then rose upon the branch.
Her tail arched up, a banner and a bow.
"I do not need to say I have returned,"
She said. "I'm here, and here is all I am."
The tree replied, "And here is what you gave—
A self that left and found the self you save."

And neither one required further phrase.
The air grew warm, the morning reached its height.
They sat, as once they had, as now they do—
But every echo held a brighter ring.
For nothing left had come back quite the same,
And still, the tree would call her by no name.

No name was needed, nor was mark or sign.
The limb she touched was shaped by her alone.
Not scratched or bent, but changed by quiet weight—
A memory that didn't need a form.
The tree would hold that pressure in its grain,
And Rosie, too, would hold what did remain.

She looked down once and watched a beetle crawl.
Its path was slow, yet sure beneath the shade.
And Rosie smiled, though not in human ways—
Her whiskers twitched, her spine grew soft with peace.
"I think," she said, "we don't return to place—
We only find again what holds our trace."

The tree agreed, and sent a scentless bloom
To rest beside the crook of her front paw.
It had no colour bright enough to name—
But shimmered like the hush between two thoughts.
And Rosie, seeing it, did not respond—
Except to stay, and not to move beyond.

She let the wind pass over, let it go.
She did not chase, and yet she did not stop.
Her stillness held the grace of all return—
A poise that said: I left, but not apart.
And in her fur, the memory had curled—
Not of a trip, but of a turning world.

The sun began to tip into descent.
The shadows stretched, and morning passed its torch.
Yet nothing in the tree or cat had dulled—
For what had deepened now began to gleam.
The quiet that they shared was not from rest—
But from the knowing that they had been blessed.

She purred again, a tone both old and new—
A sound that spoke of every path she'd known.
It resonated through the bark and wood—
And echoed where the dreams had once been stored.
The tree stood tall, and did not seek to bend—
For now it knew: the journey has no end.

She did not ask to speak of where she'd gone.
She did not need to name the places passed.
For every breath she drew beside the bark
Was filled with more than any tale could hold.
And in her eyes, the silence brightly shone—
A light that said, I leave, and yet I'm home.

And so they sat, not changed in who they were,
But deeper still in how they came to be.
The cat, the tree, the river and the sky—
No part was new, and none were quite the same.
For those who leave and choose again to stay
Return as roots that learned a different way.

The wind grew bolder, curling through the leaves,
But Rosie stayed, unmoved except in gaze.
She watched the world as if it knew her name,
Though neither voice nor call was ever made.
The tree stood quiet, offering no cue—
For being seen was all it had to do.

She stretched once more, not idly but with grace—
A bow drawn back to show the strength it keeps.
"I once believed," she said, "in sharp goodbyes.
But now I know the better way is soft.
A change so slow it looks like staying still—
A kind of leap that happens when you will."

The tree had never spoken of farewell.
It did not track arrivals, did not mark
The moments when a branch grew long or short—
It only grew, and bore what time had asked.
So when she left, it did not mourn or call—
It only kept the space where she might fall.

"I did not go to find what I had lost,"
She said, her tail curled gently round her feet.
"I went to see if I could be alone,
And find myself not wanting to escape."
The tree replied, "And what did silence show?"
She answered, "That the self is what you grow."

She leapt down low, then traced a ring of roots.
Each step she took remembered where she'd been.
She paused where once she'd whispered to the bark—
And touched it now without a single word.
The tree received her paw without surprise—
The path she'd walked was clear within its size.

The grass had changed, but not in ways she said.
Its blades were tipped in gold where once was green.
The moss had thickened where she used to sit,
The bark was darker where she leaned to dream.
And Rosie, circling once more near the shade,
Saw that the world had kept the shape she made.

She did not claim it, nor did she retreat.
She let the world become what it had missed.
A cat, a tree, the notion of return—
Not as a loop, but spiral drawn through thought.
The tree stood still, but knew what she had taught:
That presence holds more meaning than it sought.

A crow flew past, then vanished down the bend.
Its cry was sharp, but neither one looked up.
They didn't need the world to prove its pace—
They had the hush that lingered in their bark.
And Rosie, glancing once into the air,
Let go the urge to ever chase it there.

She laid once more upon her chosen perch.
Her form was smaller than it once had been—
Not shrunk in size, but folded into self,
As if the distance made her mind more whole.
And in the crook where bark had shaped her seat,
She found a calm that wrapped around her feet.

The light had turned from gold to something deep—
A tone between the blue and fading grey.
And Rosie blinked, then whispered to the air,
"I never left. I only moved through thought."
The tree, in kind, let out a gentle creak—
A sound not made for words, but just to speak.

She purred again, not loud but like a stream.
The sound slid through the roots and out the rings.
The tree, once shaped by silence more than song,
Now felt the sound as part of how it grew.
And though the purring wasn't meant to last,
Its echo settled deep within the past.

"I'll go again," she said, "but not to leave.
I'll go to grow, and then I'll come again."
The tree replied, "Then every step you take
Will press its weight in paths I've yet to feel.
I do not move, but still I walk with you—
Through shade and sound and everything you do."

She flicked her tail, then looked toward rising mist.
The Clyde was whispering of other shores.
But Rosie didn't stir, nor stretch to chase—
Her eyes were full, and still, and made of here.
"I used to think the world was mine to know.
Now I believe it's something I outgrow."

The tree let fall a seed upon the soil.
It did not name it gift, nor call it sign.
But Rosie turned, and saw it settle there—
And nodded once, as if she understood.
Some things are planted not to be a tree,
But just to show how quiet things can be.

They sat again, like how they sat before.
No speech, no game, no riddles pulled apart.
But all the depth of every dream and doubt
Was present in the silence that they kept.
And in the hush between the Clyde and cloud,
A bond more strong than any vow was vowed.

The sun dropped low, the wind began to fade.
The day was folding, petal after petal.
And Rosie lay with eyes still open wide,
As if to catch the final piece of light.
She didn't move, nor plan, nor mark the hour—
She let the moment pass, and watched its power.

She dreamed, perhaps, though still beneath the leaves.
But now her dreams were neither wild nor vast.
They curled like roots around a certain truth—
That home is not a place, but how we pass.
And when she stirred, the tree could feel the thread
That every pawstep left where she had tread.

The stars arrived, but not with ceremony.
They blinked like thoughts the sky forgot to keep.
And Rosie watched them with a knowing face—
Not wonder, but the calm of one who's seen.
"I used to ask if I would be," she said.
"Now I just ask how long I'll stay instead."

The tree, unmoving, let her question live.
It didn't try to cage it in a phrase.
For some ideas are meant to stretch and sway—
Like branches leaning out to touch the haze.
And Rosie, feeling no reply was made,
Felt fuller still within the soft cascade.

The wind returned, as if from far away.
It moved through branch and fur with quiet pace.
And Rosie blinked, then stood upon the bough—
But did not leap, and did not make a sound.
She simply stayed, like memory held true—
A thought that knew exactly what to do.

She pressed her side against the trunk and sighed.
The sound was small, but heavy with her age.
Not age in years, but in the days she'd shaped—
The ones she spent becoming what she meant.
The tree received the sigh and held it fast—
And deep inside, it planted it to last.

She said, "I will not change unless I must.
But if I do, I'll change with all I've kept."
The tree said, "That is all that growth requires—
To carry forward what the silence left."
And in that vow, though quiet and unclear,
A future bent its shape a little near.

The river slowed, though only in their gaze.
The reeds grew still, the dusk began to hum.
And Rosie, now as weightless as the dusk,
Became a shape that light could almost pass.
She did not ask for end or start or tone—
She only stayed where time had made her known.

The stars began to bloom like ancient thought.
The tree stood tall, the cat lay soft and low.
And everything between them now had grown—
A space, a thread, a soundless kind of glow.
They did not move, and yet the night was full—
As if the hush itself had grown a pull.

She closed her eyes, but not from any need.
She closed them like a door not meant to lock.
And in that gesture, all the world stood still—
For silence has a gravity of its own.
The tree, though firm, did not resist the sway—
It let the hush become the shape of day.

The moon rose slow, its face a softened coin.
Its light was not for truth, but for return.
And Rosie glowed beneath it like a tale—
One told in fur, in purr, in quiet stance.
The tree looked on and saw in every ring
The echo of her leap, her look, her spring.

"I'm not a part of you," she softly said.
"I am myself. But where you are, I rest."
The tree replied, "And I am not your path—
But where you turn, I always bend to meet."
And in that mutual shape, they found their peace—
Not ownership, but something like release.

A blossom dropped and landed on her back.
She did not flinch, nor lift her head to look.
She let it rest like thought upon a stream—
A symbol that required no debate.
And though the wind might blow it off by dawn,
The weight of it had already been drawn.

The night grew thick, but they had grown more thin—
Not weakened, but made closer to the sky.
Their boundaries dissolved in shared return—
A cat, a tree, a place that did not end.
And though the world kept turning past the shore,
They stayed inside the hush they'd shaped before.

So ends no end, and starts no formal start.
The cat will go and come, the tree will stay.
But now they share a thread not seen or touched—
A bond that bends through silence, light, and play.
For what returns is never what it seemed—
It carries all it was—and all it dreamed.

Poems of Mystery

The Breath Behind Me

Part I

I took the path beneath the ancient trees,
Where every limb was twisted out of shape.
The wind had died; the world was ill at ease,
As though the woods had closed without escape.

My dog ran free, her collar loose and light.
She darted through the underbrush ahead.
Her steps were sharp, her coat a blur of white,
A living thing where everything else was dead.

I called her name. She turned and gave a glance,
Then vanished in the bramble and the mist.
Her paws disturbed the stones in sudden dance,
The sound was soft, but something in it hissed.

At first, her presence held my fear at bay.
No ghost would walk where loyal beasts have gone.
But when she strayed too far or moved away,
The forest felt too wide, too old, too drawn.

Each rustling branch, each scatter of a stone—
My nerves would jolt and twist inside my skin.
I could not tell when I was still alone,
Nor where the breath began or I did end.

It came behind—too close, too real, too slow.
A warmth upon my neck I could not name.
It did not rush. It merely chose to show
That I was not the master of this game.

I turned. She barked. I flinched. My skin went cold.
A branch had snapped—but was it her or not?
I saw no one, no shape that I could hold—
Just trees like teeth and leaves like flecks of rot.

She sniffed the air. Her ears turned back and flat.
She didn't wag. She didn't make a sound.
She crouched. I followed. Then she froze at that—
A spot where shadows gathered on the ground.

I whispered low, "Come here." She did not budge.
Instead she whined—a long, uneasy tone.
And something in the air began to nudge—
A shape without a voice, a breath alone.

She bolted forward, silent through the brush.
I watched her tail dissolve into the haze.
I chased—but only met the timeless hush
That watches us through trees in ancient days.

I shouted once. The forest swallowed whole
My voice as if it never had been born.
I stood alone, and something took control—
The air grew thick, the dusk began to warn.

A second step that wasn't mine replied.
The leaves bent back, the soil gave a sigh.
The breath was back—beside me now, not tied
To wind or sound, but *will*—and standing nigh.

The path grew tight. The trees began to lean.
Their limbs were wrong, their trunks too smooth, too bare.
And somewhere deep beyond the twisted green,
I felt a pair of eyes beneath the air.

I walked. I had no choice. My limbs obeyed.
My body stiff, my mind a wheel of ash.
And every step I took, the darkness stayed,
And somewhere just behind, the shadows thrashed.

I felt a tug—a memory, a grin.
A voice I knew from childhood whispered low.
A presence pressed its silence through my skin—
And all I'd buried threatened now to show.

The breath grew sharp. The wind refused to move.
The path beneath my feet began to ring.
My fingers clenched. My spine forgot its groove.
The forest dared me now to see the thing.

And then—I turned. I broke the sacred pact.
The rule we learn but never know to name.
I turned. I faced what silence held intact.
I looked. I saw—
But it did not have a frame.

It wasn't beast. It wasn't wind or man.
It wasn't fog or tree or crawling night.
It *was*, and in its gaze, the stars began
To shake like leaves and tremble out of sight.

I could not move. My breath was not my own.
It stole from me, and filled me with a taste
Of soil, and rain, and time gone overgrown—
And grief that moved too deep, too dark, too traced.

And then—I blinked. It vanished like a sigh.
The trees stood still. The path returned, though cracked.
The dog was gone. The sky was whisper-dry.
And something still behind me held me tracked.

I stumbled on, though nothing made me move.
No voice. No force. Just trembling in my knee.
I felt the hush again, begin to prove
That all I'd seen was never meant to be.

Yet still it walked. It did not speak or show.
But I could hear it drawing close in breath.
Not swift. Not loud. But steady, soft, and slow—
Like someone pacing just beyond my death.

I reached the clearing. Dawn was faint and thin.
The edge of wood revealed the moor and field.
But in my chest, the thing remained within—
And would not leave, and would not be revealed.

I turned once more. I said, "Then come with me."
It did not speak, but neither did it go.
And so we walked—my shadowed company—
Together down the path that none should know.

You ask me now if I was not alone—
I say I was, and also say I'm not.
Some things are with us, even when long gone.
Some breath remains, and never can be caught.

Part II

I boarded late, the lights were humming low.
The carriage breathed a soft mechanical sigh.
The doors had closed. The wheels began to go.
Ten minutes' ride beneath a bleary sky.

My shift was done. I leaned into the screen,
A flashing scroll of texts and vacant feeds.
The world was small, the glass a glowing sheen—
Enough to blur the ache beneath my needs.

The car was near to empty. Just a few
Still hung their heads or blinked their way through thought.
A builder's boots, a woman's weary shoe—
And I, alone in webs my phone had caught.

The driver's voice announced a coming stop.
The speakers buzzed and crackled through the air.
Then silence fell again, without a drop—
No cough, no page, no shift, no breath to spare.

The checker came, a nod, and passed me by.
He vanished through the door into his cell.
The windows stared with dark and empty eye.
The train picked up a rhythm smooth and fell.

I barely moved. The rumble held me firm.
The plastic seat was neither hard nor kind.
The neon lights were cold, and every term
Of comfort felt unglued inside my mind.

It started small—a pressure, then a still.
A change in air too subtle to define.
A weight across my chest, a binding will—
The taste of dust along a broken spine.

I looked, half-sure, and yet I had to look.
The seat ahead had been, I swore, unclaimed.
But now it felt as though it somehow took
A form too blank, too near, too undefined.

The fabric bent—was that a shift? A crease?
I blinked, but still the shape refused to hold.
It stirred without a motion, brought no peace—
A silence thicker than the metal cold.

I dropped my phone. The screen went dark and blind.
My breath grew short. The ceiling pressed me down.
The tracks beneath kept hammering my mind—
A steady pound beneath the whole train's crown.

I watched the space ahead. I would not blink.
I could not hear the world beyond that chair.
My body swayed. My stomach dared to sink.
And still I saw the shadow seated there.

No face, no limbs, but not a hollow space.
It was a thing. It knew that I could tell.
Its presence leaned into the time and place—
Too dense to break, too real to dispel.

I dared not cough. I dared not lift my hand.
The air around was stitched with threads of dread.
The train moved on, a slow and ghostly band,
And I sat locked, with sweat across my head.

The lights above me flickered, dimmed, then stayed.
The walls seemed tighter than a breath should bear.
The window showed no colour, only shade—
A glaze of glass that watched me in despair.

I whispered once, then twice: "Is someone there?"
No change, no sign, no answer to the sound.
But still I felt the shadow softly stare—
As if my name were spoken underground.

I shut my eyes. I tried to count my breath.
But counting failed. My lungs began to lock.
I thought of graves, of soil, of silent death—
Of dogs long gone, and paths beneath the rock.

The metal walls seemed closer than before.
The windows stretched, the space began to tilt.
The seat across me wasn't seat, but door—
A gate to something deeper than my guilt.

My thoughts grew wild: Had I once met this thing?
A dream? A place? A night I can't recall?
Had I disturbed some depth beneath a wing
Of time, and now it hunts me through it all?

The carriage groaned. The engine's pulse grew slow.
The voice again announced a nearby bend.
But no one moved. The air refused to flow.
And I could not distinguish foe from friend.

I rose too quick. The cabin seemed to reel.
My knees were weak, my vision stretched and spun.
And still that seat, that weight, that presence real,
Sat watching me with eyes that burned like none.

It touched me not, but every nerve was struck.
A million thoughts were buried under one.
The train had stopped. The doors had screamed and stuck.
But no one moved, not even for the sun.

I faced it square. My throat was cracked and dry.
I said, "You're real."
It moved, but nothing said.
It did not rise. It did not blink or sigh—
Just lingered in the space where silence bled.

I stepped away. It did not follow yet.
It only watched, if "watching" it could do.
And something in my soul began to sweat—
A memory I never fully knew.

The doors stayed shut. The silence wrapped me round.
The figure's weight pressed deeper into space.
A pressure moved beneath, not over ground—
A slow collapse of breath, of time, of place.

But then, at once, the speakers cracked to life:
"This train will soon arrive at Gilshochill."
The voice was dull, mechanical—but rife
With something warm that bent the shadow's will.

The seat ahead grew paler, faint, and thin.
Its outline blurred, its gravity withdrew.
As if the name had burned away its skin,
And light returned where dark had fastened true.

I rose. The doors slid open with a sigh.
The scent of moss and diesel met my face.
I stepped beyond the rail, beneath the sky,
And felt the loosening of that unseen brace.

No one got off but me. The platform bare,
The lights above me blinking, weak and still.
Yet I could breathe again the open air—
The name had saved me: simple Gilshochill.

I turned once more. The train was sliding past.
Its windows dim. The haunted seat was gone.
But in the glass, one shape remained and cast
Its gaze toward me, unmoving and alone.

It watched from where I'd sat. It did not blink.
A darker patch upon the window's gleam.
Its face was lost, its edges blurred to ink—
But watching me, as steady as a dream.

The train moved on. The night fell back to black.
I stood there in the hush the diesel spilled.
I didn't run. I did not turn my back.
I wondered if that gaze would now be stilled.

Or will it ride, in carriages behind,
To other souls, when lights begin to fade?
A whisper pressing softly on the mind,
A breath across the glass that we evade.

And though I stepped into the city's breath,
And felt the ground beneath me firm and wide,
There lingers still that taste, that scent of death—
The one who rides the silence of the Clyde.

Part III

The world has changed, though no one else can tell—
The streetlight's flicker now implies a threat.
Where once the silence soothed, it casts a spell,
And shadows stretch where light and stillness met.

A peace has ruled, or seemed to, since that night
The train exhaled and left me at the hill.
Yet ever since, the corners bite with fright,
And something waits beyond my human will.

The woods have grown too quiet for the birds,
And branches arch like claws in prayer-less pose.
The wind will hiss, though never speak in words,
Its meaning smothered, like a throat that froze.

At first I walked with care and careful eyes,
My dog beside me, leash-less but alert.
I scanned the limbs that split the copper skies,
And dared believe that time had dulled the hurt.

Yet something followed—never touched the path,
Nor stepped on twigs, nor dragged across the loam,
But breathed, I swear, and carried living wrath,
And stirred the air like dreams that flee from home.

I came to love the presence in its lack.
The peace that once unnerved me now was dear.
I feared its coming but I longed it back—
To see, to know, to feel the thing I fear.

The quiet turned to habit, then to need.
A man who once was hunted now would call.
I waited in the dark and dared to plead,
But silence held its breath and gave me all.

And then it came again—a change in hue.
The autumn light was bronze, the dusk was cold.
My breath would fog the room as if it knew
That something dead had come to make me fold.

The dog was calm, too calm—no growl, no cry.
The vapour from my lips dissolved too slow.
I walked through rooms and whispered low "not I..."
But felt a pull from where I dared not go.

I searched the flat. Each drawer, each open door.
The kettle cold, the windows locked and shut.
My own reflection passed across the floor,
But in the hallway stood a deeper cut.

A crack—just that. A gap that should not be.
The space between the doorframe and the shade.
And in that gap, a presence turned from me,
Its back a cloak where dread and shape were made.

It stood. It stirred. But never once it spoke.
And though I whispered out, it did not flinch.
Its form was smoke, but shaped as if it woke
From ancient sleep and dreamt without a pinch.

I sat. I dared to match it, face to face.
No breath, no blink, no twitch betrayed its plan.
Yet something old began to fill the space—
A peace that frightens more than terror can.

The light grew dim, though none had dimmed the lamp.
The dog had vanished to another room.
The air was thick, as if with ancient damp,
And silence hummed a low and pulsing doom.

The figure turned. My heart stopped in my chest.
I wished to run, but limbs were carved
And what I saw could never be confessed—
The shadow bore the features of my face.

Its eyes, my eyes; its breath, my stolen breath;
A perfect shape that time could not erase.
It was myself, but hollowed, stretched and still.
A mask of me with nothing left behind.

Yet in its gaze I felt a deeper will,
A whisper older than the human mind.
It stepped with solemn grace and closed the space.
Its body swam like smoke in rigid lines.

No footfall rang, no tremor broke its pace—
It moved through air as ink through spilt designs.
I wept. My lips were mute with frozen fear.
The tears ran hot, but I was locked in place.

It mouthed a word, too faint to reach the ear,
And stared as if to blot me from all trace.
It spoke again, a murmur through my bones,
Like wind that swells from graves beneath the sea.

It muttered low in dry, relentless tones—
"Necessity," it said, then said to me:
"Necessity," again, and louder still.
The sound began to bloom within my head.

I tried to scream, to run, to break its will—
But I was made of ice, already dead.
It reached with both its hands and gripped my ears,
Its fingers smoke and shadow, rough with age.

I shrieked, I bucked, I burned with all my fears,
But it held tight, the poet and the page.
The dark collapsed. All sound became a thread.
And through that thread, a silver silence shone.

A point of light emerged where vision bled—
A dot that grew, until my breath was gone.
I saw a reel of moments not my own,
Yet all were mine, replayed from different view.

I saw the woods, the train, the nights alone,
And something always watching, always true.
The boy I was, with dreams too large for sleep,
Was never quite alone within his bed.

A presence lived where shadows dared to creep,
And whispered secrets in his little head.
The games I played, the chairs I pulled aside,
Were never empty—not the way I thought.

For I had made a friend who could not hide,
A silent one, whom waking time forgot.
It fed on fear but never meant me harm.
It grew when I grew restless in the dark.

Its voice was low, but always held a charm,
A single word that left the smallest mark.
"Necessity"—the curse of knowing truth.
The hunger not for joy, but for the flame.

The thirst to find the horror in one's youth,
And wear it like a skin, without a name.
I watched my life as if through stranger's eyes.
Each step I took, it followed, cloaked in dust.

The street, the wood, the train beneath the skies—
It followed not in hate, but in disgust.
It saw what I denied, and drank it in.
My failures, shame, and petty, quiet lies.

It saw me weak, and branded me in sin.
It wore my shape, but never blinked or cried.
And now, I knew. It fed, because it must.
A creature drawn to dying, soul by soul.

It waits for life to tremble, then combust,
To take what's raw and make the broken whole.
The vision burst. I fell back to the floor.
The flat returned, the dog now at my side.

But there it stood, that shape I feared before,
Repeating low the word I once denied:
"Necessity…" and closer still it came.
Its voice like winter boiling through my mind.

It bent to me, and whispered out my name—
And then I knew I'd never leave it behind.
It leaned so near, its breath became my own.
A chill, yet warm with something faintly sweet.

Like earth just turned, or seeds in soil unknown—
Decay and birth both trembling at my feet.
I could not rise. My legs had turned to thread.
My arms were numb, my lungs began to freeze.

It circled me with eyes that had not bled,
Yet knew the weight of many centuries.
"You are the one," it said, without a mouth.
"You called me with your silence, not your scream."

Its voice was wind, that wound from north to south,
That scattered sense and sense of self and dream.
"You needed me," it said, "when you were five.
You needed me again when love had failed.

You needed me to prove you were alive—
And now, you've aged, but still your heart has paled."
I shook my head, but couldn't make a sound.
It hovered just a breath beyond my skin.

Its fingers stroked the air and swept around,
As if to trace the cage I held within.
My dog, now still, no longer barked or stirred.
Her eyes met mine, and in them was a plea.

I whispered low, then failed to form a word.
The shadow cast its silence over me.
It touched the wall, and every frame fell down.
The windows darkened, though the sun was high.

The clocks all stopped, the time itself unwound.
The breath I drew came sharp, a swallowed cry.
It moved into the room as if it bled.
The shape was smoke, but full of cruel design.

It stepped where once I'd read and once I'd bled,
And claimed my chair, as if that chair were mine.
"Sit down," it said, and I obeyed its will.
It faced me like a mirror in the storm.

I saw myself, but nothing else was still—
I saw the shape of me before the form.
It mimicked me in gesture, tilt, and thought.
Each blink, each twitch, each tremble of the hand.

A copy born from something I forgot—
Or something born to break what I had planned.
"You will forget the way you walked alone.
You'll think you chose the path, but it was me.

Each door you passed, each turn you called your own,
I was the breath that made you choose and flee."
The room grew dim, the air began to thrum.
A pulse beneath the floor, behind the walls.

I heard a knocking—soft, and then it hummed—
A rhythm born from tombs and funeral halls.
It reached again and placed its hand on mine.
The hand was mine, and yet I couldn't feel.

Its nails were blackened roots of some old vine.
Its skin was dust, but also iron and steel.
It leaned and touched its head against my brow.
The tears welled up again and would not stop.

It whispered, "You have always feared me. Now—
It's time to drink, and taste the final drop."
The walls began to crack with unseen weight.
The books ignited, slow and blue with flame.

The ceiling wept with blackness, cold and great.
The mirrors shook, but still the shadow came.
It spoke no more. It merely held me still.
My breath grew faint, and all my nerves unspooled.

It pressed my mind until it bent my will—
I wept again, but knew that I was schooled.
It opened wide its chest and showed the void.
Inside were all the faces I had worn.

The smiles I faked, the moments I'd destroyed.
The hearts I'd left, the nights I'd spent forlorn.
And from that void, a thousand voices rose.
Each one a me I'd buried long ago.

They sang of loss, and pain I'd never chose,
But chose me like the tide must choose the flow.
I begged. I cried. I asked it, "Why not peace?"
The shadow grinned, or might have if it could.

It whispered, "Peace is where all hungers cease—
But even in your joy, you knew I stood."
"You danced through days pretending I was gone.
But look around—your silence grew too loud.

You mourned the dark, then begged it be redrawn.
You summoned me. Now wear me like a shroud."
I screamed, and silence broke into a bell.
The shadow shook, then sank inside my chest.

My back arched high, as if I'd drunk from hell.
My veins ran black, my heart forgot to rest.
And then, a hush. A dreadful, sacred pause.
The dog arose and licked my bloodless hand.

The flat stood still, as though the world withdrew,
And left me changed in ways I could not stand.
I stood. I breathed. My breath came white and slow.
The sun had fled, and dusk had drowned the light.

The walls were bare, the mirror ceased to glow.
And somewhere far, a train cried through the night.
I walked toward the door but did not turn.
Behind me, silence pulsed with something grim.

And in that stillness, somewhere deep and stern,
I heard a whisper, slow and frail and dim—
"Necessity," again, and in my voice.
A truth I never asked, but had to learn.

A curse that mocks the one who has no choice—
To feed, to haunt, to wait, and then return.
The night came fast. The stars were dull and few.
The wind had teeth and scraped across the trees.

I closed the door, but darkness still came through.
I knelt, and begged the shadow, "Let me be."
But there it stood, inside the glass once more.
Its hands were mine, its eyes no longer strange.

It whispered through the seams and through the floor:
"Become what must, for you will never change."
And though I tried to leave, to run, to flee,
It walked beside me, silent, step for step.

It smiled when I was crying secretly.
It held me while I dreamed and while I slept.
And now I sit. The evening folds in slow.
The breath before me dances on the air.

I feel the dark behind begin to grow.
And turn—though I know nothing will be there.
But still I turn. The fear has grown refined.
It's like a prayer, a rite, a ritual creed.
It waits for me, the tremble in the mind.

It is the want I never chose to need.
I stare into the window's paling light.
The sky is grey, the hour drawing nigh.
I feel it now—no need to look for sight—

The breath, the breath, the breath behind me.

The Woman in the Café

I stood behind the counter, calm and bright,
The day was nearing dusk, the closing hour.
A woman stepped inside beneath the light,
Her presence bore a strange and quiet power.

Of Asian cast, but not of place or time—
Her voice a citrus twist, both sharp and dry.
It snapped the air in rhythm, out of rhyme,
A tune that danced but never met the eye.

She ordered herbal tea, her gaze askew,
Unsure if she should speak or simply stare.
I helped her with the menu, patient, true,
She murmured thanks, then vanished to her chair.

My work resumed. The clatter of the tray,
The hiss of steam, the sweeping of the floor.
But half an hour in, she came my way,
And spoke again, then lingered even more.

She asked me things, her voice a glinting blade,
Too close to kind, too soft to be unkind.
A pulse of tension throbbed beneath the trade—
I smiled and hoped that she would read the sign.

She left, but only just; her feet still warm,
She hovered near, then came again to me.
This time she placed no order—broke the norm.
She came, it seemed, for conversation's fee.

She asked me of my dog—how we connect,
What words we share, what silence speaks the most.
But then her questions swerved. I could detect
A tone too smooth, too intimate, too close.

She offered me a chance to meet again,
To try a form of speechless, sacred talk.
She said she'd show me ways to pierce the brain,
To reach the soul without the need to walk.

I smiled and nodded, though my chest was tight,
I gave an email, just to end the game.
Her voice had dulled the air, had blurred the light—
And when she said goodbye, she used my name.

I never hated hearing it before,
But from her mouth it curdled in my blood.
It echoed like a hand against a door
That opens not with welcome, but with flood.

She sent the mail. I did not dare to read.
I hit delete, and told myself, it's done.
Yet still her voice would in my dreaming feed—
Like dripping taps that never see the sun.

And then one day, while serving in a rush,
Among the crowd, she surfaced like a stone.
The café roared, but time began to hush.
She looked at me, and I was not alone.

Her mouth hung slack a moment, like a mask,
Then twitched and spoke, resuming her old tone.
She asked again the things no one would ask,
And all the while, I felt she was alone.

But more than that—I feared what lay beneath.
A hollowed thing in skin that still could smile.
Her words, though odd, concealed a darker wreath,
A pressure rising slowly all the while.

She stopped, apologised, and took a seat.
She read a book, she stared into the glass.
But moments passed before I heard her feet,
And she was there again—she would not pass.

My colleagues asked if I had known her well.
Their voices held concern, a quiet dread.
They saw the way she walked, the things she'd tell,
The things that made the colour leave my head.

And I began to fear what she might do.
Would she appear alone beneath the moon?
Would she step past the counter, past the queue,
And stand too close, and whisper of some tune?

Would hands that never trembled take my wrist?
Would eyes that never blinked begin to burn?
Was all of this some nightmare in a mist—
Or worse, a truth from which there's no return?

The hours passed. She'd come, then drift away.
And though she never raised her voice or hand,
Her gaze began to peel my guard away—
Like waves that wear the sharpness from the sand.

I watched her once upon the CCTV.
She sat alone, and stirred her cup of tea.
She stared outside as if she meant to leave—
But something held her still and fast and free.

Her mouth moved once, though no one sat nearby.
She spoke to air, or something I could not.
And then she laughed—a single note, too dry.
It snapped the wire of calm within the spot.

She vanished with the dusk. The air was clear.
The tea had cooled. Her cup still bore a ring.
But something darker settled in my ear—
The echo of a song I shouldn't sing.

And since that day I flinch at every sound,
At every door that opens with a creak.
I sense her steps upon the mottled ground,
Her voice that waits each time I start to speak.

She might be gone, or hiding in the rain.
She might be close, or watching from the street.
But I have learned to live with silent strain—
And fear the day we ever truly meet.

A Dinner Invitation

One afternoon, beneath fluorescent light,
We wandered through the aisles, hand in hand.
A couple smiled, their presence warm and bright,
Their charm as smooth as waves upon the sand.

We chatted there, amidst the fruit and bread,
Exchanged our numbers, laughter in the air.
Their ease and grace, the friendly words they said,
Invited us to dine without a care.

The day arrived; we drove through winding lanes,
Past gates that gleamed with ornamental pride.
Their mansion stood, where wealth and taste remains,
A palace where the finest dreams reside.

Inside, the halls were lined with art and gold,
A butler bowed and took our coats away.
The air was rich with stories yet untold,
As twilight danced and turned the skies to grey.

They led us to a room with candlelight,
Where crystal glasses sparkled on the board.
We sipped on wine, the red as dark as night,
And praised the hosts, our gratitude outpoured.

The starters came, a symphony of taste,
Each bite a note in culinary song.
We marvelled at the chef's refined embrace,
Unknowing of the path we walked along.

Then silver domes concealed the main affair,
Unveiled with flair, revealing meats unknown.
The hosts observed with penetrating stare,
Their smiles fixed, their eyes as cold as stone.

We tasted flesh so tender, rich, and rare,
The flavours danced, yet something felt amiss.
My husband paused, his brow began to wear
A furrowed line, disturbed by what was this.

He asked, "What meat is this upon our plate?"
The lady laughed, her voice a chiming bell.
"Why ask, dear friend? Does not the flavour sate?
Enjoy the feast—there's more than we can tell."

Their laughter grew, a chorus strange and deep,
A melody that chilled us to the bone.
The room grew still, as if it fell asleep,
Yet shadows moved with lives unto their own.

My heart began to race, my hands grew cold,
The wine now tasted bitter on my tongue.
The hosts' demeanour shifted, uncontrolled,
Their faces twisted, songs of madness sung.

"Is this... is this meat human?" I inquired,
A tremor in my voice I could not hide.
The lady's eyes with wicked glee were fired—
She nodded once, her joy she did not bide.

A scream escaped, my husband rose in haste,
But swift the lady lunged with gleaming knife.
She struck his side, his blood a crimson paste,
She carved with glee, as if it were her life.

She feasted on his flesh with savage grin,
Her teeth tore through, her eyes alight with fire.
I stood in shock, my mind a storm within,
As horror played upon this cursed lyre.

The husband raised a toast and drained his glass,
Then wiped his lips and threw his head in glee.
He said, "The rites have started. Let them pass—
Tonight we dine in full eternity."

The walls began to throb and hum with sound,
A rhythm deep, not heard but only felt.
The floor beneath me cracked the polished ground,
As something vast and ancient there did melt.

A voice arose from under skin and floor,
A whisper first, then something more profound:
"Consume, consume. There's always room for more.
The meat you eat shall soon become the ground."

I saw the wine ferment to clots of blood,
The portraits on the walls began to scream.
The chandeliers wept wax in steady flood,
And time itself fell out of waking dream.

The couple circled me with ghastly steps,
Their feet did not disturb the haunted rug.
The lady, grinning wide, her dress in sweats,
Came close and gave my cheek a tender tug.

She said, "You came to us with joy and light.
How sweet you are—how sweet you are inside.
We loved you from the start. You taste just right."
Her teeth shone red. I had nowhere to hide.

I stumbled back and found the hallway wide,
Yet bent and shifting as I tried to flee.
The house itself was breathing, satisfied,
Its walls exhaling meat and memory.

Each room I passed was deeper, blacker still.
No door would lead me to the world I knew.
Each corridor consumed my hope and will,
And voices laughed in halls I stumbled through.

My husband's scream still echoed in my head,
A strangled sound, a blade dragged through the core.
I whispered prayers to saints and to the dead—
But none would breach the house's bloated door.

At last I found a room with curtained glass,
And forced it open with a silent shout.
I leapt, the hedge below like brittle grass,
And crawled my way from that infernal house.

I found him, bleeding, breathless but alive,
Collapsed upon the drive with widened eyes.
We looked at one another, hearts revived,
And fled beneath the choking, burning skies.

We reached the car. Our fingers shook with dread.
I started it and roared into the night.
Behind us roared the house where we had fed—
Its flames erupting like a soul's last fight.

I turned to look, compelled against my will,
And saw them in the window, hand in hand.
Their flesh was charred, but smiling still and still—
They waved to us as though they'd understand.

The house collapsed into a grave of flame.
The trees around it hissed with ghostly breath.
The sky above it whispered out my name—
And silence fell, the silence known in death.

We drove and drove through backroads old and grey,
Not speaking of the terror we had seen.
Our hands were red, though washed a hundred ways,
Our hearts forever darkened by the scene.

The nights that followed bled into my dreams.
I saw her face behind each eyelid's veil.
And in the wind, her laughter split the seams
Of sanity that tried but failed to scale.

My husband, too, was distant from that night.
He rarely spoke and hardly met my eyes.
The trauma etched in him like cuts in light,
His voice a ghost, his dreams reduced to cries.

We moved, we ran, we tried to cast it off,
But evil clings to memory like skin.
We scrubbed our minds, but madness loves to scoff—
And darkness grows forever from within.

Each time I see a stranger smile with grace,
I wonder what they cook, and what they hide.
What lies beneath the surface of their face?
What meat they keep, what hunger swells with pride?

Beware the house where wealth and charm entwine.
Beware the plate too perfectly prepared.
Beware the wine that tastes too rich, too fine.
Beware the ones who feast and always stared.

For evil walks with grace upon the tongue,
With laughter smooth, and hands that pour your glass.
And you, like us, will find your praises sung—
Until you're meat, and watched as others pass.

The Box

The rain had barely kissed the cobbled street
When I first saw the shop through smeared glass.
A crooked sign swung slow in air and sleet,
Its letters etched by time too dark to pass.

Inside, the air was thick with mold and smoke.
Each shelf bent low with things no hand should touch.
A smell like wilted roses made me choke,
And dust clung close with memories too much.

My steps were slow, as though the floor might break,
Each creak a whisper deep beneath my feet.
I felt the space around me stir and wake,
As if the walls could hear my silent beat.

And there it was, beneath a cracked glass dome,
A box too bright to rightly call antique.
Its surface danced like fire carved in chrome,
With paints that shimmered purple, green, and bleak.

The lacquer shone like wet and living skin.
Its corners curled like lips that hid a bite.
It seemed too warm to merely hold within—
A thing that fed upon the breath of night.

I swore it whispered softly through the din,
Not words, but syllables of something more.
It said my name—or something deep as sin—
And reached across the room from where it swore.

I touched the glass. My fingers turned to ice.
A thousand voices screamed beneath my palm.
Yet still I felt its pull—a luring vice
That made the world outside dissolve to calm.

The keeper smiled. "You hear it call you too,"
He said, and brushed the dust from off the dome.
"It waits for one whose blood runs cold and true.
You take it now—it's time to bring it home."

I didn't think. My body paid the cost.
I held the box, and felt it breathe and twitch.
Each heartbeat like a deal already lost,
Each second like a tightening of the switch.

He wrapped it slow in paper black and dry.
The twine, once tied, grew wet with pulsing red.
The box beneath it gave a humming sigh,
As though it knew the path on which I'd tread.

I left the shop, but never found the door.
The world had changed, or I had lost its thread.
The sky looked bruised, the air no longer sure.
The street behind me choked on things unsaid.

At home, I set it gently on the floor.
Its colours writhed beneath the lamplight's beam.
It didn't move, and yet I felt it pour
A presence into me, like blood through dream.

I tried the lid—it wouldn't budge at all.
I used a blade, I scorched it, pulled and screamed.
It stayed shut tight, though whispering did call
And fed me thoughts that slithered where I dreamed.

I pressed my ear against the painted side.
A breath exhaled, not mine, from deep within.
It whispered: All your hopes must now have died.
I am the start of rot, and guilt, and grin.

Its voice was old and cruel, both sharp and slow,
Like language lost to stone and fire and ash.
It whispered: What you seek, you'll never know,
But still you'll beg me for the final crash.

Each night I sat and listened to it hum.
It crooned of gods defiled and saints betrayed.
It sang of mothers slaughtered by their sons,
Of children raised in silence, dark, and blade.

The days turned pale. I did not leave my bed.
The box grew warm and pulsed against my skin.
It fed on everything I'd left unsaid,
And birthed a storm of silence deep within.

I locked it up inside a chest of pine,
But still its whispers found my every thought.
It told me: You are mine. Your blood is mine.
And all you've loved will now decay and rot.

My dreams turned black with shapes I couldn't name,
Each night a film of screams that stained my sight.
I saw the box in halls of endless flame,
Its lid ajar, yet sealed in sacred blight.

I woke with blood beneath my clawed, clenched nails.
My lips were split from whispering too long.
My breath would frost, though summer's heat prevailed,
And every mirror showed a face all wrong.

My friends came by, their faces drawn with care,
But I could see the falsehood in their smiles.
They eyed the box. I saw their hungry stare,
And kept it close through all their well-phrased trials.

My family pleaded, begged me, wept and swore
That something wasn't right inside my home.
But I had locked the box behind a door
And feared they'd steal it, leave me all alone.

Their voices joined the whispers in my head.
They'll take it, hissed the box, you must beware.
They envy you, and wish that you were dead.
Don't let them touch, not even breathe your air.

I stopped replying. Let the phone go dead.
I boarded windows, let the garden die.
Each night I lay with box beside my bed,
And listened to it murmur, sob, and sigh.

It spoke of plagues, of kingdoms crushed to sand.
Of popes who drank the blood of fettered youth.
Of angels strangled by a newborn's hand.
Of worms that learned to mimic love and truth.

By week's end, all who knew me had gone still.
They would not knock again, nor call, nor pray.
The world outside was ash, and I was ill,
Yet stronger near the box from day to day.

I carved strange marks along the kitchen wall—
Not symbols I had seen in books or lore.
They came to me at night, a creeping scrawl
That made my tongue bleed just to speak them more.

I knew the box would open once I'd learned
The price of faithless longing and despair.
It pulsed. It shivered. Still, I never turned.
My soul was bent, and still I did not care.

I laid beside it, pressing close my cheek,
And whispered secrets I had never told.
The box responded in a foreign squeak
That chilled the room though firewood turned to gold.

It mocked my tears, then sang in lullaby:
A child was born with serpents in his hair,
Who fed on men and watched the mothers die,
And crowned himself with skulls stripped clean and bare.

I laughed at first. But soon the laugh decayed.
The sound I made was hollow, burnt, and foul.
I wandered rooms, each hallway smeared and grayed,
And kept the box wrapped tight in robe and cowl.

It owned me now. I did not try to hide.
I drank no more. I ate no meat or bread.
I only stared and listened, mouth all wide,
While thinking thoughts no sane man ever said.

The box began to throb with every hour.
Its colours changed, grew deeper, black with flame.
I felt it gathering some awful power,
And wept in joy each time it spoke my name.

And then, one night, the silence dropped and broke.
The box began to tremble, hiss, and sing.
It split the dark with words no man had spoke,
And pulsed like some infernal living thing.

Its lid creaked loose, though no hand touched its frame.
The colours bled into a screaming light.
I knelt, ecstatic, whispering my name,
And welcomed madness in that sacred night.

From out the box, two children came to be—
No eyes, no mouths, no features carved or grown.
They stretched thin arms as if to comfort me,
And held out hands as cold and hard as bone.

Their skin was wax, their fingers made of clay.
They moved with grace that didn't match the flesh.
No breath disturbed the air, and yet they'd sway
Like reeds that bent in winds both foul and fresh.

They didn't speak, but still they pulled me near.
I wept with joy, my life's desire fulfilled.
The box had opened; all I'd known was clear:
That truth and pain and awe are made to build.

They took my hands, and though I felt the pull,
I did not flinch or question where I'd go.
My mind was hollowed, thirsting to be full—
And what they brought, no man on Earth could know.

They led me down through shadow, through the grain
Of matter peeled from everything I'd been.
My heart was ash, my thoughts no longer sane.
I walked into the void, devoid of sin.

And still I hear the whispers in the dark.
The box remains, though I am not the same.
The ones who seek it now will feel the spark—
The curse, the need, the call that speaks their name.

Perhaps I breathe within its lacquered shell,
Or sleep between the folds of time and fate.
Perhaps I am the thing it learned to tell,
And guard the gate for others drawn by hate.

You reading this may hear its beckoning cry.
You may walk past that shop some fated day.
And should you see it shine, do not ask why—
You'll want it more than breath, and you will pay.

The Hundred Rooms

The Arrival

The storm had swallowed sky and road alike.
Its throat was wide with wind and hungry breath.
Our tires skidded through a slurry bend,
Then stopped beneath a tree like grasping death.

We were a group of six with fading phones,
No bars, no lights, no signal in the haze.
The rain had turned to needles on the glass,
And dusk was folding into blackest phase.

We left the car and wandered through the mire,
The woods around us thick with crooked yews.
The branches groaned like gallows in the fog,
And every path dissolved beneath our shoes.

Then through the trees a glimmer blinked alive—
A house, immense, with torches on its face.
Its roofline cut the clouds like rusted blades.
Its windows glowed with neither warmth nor grace.

The gates were open, wrought of iron teeth.
The hinges sighed like lovers close to death.
We crossed beneath a broken arch of stone,
And met the windless hush with baited breath.

The garden had been strangled long ago.
Its statues leaned like mourners in the rain.
A fountain, cracked, held nothing but a bird
With eyes removed and wings that dripped with stain.

The steps were warped, the porch was rimmed in moss.
The knocker hung in chains it could not shake.
The door was wide—unlocked, unmanned, and still,
As if the house had dreamt we would awake.

One glanced behind. The car was out of sight.
Another tried to speak but found no voice.
We had no choice but forward, and we knew—
Though none had said it, none had called it choice.

Inside, the air was thick with polished dread.
The walls were dressed in velvet soaked with dust.
A chandelier above us swung in stills,
Its arms like bone, its crystals flecked with rust.

Each sconce along the hallway breathed a flame,
But none gave heat, just flickering unrest.
The carpet muffled every foot we placed,
And muffled, too, the questions in our chests.

The foyer led into a grander hall,
Where portraits stared with eyes that seemed too real.
Each face was cast in shadow more than paint,
Each frame a shrine for something none should feel.

A woman held a child made of teeth.
A man sat posed with half a hand and grin.
A boy whose mouth was sewn in looping thread
Still seemed to whisper, "Don't let them begin."

We passed through doors and arches dressed in gold.
The ceiling murmured downward with a moan.
No clocks, no phones, no stairs that led back out.
The house was larger than its outer stone.

A dining room lay set with seven chairs.
The silver gleamed, untouched by time or air.
But dust lay thick across the empty plates—
And wax dripped slowly down through silence bare.

A hallway stretched beyond with numbered doors.
One hundred strong, each painted with a glyph.
No two the same. Some locked. Some barely closed.
The nearest cracked, and through it sighed a whiff—

Not air, not wind, but something close to grief.
A sob, perhaps, from someone still inside.
The dog we'd brought began to pace and bark.
Its growl turned low, and then it tried to hide.

We stood before the first door in the line.
Its knob was brass, its surface faintly warm.
And though we feared, we knew we would proceed.
The house had drawn us inward from the storm.

One turned away. Another reached to knock.
A third just breathed and stared into the grain.
The fourth said, "If we stop, we'll only freeze."
The fifth, "It's not the house. It's all our pain."

The sixth was me. I said no single word.
But in my chest, the beating had begun.
Not heart alone, but something just beyond—
A sense the house would not be overrun.

We turned the knob. The room beyond was dark.
A hallway like a throat without a light.
We stepped inside. The door began to hum.
And sealed us in the mansion for the night.

The First Room

The door was bare of markings, pale with rot,
Its knob engraved with roots that spiralled tight.
The frame was bowed as though it bore a weight,
And every nail within it pulsed with blight.

We opened slow. A breath escaped the dark,
So cold it set the dog to tail and whine.
A thread of scent—like vinegar and salt—
Crept out and slid like thought along the spine.

The room beyond was square and far too still.
Its corners leaned, its ceiling sloped and low.
The walls were lined with paper once ornate—
Now flaking like the skin of things below.

A table sat alone, a single chair.
Upon the cloth, a plate with bloodstained rim.
A fork and knife, both bent, lay side by side.
A candle, lit, began to slowly dim.

A man sat there. His posture poised and prim,
His clothing neat, though dust clung to his sleeve.
His eyes were glass, unblinking in the glow.
He did not stir, nor speak, nor blink to grieve.

His mouth was stitched with thread, yet not quite shut.
He moved his hand to gesture toward the seat.
The woman gasped. The rest of us stood back.
The flame grew high, then lowered at his feet.

He placed a hand upon the table's edge,
And then, with care, drew out a folded sheet.
It bore no words, just stains of reddish-brown,
But somehow told us all we feared to meet.

A whisper curled around the seated man,
Not heard aloud, but pressed into the brain:
"The price of entry is a piece of you.
A truth unvoiced. A memory. A name."

The woman stepped, compelled by silent call.
She took the seat across the rigid frame.
Her hand reached out to touch the tattered cloth—
And when she did, the man began his claim.

He reached with needle, thread still through the eye,
And drew it slow across his lips once more.
The thread dissolved, and with a pop of flesh,
He grinned and spoke like wind through cellar door.

"I held her down. I told myself she lied.
She begged, but I had heard it all before.
I turned the lock and let the fire grow.
She burned too fast to scream, but not to score.

The walls are marked with fingers even now.
Her shadow lives between the bricks and bone.
I stayed. I watched. I wrote the note in ash—
It's folded still beneath the dining stone."

He pointed to the slab beside his feet.
The stone was cracked. A soot-black note was there.
The woman reached—but as she neared the stone,
The air grew thick with murmurs in her hair.

She dropped her hand. The whisper ceased to rise.
The man let out a breath like years ago.
His hands collapsed into the folds of cloth.
The candle flared once more, then burned too low.

The woman rose. Her eyes had changed their light.
She did not speak, but something in her swayed.
The figure slumped, his back against the chair,
And from his lips a final echo played:

"There's more of me in all of you than not.
You'll see me in the halls, the glass, the fire.
This room remembers all you ever were.
Now leave. The House is waiting to inquire."

The door behind us clicked into its frame.
We turned to see a hallway curling wide.
The air was still, but every wall had moved.
The dog stood tall, its gaze upon the side.

A mirror now replaced the open wall—
And in it, all of us were shown with blood.
Not dripped, but stained. Not scattered, but engraved.
The room was done. The house had tasted flood.

We walked again. Our group still held at six.
Yet one among us shivered in her steps.
We did not name it then, but we had seen—
The room had touched her past with spectral depths.

Another door appeared beside the next.
Its carvings bore the shape of tangled roots.
We paused and breathed, then stepped into the hall,
Where waited Room Three's long-forgotten truths.

The Second Room

The hallway wound like something breathing slow,
Its plaster damp, its corners weeping pitch.
The dog stayed near, but whimpered when we turned—
Its nose against the seams that twitched and itched.

The second door stood taller than the rest,
Its grain was dark, its varnish smeared with black.
Upon its face, a carving had been burned:
A cradle, cracked, with serpents in the slack.

No knob was fixed—just nails driven in.
To open it, we had to tear it wide.
The wood moaned low, a groan of wood and grief,
And then we crossed the rotten threshold's side.

Inside, the walls were painted soft and pale—
A nursery, in hues that dulled the mind.
A rocking chair still moved, although the air
Was tight as cloth and laced with sour rind.

A crib stood high with blankets oddly white.
A lullaby rang faint from somewhere near.
No source was seen—yet still it played and played,
And every note felt sharpened by a sneer.

The mobile hung with birds too limp to swing,
Their paper wings now drenched with something old.
A bottle stood beside a ragged bear—
Its nipple sealed with wax and melted gold.

We did not speak. The room was made for hush.
The dog sat down and whined into the floor.
Then, slowly, from the crib, a shape arose—
Too small for child, too twisted to ignore.

Its skin was grey and stretched across the bone.
Its eyes were pearls with maggots in the whites.
Its voice was hoarse and old despite its size.
It said, "At last. The House has turned the lights."

It clambered down with arms like broken sticks.
Its feet were hooves, or claws, or neither one.
It dragged a rattle made of someone's teeth,
And with its song, it called the room begun.

It pointed at the crib, where more now stirred—
A shape like blankets shifting on their own.
We leaned to see—then staggered back with cries.
A face appeared. And every inch was grown.

A grown man's head within a newborn's frame,
Its mouth too large, its tongue a bloody glove.
It smiled. It blinked. And then it softly cooed:
"My name was taken, but I kept my love.

She bore me once. She left me in the well.
She said I cried too loud, too long, too wrong.
I made a deal to keep my eyes and teeth.
And now I sing. I sing the Ending Song."

The rattle shook. The floor began to crack.
The rocking chair spun wildly out of tune.
The walls peeled back like pages of a book—
And in the cracks, we saw a second room.

Another crib. Another set of eyes.
Each child the same, each grin a mirror's twin.
The ceiling split. The lullaby grew sharp—
A wail of knives to cut away our skin.

The dog leapt up and barked into the air.
The rattles shrieked. The thing began to dance.
We turned to flee—but one among us fell.
A woman, caught in sleep's unwilling trance.

She cried, "I dreamed this! I remember now!
This is the room I saw when I was five!
The songs! The crib! The hands beneath the rug!
I think—I think—I think it's still alive!"

We pulled her back. The air had grown too thick.
The thing crawled fast, its limbs too many now.
It hissed and reached, its eyes alight with flame.
The woman screamed and bit her own wrist down.

We dragged her through as crib and rattle wept.
The door slammed shut. The hallway howled behind.
The dog had fled. The floorboards hissed with steam.
And from her mouth, she coughed a lullaby.

The second room was sealed. Its hunger fed.
The hallway bent, then straightened in its rest.
Our group now five, though one had left her voice
Behind, along with hope and needed rest.

A new door formed where none had been before.
Its frame was stitched with wax and human hair.
We did not speak. The House had set the pace.
And Room Three breathed. And Room Three waited there.

The Third Room

The hallway pulsed as though it bore a wound,
Its walls now warm and slick with unseen sweat.
We wiped our hands along our trembling sleeves—
But still the air clung thick with black regret.

The dog returned, but would not walk ahead.
Its hackles rose. It stared into the door.
A murmur passed beneath the boards like breath.
The knob was bone. The frame was spattered o'er.

The third room opened inward, slow and wide.
The scent of oil and polish struck the chest.
At first, it seemed a study made with care:
Tall shelves of books, a desk, a hearth at rest.

A phonograph stood idle on a stand.
A map of seas adorned the peeling wall.
And on the desk, a folded flag lay still—
Its corners crisp, untouched by time or squall.

A figure sat, half-draped in officer's blues.
His chest was sunk, his mouth a sunken slit.
One eye was glass, the other black with mold.
His hands were clasped as though he prayed and quit.

We stood in silence, waiting for a sound—
The dog gave low and guttural dismay.
Then came the creak, not from the man, but floor.
A trapdoor opened where the lanterns swayed.

He did not rise, nor blink, nor seem to breathe.
But still his voice emerged, like metal dragged.
"I sailed a war across the inland seas.
I called it just, but justice long had lagged.

They made me keep the ledger of the drowned.
I signed each name and numbered every sin.
But when the wind grew sharp and tore the sails,
I struck the mast and let them all fall in."

He gestured toward the phonograph, then sighed.
The needle dropped though no one turned the crank.
A song began to warble from the horn—
Not music, but a list of names that sank.

A drumbeat rose, a march of hollow tone.
Each name grew louder, echoed off the beams.
A woman's voice. A child. A stuttering plea.
A gurgled cry between the twisted screams.

The man still sat. A tear rolled down his cheek.
But what emerged from it was not like brine.
It shimmered, thick, a golden drop of pitch,
And hissed when falling on the map's faint line.

"The sea took them," he whispered, "but I watched.
And I remain, the scribe of what I sunk.
They do not sleep. They walk within the tide.
They wear my name inside their bellies' trunk."

The trapdoor hissed. The floor began to rise.
A hand emerged, bloated and blue with ropes.
Another followed, thin and webbed and long,
And grasped the air as if to choke out hope.

A sailor's cap was floating near the desk.
A jawbone clacked beneath a tide of smoke.
The woman we had dragged from lullaby
Began to sway, then pointed to the oak.

"He's not alone," she said, "they're all still here.
They never left. Their boots are full of bones."
A boot appeared, still tied, without a leg.
Another stepped, and then the room gave groans.

We ran toward light, but found no knob or lock.
The window cracked and moaned against the weight.
The officer now raised his hand in prayer—
But every word he mouthed came far too late.

"You leave this room with blood beneath your feet.
Each drop you hear was once a name I kept.
This House will make you catalog your dead.
This House will show you where and when you wept."

The trapdoor slammed. The song at last went still.
The names were gone. The silence hurt the ear.
We fled, and from the hall we heard a tide—
The sound of drowning souls that do not fear.

The hallway twisted backward on itself.
Its lamps now swayed in time with unseen waves.
Our group was five—but silence held one more.
Her lips moved not, her eyes were storm-filled caves.

The dog returned, its fur now soaked with brine.
It barked but once, then turned its gaze aside.
A door appeared with rivets shaped like rings.
It yawned for us. It whispered, "Room Four. Hide."

The Fourth Room

The door to Room Four breathed a steady pulse,
Its wood damp-dark, its hinges bound with tar.
Around the frame, the symbols shifted shape—
Then settled into letters spelling scar.

No wind had touched the hall in many hours,
Yet still a draft slid out between the cracks.
It smelled of linen buried under stone,
Of rusted steel, of walls with painted backs.

We pressed it wide. The room was long and low,
With narrow beds arranged in ordered rows.
Each one was made, with linens tightly stretched,
Their corners sharp, like coffins left exposed.

The walls were tiled in green, the ceiling pale,
A light above buzzed gently without source.
We stepped inside and heard a hush too pure—
The kind that warned of punishment or force.

A figure stood, starched white from head to sole,
Her gown unwrinkled, hands clasped at her waist.
Her mouth was gone, replaced by stitched-up skin,
Her eyes twin holes of sterile, ancient haste.

She didn't turn, yet still we felt her gaze.
She motioned once—a gesture downward slow—
And from beneath the beds there came a scrape,
A shuffle soft, like something dragged below.

"The ward is clean," a whisper filled our heads.
"The cure is pain. The wound must be revealed."
She pointed at the nearest empty bed—
And on its sheet, a fresh red mark congealed.

The woman closest to it shook and stared.
Her feet began to move without her will.
She sat upon the mattress, pale and blank—
And all the others backed away and still.

The nurse approached, her steps without a sound,
Her heels like needles clicking on the tile.
She reached into a pouch upon her side,
And drew a knife as long as measured trial.

No blood was on it—only hair and lint.
Its blade was clean, but smelled of salt and screams.
She raised it slow, then pressed it to the air—
And every bulb above began to gleam.

The patient cried, but still did not escape.
Her limbs were limp, her breath was turned to stone.
The nurse now cut, but not into the skin—
She sliced through shadow, bone, and time alone.

And from the wound, a whisper spilled like silk:
A voice from childhood begging not to die.
A father's shout, a crash, a muffled sob,
A drawer unlocked, a lullaby, a lie.

The bed turned red, though not from bleeding flesh.
It soaked in sound, in grief, in cries unsaid.
And when the knife withdrew, the woman screamed—
A scream that cracked the glass above her bed.

She leapt to floor, her lips now slack and wild,
And shouted words no others dared repeat.
The nurse turned slow, her mouth still sealed and tight,
And vanished like a whisper on retreat.

The rows of beds began to shake and moan.
Each one revealed a secret wrapped in sheets.
A mother swaying, cradling a void.
A boy with bites too small for human teeth.

A man who wept into a bloodstained shoe.
A girl who carved her wrists into a name.
They all lay still, and yet their voices rang—
A chorus built of shame that had no claim.

We fled. We pulled the woman to her feet.
The hallway burst with light from wounds unseen.
We heard the nurse's heels behind our steps—
A ticking time, too calm, too sharp, too clean.

The door slammed shut. The pulse grew faint again.
The tile beneath our shoes was pale with sweat.
We'd entered Room Four clean and mostly whole—
But now, we knew what even scars forget.

The walls were close. The ceiling bent with grief.
A single lamp swayed gently in the dark.
We did not speak, but all of us had seen—
The wound is where the House leaves its first mark.

Another door appeared, now split in two,
Its wood still fresh, as if it bled with bark.
The number five was carved with curling ends.
The dog sat down. It would not cross the mark.

The Fifth Room

The fifth door sighed and swung before we knocked,
Its hinges whispering like breath through teeth.
The scent of rot was thick, but sweet with spice,
Like meat long stewed beneath the floorboards' sheath.

We entered slow—the room was draped in red,
With curtains hung to mask the window's eye.
A fire roared too loud for such a space.
The walls were tight, the ceiling hung too high.

A table stood with velvet seats for two,
A crystal vase with roses black and curled.
The wine decanter trembled where it sat,
Though no one poured, and none had touched its world.

A phonograph began without a hand—
A waltz, too slow, with moaning from the strings.
The chairs pulled out, then slid toward the floor,
As though inviting guests to darker things.

A man stepped forth. Or rather, something once.
He wore a suit that moved like skin too loose.
His face was pale, his mouth too close to grin,
His fingers long as truth without excuse.

He took a seat and folded one long leg.
He beckoned with a glance and raised his glass.
The wine inside did not reflect the fire—
Instead it swirled with scenes that came to pass.

"I used to dine," he said, "with finer guests.
But hunger makes no room for dignity.
My wife, she left before the plates were cleared.
So now I toast to what the House feeds me."

He sipped and set the glass down with a clink.
"Would either of you care to try the veal?
It's not quite lamb, nor pork, nor anything—
But once it begged. I find that gives it feel."

We shook our heads. The woman stepped away.
The dog let out a growl too low to last.
The fire flicked its tongue toward her pale coat—
And in the flames, a vision flared and passed.

She saw herself, or something like her face,
Bent at a table, knife and fork in hand.
Before her lay a meal still twitching faint,
Its shape too small, too human to withstand.

She screamed and blinked—the fire snapped away.
The man stood up and dragged a chair aside.
"You judge," he said, "but hunger is a hole.
We fill it how we must to stay inside.

I chewed my vows. I carved them from her back.
Her hands I kept, for soup. Her teeth, for dice.
Her tongue I dried and tacked above the sink.
And still I dream of seconds every night."

The walls grew close, as if they leaned to hear.
The carpet squelched like flesh beneath our tread.
The roses turned to mouths, and from their stems
Spilled laughter steeped in vinegar and dread.

He lunged—but not to harm, just to invite.
He pulled a chair for her with courtly pride.
"One bite," he said. "Just one, to taste the House.
And afterward, I'll let the fire decide."

She turned and ran. We followed through the smoke.
The chairs flew back and slammed into the floor.
Behind us, knives rose up and danced midair—
Their points all aimed to chase us through the door.

We passed through flame, through screams that licked our backs.
The room behind collapsed into a feast.
The music played its last, then broke in glass.
And on the walls, the blood became a priest.

The door slammed shut. The hallway twisted left.
The woman shook and stared down at her hands.
They bled, though she had touched no knife or flame—
As if the House had fed her other plans.

We stood in silence. Then the dog gave voice.
It barked once more and pressed against the frame.
Another door was rising from the stone—
Its number six inscribed in ash and shame.

The Sixth Room

The door to Room Six creaked before our touch.
Its hinges sounded like a child's moan.
The number burned above in dripping wax—
A makeshift candle jammed into the stone.

The dog lay down and growled, but would not bark.
It stared as if it saw through wall and flame.
We opened slow, and air as cold as glass
Spilled out and laced our mouths with guilt and name.

The room was bare, or so it first appeared.
Just concrete walls, no windows, and no bed.
But all around the floor were tiny shoes—
Each turned askew, each marked in white or red.

They were of every kind and size and time—
Leather boots, silk slippers, woven straw.
And written on the wall in charcoal hand:
"We count because the world forgot the law."

The door swung closed and bolted from behind.
The lights above began to hum and spin.
We stood in place, afraid to cross the floor,
Afraid of what might crawl from under skin.

A voice began—not one, but several more.
A chorus low, from walls, from shoes, from dust.
And though the mouths were gone, the words were clear:
"They took from us. Now take, because you must."

Then from the farthest wall there stepped a form.
A child in stature, yet no child's face.
It wore no eyes, just sockets full of nails,
And where its heart would beat, it left a space.

Its voice was faint, as if it knew the end—
But still it spoke, and every line was true.
"I asked for warmth. They gave me to the frost.
I learned to dig with hands too cold for you."

It stepped aside, revealing then a well,
A square cut deep into the cement floor.
Inside it, more of them began to climb—
Not fully formed, but not quite dead before.

One had no jaw. Another missed its skin.
They moved with grace, as if they'd never stopped.
Their tiny feet made tapping sounds on stone,
A beat of grief the House had never dropped.

"We came back here," the eyeless one now said,
"Because the world moved on without our names.
They left us cold. They left us full of worms.
And now we count our silence into flames."

The shoes began to move along the floor.
They danced, but not with joy—this dance was wrong.
Each step aligned with screaming from the wall,
And every note reeked vengeance steeped too long.

We tried to move, but all the ground was death.
Each footfall echoed back a whispered sin.
A girl among us stumbled on a boot—
And when she screamed, it sounded deep within.

A pair of hands emerged and grabbed her calf.
Another gripped and tore with joyless speed.
They dragged her down into the writhing well,
And as she vanished, all the shoes would bleed.

The rest of us had run before the end.
The door was gone. The walls began to bend.
We screamed. The floor cracked wide and spilled with ash.
A hundred names rose up, all left unpenned.

Then just as fast, a door appeared in smoke.
We crashed through it and landed in the hall.
Our friend was gone. Her shoes remained behind—
Now lined outside the door along the wall.

The hallway turned. The lights were dimmer still.
The woman sobbed but could not name her thought.
The man just stared and whispered things too low.
The dog walked on, its growl the only knot.

The next door formed of leather stretched and thin—
Its hinges stitched, its frame too warm to be.
The number seven burned from under skin.
We breathed once more, then left our grief to see.

The Seventh Room

The seventh door was pulsing in the dark,
Its leather skin drawn tight across a frame.
No wood, no steel, just something once alive—
Now bound in straps and stitched in rows of flame.

We hesitated, but the hallway swayed.
The ceiling wept with drops like clotting breath.
The floor beneath began to flex and shift,
And stepping back felt closer now to death.

So in we went. The room was red and dim,
Its walls composed of parchments sewn as skin.
Each bore a script in languages unknown,
In blood or ink or things that moved within.

A single lightbulb swung from up above—
A noose tied to its cord just out of reach.
The air was hot and thick with candle soot,
And something scrawled across the floor like speech.

A desk stood tall, a lectern stacked with bones.
Upon it, books were open, writing slow.
No hand was near, no pen or author seen—
The text appeared as if the room would know.

A man emerged from shadow near the wall,
His spine bent low, his teeth too sharp to show.
His robes were stitched from scalps and torn-out spines.
His eyes were made of pages wrinkled so.

He spoke in tones too measured to be kind:
"The House is built of stories never told.
Each guest must leave their name upon its flesh,
Or else it writes them out and keeps the soul.

I am the scribe. The ink is what remains.
You see this robe? I wore it once with skin.
Now every tale I never dared to speak
Has taken form and dressed the guilt within."

He pointed to the nearest stitched-up sheet.
It bore a tale in looping, frantic scrawl.
"She drank too much. She drove. She hit. She ran.
She told herself it wasn't her at all."

Another page now curled along the wall—
"He knew the boy was crying down the hall.
He turned the sound up louder. Played the game.
He figured that the bruises weren't his fault."

We tried to flee, but parchment gripped our hands.
It coiled up our arms like living thread.
The dog began to bark and gnaw the strands.
The woman shrieked as words bloomed on her head.

They wrote her thoughts, exposed them without end:
A kiss she lied to take, a life she stole.
Her skin grew thin as letters carved within.
The scribe looked on, and fed upon her soul.

"Each guest becomes a page," he said with glee.
"Each tale they bury writes itself in blood.
There is no lie that will not take a root.
There is no truth that does not end in mud."

He opened up a book that bore no spine—
Inside, a scream began to leak like gas.
We tore her free, though letters clung like vines,
And fled again across the writhing grass.

Behind us, every page began to sing.
A thousand voices crying out in print.
The lightbulb burst. The lectern cracked in half.
The scribe let out a shriek of sulphur's tint.

And just before the door could close us in,
We saw our names now etched along the seam.
We slammed it shut. The hallway curled again—
The dog still shaking, caught inside the dream.

Now only four of us remained to walk,
The others lost to ink and death's design.
The next door bloomed like fungus from the wall—
Its number eight formed perfectly in twine.

The scent of lilies touched the air like skin.
The knob was cool, like silver dipped in sleep.
We did not ask what lay beyond that mark.
We only knew the House had depths to keep.

The Eighth Room

The eighth door opened slow, with no complaint.
Its hinges whispered like a breath let go.
The scent of lilies floated through the gap—
Too fresh, too strong, too solemn, and too slow.

The hallway hushed, as though it feared this room.
The dog refused to move and whined instead.
We crossed the frame, our shadows trailing long,
And entered where the house remembered dead.

The space was soft—too soft for earthly things.
The walls were padded thick with satin pale.
No windows pierced the room, no fire burned.
Yet still, it glowed with moonlight faint and frail.

A dozen chairs stood wrapped in funeral cloths,
Arranged in half a circle, all well-worn.
Atop each seat, a flower fresh and still.
Beside each bloom, a name engraved in thorn.

An altar sat beneath a draped motif,
Its shape unknown, a body or a box.
A music box played somewhere far away,
Its notes repeating like the turn of locks.

And from behind the cloth, a figure rose.
She wore a veil as black as widow's grief.
Her face was pale, but lovely in its rot,
Her gaze unread, her presence wrapped in thief.

She did not speak, but motioned to the seats.
We sat—or rather, found we could not stand.
The chairs had claimed us softly at the thighs,
Their velvet grips as binding as a hand.

She walked between us, trailing silent steps.
Her veil dragged over stones we could not see.
She stopped before the altar's draped embrace,
And murmured words not meant for memory.

"You mourn the wrong," she said, "you bury guilt.
You dress regret in white and call it rest.
But death is not a vessel made for grace.
It festers when unspoken sins infest."

She pulled the cloth, revealing what we feared—
Not corpse, not ash, but mirror framed in black.
It showed not her, nor altar, nor the dead—
But each of us in time we can't get back.

The man among us gasped and looked away.
The woman wept. Her face began to drain.
My heart grew tight, for what I saw was this:
My father's belt. A fire. And the rain.

She spoke again, now louder in her tone:
"You came to mourn, but never bore the weight.
You left them buried deep behind your eyes.
But every tomb you build becomes a gate."

The room began to twist with static sound.
The music box cracked open in a shriek.
The chairs grew hard, their arms now chains of bone.
The flowers wilted. One began to speak.

"I was the friend you told would be okay."
"I was the mother left without a word."
"I was the child you promised not to break."
Their voices stacked in agonising chord.

The mirror now grew dark, then bloomed with flame.
Within its glass, the woman we had lost
Appeared again—but not as we recalled.
Her eyes were gone. Her limbs were shaped in frost.

She mouthed a phrase, but we could not make sense—
Until the widow hissed, "She's here. She sees.
You brought her here by failing to let go.
The dead can't sleep when memory deceives."

We broke the chair, the dog began to bark.
The veil caught flame, the altar split in half.
The widow laughed, but not from joy or hate—
Her laugh was grief, then silence, then a gasp.

We fled the smoke, our heads too full to breathe.
The hallway wrapped us back in weighted cloth.
We didn't speak. We couldn't hold the loss.
The room still wept, the lilies cold with moth.

Another door now grew from out the floor.
Its number nine was carved in candlelight.
We did not rest. We stepped where shadow leaned—
And carried with us grief that stole the night.

The Ninth Room

The door to Room Nine hissed as it arose,
Its number flickering like moths in flame.
The floor beneath it trembled as with breath,
And every step we took betrayed our name.

The wood was soaked—though none could say with what.
The grain was warped, as if it tried to flee.
The knob was cold and slick with some old sweat.
The dog began to growl, and stared at me.

We pushed the door. It stuck, then slid apart.
A sudden heat spilled out like furnace breath.
We entered to a red and dripping space,
Alive with rust and long-forgotten death.

A factory, or what remained of one—
Its rafters bent, its pipes all choked with hair.
A wheel spun slowly near a vat of sludge.
A chain hung down and shivered in the air.

The air was thick with iron, soot, and meat.
The scent of burning oil laced with bone.
And in the centre, strapped against a beam,
A figure toiled with hammering alone.

He struck the wall, though nothing he repaired.
He pounded steel with purpose none could name.
His back was broad, his arms were stitched and black,
And every blow spelled out another shame.

"I forged the locks," he said, and turned to us.
His eyes were soot, his face a mask of ash.
"I built the bars for cells you never saw.
You think you've never jailed—but burned the lash.

You kept a brother poor. You turned your cheek.
You signed the deed, then left the blood to dry.
You locked your neighbour in a cage of debt.
You let them rot while you learned how to lie."

He raised his hammer high and let it fall.
A spark leapt up and caught upon the wall.
The pipes began to moan like dying whales.
A furnace hissed, a scream too thin to stall.

Then chains dropped down from rafters thick with grime—
Each one alive, they slithered like a snake.
They wrapped the dog, who barked in sudden pain,
Then lunged at us and snapped a chain with break.

We scattered fast, but not before the man
Reached out and caught the woman by her braid.
He held her up and whispered near her ear:
"What did you sign when others wept and paid?"

She screamed and kicked. Her boot struck down his jaw—
It burst apart, a bell of molten coal.
The room itself began to twist and roar.
The chains all writhed, as if they had a soul.

The hammer flew, and struck against the steel—
The floor gave way, revealing fire below.
The man fell in and laughed with choking joy,
And through the smoke he roared: "Now you all know!

The locks are made from silence, not from law!
The cages built are built by what you don't!"
His voice was lost beneath the molten pitch,
And with his fall, the factory's grip broke.

We dragged the dog, now wounded in its side.
The woman coughed, her hair still stinking flame.
We leapt through smoke and found the hallway cool—
Though now the walls were scorched and not the same.

They bore the handprints of a hundred ghosts,
Each burned into the plaster like a stain.
We did not count. We did not ask or cry.
We only moved, and braced for more of pain.

A door emerged. Its brass was clean and new.
The number ten was etched in cursive white.
It gleamed like it had never known a guest—
But we had learned that beauty was a fright.

The Tenth Room

The tenth door bore no grime, no blood, no mark—
Its varnish gleamed, its hinges bright and bare.
It stood as if untouched by all decay,
A lie too smooth, too polished to beware.

The dog lay down, still licking at its side,
Its fur scorched black where fire had seared the skin.
We did not wait to guess what calm might hide.
We touched the knob and let the house pull in.

Inside, the light was golden, soft, and still.
The floor was marble, veined with pearly green.
Tall mirrors hung in pairs along the walls,
Each set so clean they blurred the space between.

A table stood with porcelain and tea,
The cups arranged for guests not yet arrived.
The scent of sugar hung upon the air—
A sweetness that no fruit had ever lived.

The woman stepped, and found her face in glass—
Reflected once, then twice, then far too deep.
Each mirror showed a version not quite right:
Her mouth too still, her smile a wound asleep.

The man stood still, his breath caught in his throat.
His face was young, then old, then lost to time.
His eyes looked back but carried other thoughts—
As though the glass knew better than the mind.

A host appeared, not ghost and not quite man.
He wore a tailcoat brushed with perfect care.
His eyes were stitched, yet somehow still they saw.
His skin was flawless, waxen, pale, and bare.

He spoke with ease, his voice like syrup thin:
"You've come at last. Your seats are well-prepared.
The mirrors miss you more than you have known.
Please sit. It's time to see what you have shared."

We did not move. The mirrors whispered close.
Their silver surfaces began to breathe.
We saw our lives in fragments played again—
A birthday drowned in silence. Bruised beliefs.

A wedding night where someone cried alone.
A letter burned before it reached a friend.
Each cup on that fine table bore our name.
Each drop inside would mirror to the end.

The woman gasped. Her cup had filled with hair.
She tipped it once, and saw her father's eyes.
The man's had blood, but also bits of gold—
The cost of lies wrapped up in lullabies.

We backed away. The host just bowed in peace.
"You do not want to drink?" he said, still kind.
"Then let the House take what you would withhold.
Its thirst is just. It drinks the hollow mind."

The mirrors cracked—not broke, but stretched instead.
They thinned and opened like a wound through space.
And from within, our other selves stepped out,
Each bearing grief behind a perfect face.

They mimicked us with flawless, mirrored grace.
They smiled too wide. They knew the things we'd done.
The dog began to bark and leap with fear—
It snarled as if it saw what we'd become.

The mirrored man was calm and walked ahead.
He held a cup and raised it to the air.
"To all the lives we live inside a mask—
To all we lose by saying we don't care."

He drank—and then dissolved into the floor.
His skin became a gleam upon the tile.
The host clapped once. The mirrors turned to dust.
"No masks?" he said. "Then stay a little while."

We fled. The hallway met us like a breath—
Too soft to trust, too silent to explain.
The dog looked back and growled toward empty glass.
The woman wept. The man just spoke one name.

A door appeared, its surface warped and blue.
The number eleven scratched with broken thread.
We dared not knock. The House had shown us now—
It kept the living closer than the dead.

The Eleventh Room

The door was stitched from coats of deepest blue,
Each patch a sleeve, a collar, button, seam.
The number "11" etched in looping thread,
Its outline frayed as if disturbed by dream.

We touched it lightly—fabric pulled away.
The door swung wide to sounds not made by feet.
A ticking echoed deep within the dark,
Like clocks that paced instead of marked retreat.

Inside, the room was vast and poorly lit.
Its ceiling curved in arches slick with dust.
Around us stood tall cases made of brass,
Each filled with clocks now choked with webs and rust.

A pendulum swung gently at the heart—
Not fixed to wall, nor tethered to the floor.
It moved through air as though it split the world,
And made the space behind it something more.

The clocks all ticked, but none in time or tune.
Some rang too fast, some never moved at all.
A cuckoo cried and bled against its spring.
A grandfather had cracked against the wall.

Then came the sound of boots upon the wood.
A soldier limped into the trembling light.
He wore no eyes—just sockets packed with mud.
His jaw hung loose, unhinged by endless fight.

"I kept the time," he said, in voice like gears,
"For every soul the house would choose to end.
Each tick a gasp. Each chime a fading name.
Each war within. Each hour I couldn't mend."

He pointed to a smaller ticking box—
A pocket watch with hands that turned too slow.
"You see this one? This marks the ones who lie—
Who die but never say the things they know."

He wound the spring, and all the room grew still.
The clocks went mute. The floor began to quake.
A mirror fell and shattered into screams—
And from the shards rose up another ache.

The woman clutched her chest and gasped aloud.
The man fell to his knees and spilled a prayer.
The soldier smiled with blood along his teeth.
"You're right on time," he said. "It ends in there."

He pointed to a door within the room,
A hidden frame behind the pendulum.
It swung as if to grant one fleeting pass—
Then snapped to block the path, its rhythm numb.

"To pass," he said, "you must confess your mark.
The second sin. The one you left too deep.
You think the house will free you once you speak?
It won't. But silence is the thing it keeps."

The woman sobbed, then reached into her coat.
She pulled a ribbon—pink and torn with ash.
She kissed it once, then dropped it to the floor.
The clocks resumed their discord and their crash.

The ribbon turned to dust, the door swung wide.
The pendulum drew back to grant a thread.
The soldier bowed, then fell into a heap—
His bones now still, his ticking left for dead.

We passed through quick, before the chance was gone.
The air beyond was colder, grey with chalk.
Behind, the clocks rang out a single chime—
A bell that cracked the hallway's painted walk.

The dog now barked at shadows yet to fall.
The next door bloomed like bruises left too long.
Its number bled across its wooden grin.
And Room Thirteen began to hum its song.

The Twelfth Room

The door was darker than the space around—
A shade that swallowed torchlight as it grew.
Its number scratched by fingernail or knife,
No paint, no brass, no ink, no blood, just rue.

The frame was warped, as though it tried to flee.
The floor before it bore a subtle slope.
The dog sat down and would not raise its head.
We breathed, then stepped beyond the door's faint hope.

Inside, the room was bare, but never still.
Its walls were papered in a muted grey.
The sound of scratching ticked beneath the floor,
As if a hundred nails had lost their way.

A single chair stood centered on the tile.
A bulb swung slow from wire over head.
A bucket sat beneath the rusted light,
Half full of brine and something black and red.

We did not speak—the air forbade all words.
Each breath we took came back too thin and sharp.
Then came the click: a lock not made by hand,
A latch that closed without a single spark.

The wall slid open on its leftmost seam.
A woman stepped, though wrong in limb and pace.
Her arms were bound in cloth, her mouth sewn shut.
And eyes were drawn in charcoal on her face.

She faced the man and tilted like a clock.
She raised her chin as if to point and name.
He took a step, but then the dog let out
A low, sustained and pleading, broken blame.

Another step—the chair began to creak.
The walls began to narrow from the sides.
The bulb above grew brighter, pale and thin—
And then it popped, and black consumed the light.

From somewhere deep, the whisperings began—
Not language, no, but sobbing, fractured low.
They throbbed like memories you never made,
And all at once, you know you still must know.

The woman moved with steps that scraped the floor.
She reached into the pail and pulled a shard—
A mirror piece, but blackened on its face,
Still wet, still sharp, still humming something hard.

She placed it in the man's unwilling hand.
He stared. He shook. He dropped it, gasped, and wept.
"I know this place," he said, "I built this room—
Not with my hands, but lies I never kept."

He looked again, and all the walls showed scenes:
A time he beat a dog for stealing bread.
A time he let his sister take the blame.
A night he watched, then walked away instead.

The scratching grew. The mirror crawled with eyes.
The floor turned slick with things we could not see.
He dropped his coat and fell upon his knees.
He said, "I left her there, and watched her bleed."

The stitched-up woman reached and touched his face.
She nodded once. Then slowly came undone.
The thread across her mouth snapped strand by strand,
And when it broke, the room began to run.

The walls retracted. Light returned in bursts.
The bulb swung mad. The bucket tipped and spilled.
The woman sank back into shadow's mouth—
And from the dark, a final whisper chilled:

"You knew the truth. You made the room your own.
The House remembers what you never said.
You cannot hide from what you choose to lock—
The doors you build are where you'll one day tread."

We fled. The hallway stretched with cruel delight.
The floor was tiled with names that hadn't slept.
The dog now limped. The woman held her chest.
And all of us had bled from what we kept.

The next door rose with hinges lined in bone.
The number thirteen scorched into its grain.
We did not breathe before we walked once more—
And gave the House our memories for pain.

The Thirteenth Room

The thirteenth door stood jagged in its frame,
Its planks mismatched, its nails all driven wrong.
The numbers carved with trembling, failing hand,
Still fresh with rust not absent from the tongue.

No knob, no hinge—just splinters pointing in.
A smear of soot beneath where fingers slid.
The dog began to growl a deeper note,
And barked once loud, then cowered low and hid.

We touched the wood—it shuddered at the palm,
Then cracked apart and creaked an inward breath.
The dark beyond was not a lack of light—
It was a weight, a silence close to death.

A single lamp swung crooked from the wall,
Its chain too short to reach the room's far end.
Its glow revealed the outline of a bed—
And something tied to it by knees and wrists.

The figure groaned but did not raise its head.
A woman, maybe, bones beneath the skin.
She whispered words, or else she only breathed—
Too frail for screams, too dry for any sin.

The man stepped near, then halted with a hiss—
The air around her pulsed and pulled away.
Her skin was black with bruises none could name.
Her mouth was gone. Her teeth had fled the clay.

And yet she wept, though neither eye was whole.
Her tears like ash, like soot from chimneys deep.
We saw the lashes stitched into her limbs,
We heard the sound of chains dragged in her sleep.

Then on the wall, a shadow moved and swelled—
A silhouette, too large to match the shape.
It loomed across the floor with twisted arms,
Its fingers smeared with oil, and cold escape.

It did not speak, but scratched into the wood.
Its nail-carved letters glowed with sickened light:
"She did not beg. She waited. That was all.
She asked to be remembered every night."

The woman moved her head toward us, then back,
As though she knew we wouldn't say her name.
We didn't know it—but the House, it did,
And somewhere in its walls, it screamed the same.

The man among us whispered soft and hoarse:
"I dreamt her once. I knew a girl like this.
She died—no, worse—she lived, then disappeared.
They said she ran. They lied. I said she did."

The shadow stirred. Its arms began to rise.
The lamp swung high and threw a world of flame.
The woman on the bed began to glow—
And all at once, we felt the House inflame.

A voice erupted, not from her but us:
A cry too loud to come from just one throat.
A guilt too vast to fit inside the ribs.
A scream that echoed down the halls we wrote.

We pulled him back. The woman turned to dust.
The shadow laughed and slithered through the wall.
The door behind us slammed with silent force.
The ceiling cracked. The floor began to crawl.

We ran. We did not wait to name the hurt.
The hallway now was red with pulsing seams.
The walls beat like a heart too bruised to stop,
And every breath we took returned with screams.

We left that door behind like one forgets
The truth they helped to bury in a grave.
The next door shone with copper polished clean—
A number fourteen shaped like fingers shaved.

The Fourteenth Room

The copper door was cold beneath the skin,
Though firelight flickered from its seams below.
The dog now whimpered low and looked away.
It would not move, though still it seemed to know.

The number fourteen gleamed in polished arcs—
Too fine, too neat, like something rich and dead.
The frame was warm, as if it pulsed with life.
We braced, then stepped inside, with growing dread.

The chamber stretched beyond what eyes could take,
A ballroom vast, with mirrors on the walls.
The chandeliers hung low and weeping wax,
And from above dripped laughter down the halls.

The floor was gold, but dulled with steps long past—
With heel marks smeared like blood beneath a shoe.
A music box stood broken on the stage.
And yet it played—its gears compelled it through.

The waltz began, a strained and aching sound.
And from the corners stepped the ballroom's ghosts.
They wore fine clothes, their mouths all full of ash,
Their eyes like sockets carved for hollow hosts.

They spun in pairs, though none held hands or smiled.
They twirled in loops, their heads a stuttering sway.
And each one whispered something on each turn—
A name, a plea, a curse they couldn't say.

A woman glided forth with shattered feet,
Her shoes too tight, the bones within too torn.
She bowed toward me and raised a splintered hand.
Her skin was laced with lace and grief and scorn.

I stepped away, but she still danced in place,
Her body moving as the music bled.
"They made me twirl until my limbs gave out.
They taught me grace was better learned when dead."

Another spun, his neck too loose to stand.
He dragged behind a broken cello's bow.
He scraped it on the floor and shrieked a note—
A single sound of agony and woe.

He wore a suit, too fine for one so young.
His boutonnière was stitched into his skin.
"I waltzed into the room that had no door.
They told me love. It turned to discipline."

The woman by my side now broke from thought.
She looked upon a ghost with wide, wide eyes.
She gasped, then stepped—her hand out in the dark.
She whispered, "Mother?" once, and then, "You lied."

The ghost approached, and now we saw her face—
Too like the woman's to be someone else.
She danced alone, but reached with final grace.
Then broke apart into her younger self.

The floor grew hot. The music box spun fast.
The dancers shrieked but would not break their line.
The chandeliers dropped wax like melting flesh.
The ceiling howled and shook in perfect time.

We turned to run, but one had joined the dance—
The woman whirling, pale and wide of eye.
The dog leapt in and barked her out of trance.
She screamed, and then the mirrors cracked the sky.

Each pane exploded, spraying molten glass.
The dancers stopped and vanished into black.
The music box let out a final sigh—
A note so sharp it nearly split the back.

We slammed the door and held our breathing still.
The hallway groaned as if it, too, had danced.
The woman's skin was scorched with looping scars,
In circles where the music's ghosts had pranced.

We did not speak. We knew the steps by now.
The House was waltzing us to deeper things.
The next door rose with velvet red and nails.
The number fifteen burned with blackened rings.

The Fifteenth Room

The fifteenth door was wide before we neared,
Its hinges torn, its lock split down the grain.
The velvet draped across its frame was damp,
And smelled of something copper-rich with pain.

No wind, no breath, no sound behind the crack—
Yet every step we took made echoes bleed.
The dog went still, its hackles raised in fear.
We crossed the frame, compelled by House and need.

The room was circular, a dome of brass,
Its walls engraved with names in winding script.
Each name was scratched as though by blade or claw,
And some were smeared as if the hands had slipped.

The ceiling pulsed with crimson, faint and dull,
A heartbeat barely thumping overhead.
No furniture, no window, not a thing—
Except a cage, and something there half-dead.

It sat within the bars like twisted wool,
Its limbs all wrong, its posture bent with age.
Its face was wrapped in sackcloth, smeared with ink.
Its fingers curled around the iron cage.

It rocked a little, murmuring to none,
And scratched a line along the brass-tiled floor.
Then slowly stopped. And raised its head to speak—
Though from its mouth came something much, much more.

A whisper not of words but full of weight.
A voice that felt like pressure on the ribs.
It said our names without a single breath—
Then told us things we kept behind our lips.

It told of nights where envy shaped our fists,
Of secrets traded for a moment's pride.
It said, "You thought confession might bring peace,
But silence built the cage where shame must hide."

It stood, though it was far too bent to rise.
Its feet were hooves, its back was stitched with wire.
It gripped the bars and smiled through sackcloth folds,
Then blew a breath that reeked of grave and fire.

The names upon the wall began to burn.
The brass grew bright, and from the cracks came moans.
Each letter hissed and tried to twist away—
Too late, too deep, too carved into the bones.

"The ones you buried here still have their names.
The ones you left behind—they leave you too.
You wear the echoes each time that you lie.
The cage is yours. This room remembers you."

The floor began to turn beneath our feet.
The circle spun as if it wished to grind.
The cage grew tall, its bars now sharp and black,
And from it poured the echo of the mind.

We saw within its shape not beast or ghost—
But forms that matched our own in twisted flesh.
Reflections melted, hollow-eyed and bare,
Still mouthing sins we'd never once confessed.

We ran. The walls reached inward as we fled.
The air grew thick and clutched at heel and waist.
The dog barked once, then leapt ahead and bit—
It dragged the woman back toward hallway's grace.

Behind, the room collapsed into a ring.
The cage was gone. The names had turned to fire.
And in the brass, before it cracked and fell—
Was written now the one thing we'd conspired.

We sealed the door. The hallway met us damp.
The floor was cold, the walls too close to trust.
Our breathing synced in silence we had earned—
Each step ahead now heavy with disgust.

Another door appeared, this one of glass.
Its number sixteen frosted on its skin.
We felt the House grow hungry once again,
And knew it meant to feed on what's within.

The Sixteenth Room

The glass was cold enough to crack the skin,
A single pane set in a frame of brass.
Its number floated under sheets of frost,
As though it watched us through the mirrored glass.

The dog growled low, then whimpered at the floor.
The woman shook her head, but still she turned.
We stepped into a chamber made of ice—
And felt the breath of every sin we'd earned.

The room was silent, save a sound like wind,
Yet none could feel it moving on their face.
No draft, no stir, and yet we heard it howl—
It rang like grief confined in frozen space.

The walls were sheets of crystal, veined and black,
Reflecting not ourselves, but shadows past.
The ceiling wept in icicles of sound,
And every drip arrived too slow to last.

A table stood, encased in frozen glass.
Upon it, photographs were caught in frost.
Each one half-seen, obscured by ice and blur,
Each face familiar, yet forever lost.

The woman gasped and pointed at a shape—
A tiny boy, his eyes wide, lips turned blue.
"That's him," she said, "my cousin—no, my—God—
I left him there. I shut the door. I knew."

A whisper stirred, like boots upon the ice.
A figure rose from underneath the floor.
His hands were black, his skin in shards of frost,
And silence wept around him evermore.

He did not speak. He pointed at the frame—
The one that bore the boy inside the snow.
Then reached into his chest and pulled a rose—
Too dead to bloom, too wrong to ever grow.

He offered it. The woman stepped away.
Her hands rose up to shield her from the cold.
The flower bloomed with blood that trickled down—
Then shattered on the floor, too cruel to hold.

The man stepped in and shouted "What is this?"
The figure raised a hand and touched the glass.
And there, a face appeared behind the frost—
The man's own mother, screaming through the past.

The ice began to stretch and hum with grief.
The walls closed in like coffins carved in white.
A memory began to twist in flame—
A fire that never reached the morning's light.

"You locked us out," the mother's image cried,
"You turned the bolt, then walked into the dark.
We froze that night while you stayed safe and warm.
And now you bear the House's coldest mark."

The ceiling cracked. A blizzard shrieked to life.
The dog howled once, its paws now slick with ice.
We clutched each other, stumbled to the wall—
And found a door now coated thick and white.

We forced it wide, the frost clinging like skin.
The chamber screamed and tried to pull us back.
But just before the snow could seal our lungs,
We burst into the hall—a freezing crack.

The warmth returned too slowly to our bones.
Our skin was red, our breath too thin to last.
We held the dog and watched the wall seal shut.
Another room devoured by the past.

The next door crept into the hallway's turn,
A thing of slate, too smooth, too round, too still.
Its number seventeen was etched in bone.
We did not pause. We walked toward deeper will.

The Seventeenth Room

The seventeenth door pulsed like living skin,
Its surface smooth, yet breathing slow and wide.
The number wasn't carved or set in brass—
It throbbed beneath, as though it lived inside.

We touched it once. It quivered, then withdrew.
The dog refused to pass the threshold line.
The woman stared, her face a mask too thin.
We pressed ahead, the hallway's light in spine.

Inside, the room was darker than the rest.
Its walls were cloth, like curtains soaked in ink.
The floor was leather—stitched with laces thick—
And from above, hung ropes like thoughts on brink.

The air was heavy, dense with perfume stale.
A scent of sweat and something sweet, then sour.
A record turned upon a phonograph—
Too slow to sing, too warped to keep its hour.

A figure stood beside the farthest rope—
Tall, dressed in black, its hands wrapped round a cane.
Its hat was wide, its face was made of veils,
Its voice too low to separate from pain.

"You've wandered far," it said. "You're near the core.
But here, the House remembers what you paid.
The pleasures you denied, the things you took—
The rules you broke and never truly weighed."

It snapped its fingers. All the ropes dropped down.
Each one revealed a dangling, shrouded shape.
They swayed in time, suspended not by noose—
But by their tongues, drawn out beyond escape.

Each mouth was wide, yet none could seem to speak.
Their eyes were shut, though every head still wept.
Their limbs were limp, their bodies bruised and red—
And through their teeth, their memories still crept.

The man among us stepped but could not breathe.
He stared at one and gasped, "I know this face…"
A boy he knew, or broke, or once betrayed—
Now swaying here in silent, strangled grace.

The figure nodded. "Lust, and shame, and pride—
You called it games, but what you meant was rule.
You bent the want of others to your own.
Now watch them swing. And know you were the fuel."

The ropes began to twitch like worms in fire.
The cloth on every wall began to crawl.
From each dark corner, laughter thick and raw
Rose up and filled the chamber wall to wall.

A woman stepped from shadow, eyes sewn shut—
She wore a dress of knives, and nothing more.
She pointed once toward us and softly moaned—
A note that made our stomachs twist and soar.

"We danced," she said, though stitched through every lip.
"You said you'd love. You only loved control.
You learned to take, then blamed us when we bled.
The House remembers. Every cut. Each role."

The ropes swung harder, striking at the floor.
The phonograph now whined like rusted steel.
We turned to flee, but veils came drifting down—
Each one a face we hadn't meant to feel.

We tore through gauze and stumbled to the door.
The walls now hissed with heat and dripping shame.
The dog was barking wild, its fur on end—
It clawed the seams and called us back to name.

We burst back out. The cloth wrapped round my leg.
I screamed and kicked until it slid away.
Behind, the ropes all danced a final time—
Then snapped with glee, as if they'd had their say.

We fell into the hallway's aching chill.
The air was dry, but every wall looked damp.
The man was pale. He did not speak at all.
The woman sobbed, her eyes two haunted lamps.

The next door bloomed in rust instead of wood.
The number eighteen curled like thorn and nail.
We did not wait to catch our broken breath.
The House had more. The House would never fail.

The Eighteenth Room

The eighteenth door was built of rusted steel,
Its hinges fused with grime and flaking red.
The number scratched upon its dented face
Looked carved by nails or claws from something dead.

No warmth came through the frame, no hint of sound—
Just silence dense, as if the room had drowned.
The dog stepped back and growled into the dark.
We touched the latch and felt the House surround.

The door gave way and groaned a metal song.
Inside, a prison cell of iron grew.
The bars were bent, though none had forced them wide.
The walls were grey and sweating rusted dew.

Each inch was scarred with names and dates and pleas—
All etched in haste by hands no longer near.
A single light blinked overhead, then stilled.
And in the farthest cage, sat something queer.

It had a face, but barely, blurred and warped.
Its head was shaved, its eyes replaced with thread.
It wore a uniform of ash and belts,
And bled a silent wound not wholly bled.

Its hands were bound, yet still they twitched and signed.
Its tongue hung low, a knotted, rubber thing.
It looked at us, then to the wall behind,
Where chains hung loose but hummed as if they'd sing.

"This is the jail," it croaked in guttural tone.
"The one you built with every word unmeant.
The House has kept the sentences you gave.
Each punishment you whispered—where it went."

It pointed to the cells that flanked the wall—
And there we saw the ones we'd cast aside:
A brother locked for truths we couldn't bear.
A friend condemned for when we never tried.

A girl we mocked when silence was her shield.
A boy we let be cornered into shame.
A teacher beaten down with sharpened words.
A stranger jailed for bearing just a name.

The cells grew loud with echoes from the past.
Each ghost arose, still shackled, still confused.
They asked no why, for we had made it clear—
We'd written laws in fear, then left them bruised.

The woman cried, her mouth too weak to pray.
The man began to claw at his own skin.
The figure in the cage laughed once and rose,
Though bound, it floated, shivering within.

"You think the House forgives the prisons made?
It keeps them warm. It keeps them full and fed.
You made these locks. You wound the time so tight.
Now count the bars and hear what never fled."

The chains came down and wrapped around our feet.
The air grew hot, each breath a gasp of flame.
A bell began to ring from nowhere clear—
Each chime a verdict, cruel, without a name.

The dog leapt up and bit the nearest link.
It shattered once, then dragged us to the floor.
The figure screamed and burst into a cloud—
Of keys, of cuffs, of judgments we'd ignored.

We fought our way toward light beyond the bars.
The door now swung with rust that peeled and hissed.
We crashed into the hall, our backs on fire,
And knew what other broken rooms we'd missed.

The metal howled behind us, snapping shut.
A silence deeper still replaced the screams.
We breathed, but barely, weighed with things we knew—
Of words that trap, of laws that ruin dreams.

The hallway stretched with walls too thin to trust.
A new door sprouted from the hallway's bend.
Its number nineteen smeared like blood in frost—
And we marched on, though none could name the end.

The Nineteenth Room

The nineteenth door was made of weathered stone,
Too old to hold its frame without a groan.
Its number chipped and fading from the arch,
Yet still it pulsed as if it breathed alone.

The threshold bore a crack that split the floor,
Where roots grew up through soil left long unturned.
The dog growled once and scraped against the wall—
Its eyes were fixed, its instincts newly burned.

We stepped across into a world gone still,
A chapel drowned in moss and muted air.
No pews, no altar—only shadowed walls
And columns shaped from hands that formed a prayer.

Above, the ceiling wept with candle soot,
And vines hung down like sins we failed to name.
A single bell swung gently, though unstruck,
Its silence heavy, echoing with blame.

A hooded figure knelt where light should fall,
Its robe of burlap torn by thorn and thread.
Its breath was wet, as though it drank the dark.
Its arms were chained and wrapped around its head.

We did not speak. The silence was a weight.
The very air condemned the wish to cry.
Then with a groan, the figure raised its face—
Two sockets wide, two lips too cracked to lie.

"You prayed," it said, "but not to offer thanks.
You bent your knee to take, not give away.
You sought no light, no peace, no higher will—
You asked for punishment to pass your way.

You cursed the gods when they denied your pride.
You blamed the stars when hunger came too near.
And every time you whispered for escape,
You fed the House your bargains soaked in fear."

Its arms unwrapped. The chains began to fall.
Each link clinked down like guilt too dense to float.
The vines upon the ceiling started twitching,
Then curled into the shapes of hood and coat.

A second figure dropped from overhead—
No face, no hands, just breathless, weeping cloth.
It crawled along the floor like blighted thought,
And muttered truths that shattered inner oaths.

We could not move. We saw our former selves—
Each kneeling in some pew, in silent prayer.
Not to forgive, but for a chance to win.
Not out of love, but out of quiet despair.

The woman fell to knees and shook with shame.
The man backed up, his throat too tight to yell.
The bell above gave one reluctant sway—
Then sounded once, a toll too loud to quell.

The figures turned and pointed toward the cracks.
The walls split wide, revealing more than stone.
They showed a void, a tunnel of the self,
Where every echo begged to die alone.

We heard our voices screaming in the past—
A thousand prayers returned and turned to knives.
The chapel cracked. The ceiling caved in slow.
We stumbled through the smoke, still clutching lives.

The hallway met us like a coffin's mouth.
The dog was first to run, and bark no more.
The woman sobbed, the man began to bleed—
Not from a wound, but from a vow he swore.

The House had peeled another layer back.
Our faith now torn, exposed for what it was.
Another door began to creak and bloom—
The number twenty, shaped like thorn and gauze.

The Twentieth Room

The twentieth door was pale and dressed in silk,
Its fabric stained with browns and faded rose.
It swung not open, but it parted slow—
As if the room behind already knows.

The dog refused to pass and whined instead,
Its tail low, its stance against the floor.
We stepped beyond the veil without a breath—
And felt it seal, like skin around a sore.

Inside, the walls were draped in children's clothes.
Too many, sewn together seam by seam.
A rocking horse stood tipped upon its side,
And every doll was frozen mid-extreme.

Some screamed, some wept, some smiled with sharpened teeth.
Their glassy eyes were set in twisted paint.
A mobile turned with blades instead of stars,
Above a crib too clean, too still, too faint.

A woman stood beside it, pale and thin.
She wore a nurse's gown, but not with pride.
Her apron bore dark handprints, small and red.
Her lips were stitched, her eyes so open wide.

She rocked the air where something should have been.
And when she turned, she showed her hollow chest.
No heart remained—just cribwood carved within,
And lullabies too drowned to ever rest.

She pointed at the dolls, then at the bed.
We dared not move. The woman simply swayed.
Then from the crib, a breathless giggle came—
Not joy, but hunger learning how to play.

A tiny hand rose up from underneath.
Its fingers bent too many times, too wrong.
Its nails were black, its palm too wet and raw.
It waved once, then it pulled the light along.

The bulbs grew dim. The dolls began to twitch.
Their limbs moved soft, like dancers in a grave.
A tune began to warble through the room—
A lullaby no infant soul could brave.

The rocking horse let out a wooden shriek.
The mobile spun so fast it cracked the air.
And then the woman wept from stitched-up eyes,
And opened wide her chest to show us where—

Inside, a hole had formed that sucked all sound.
We staggered back. The man began to scream.
The dog leapt forward, barked and broke a doll.
But still they crawled—like spiders built from dreams.

The crib stood up. It moved without a wheel.
It chased us like a cradle sent to feed.
We pulled the woman back from nursing arms,
That tried to hug but only sought to bleed.

The walls collapsed. The fabric turned to ash.
The rocking horse split down the centre seam.
The lullaby sped up, then burst apart,
And woke the dolls to cries too sharp to scream.

We found the door, though now it pulsed with heat.
We fled. Behind, a lull returned to wrong.
The House had nursed a memory in cloth—
And stitched us all into its dying song.

The hallway met us short of breath and skin.
The woman bled, the man was grey with fright.
The dog now limped, but would not leave our side.
The House had taken rest, but not its bite.

Another door emerged, its frame was cracked.
Its number twenty-one, just barely lit.
We moved, for choice had left us long ago—
And deeper still, the House would never quit.

The Twenty-First Room

The twenty-first door breathed a quiet steam,
Its wood damp-warped, its surface blistered grey.
The number etched by finger, not by blade—
And smeared as though the hand had slipped away.

The frame was soft, like pulp from rotted trunks,
And swelled with moisture bleeding from the grain.
The dog stepped back, its paws upon the tiles,
Then whimpered once, and would not step again.

We pushed inside. A mist caressed our skin.
The room was dense with heat and heavy air.
A bathhouse once—or something near to one—
With veils of steam and broken marble stare.

The floor was lined with slats of sodden wood,
The walls of tiled glass in fractured tones.
And in the midst, a pool lay still and wide,
Its surface black, as smooth as polished stones.

The scent was salt and rot and woman's breath—
A perfume faint, yet clinging to the chest.
No sound came first, just dripping from the vents,
And then a ripple, soft, disturbed the rest.

From in the pool a figure rose and swayed—
A woman wrapped in seaweed, slick with brine.
Her hair like ropes, her face a barnacled mask,
Her body blue from drowning out of time.

She didn't speak, but hummed a single note,
A hum that made the water pulse and part.
The ripple touched our shoes and made them ache,
A call that wrapped around the throat and heart.

She gestured once and turned beneath the waves,
Her form dissolving in the gloom below.
And all at once, the surface burst with hands—
Pale fingers reaching upward, row by row.

They clawed the air but grasped at nothing real,
Just memories, and dreams that had no names.
A voice began, like someone deep in sleep—
"I pulled them in. I told them they'd be clean."

The man stepped back, his eyes wide in the steam.
The woman froze and whispered, "This is mine."
She stepped toward water, as if half-aware.
The surface shone her face, but not her time.

"I came here once," she said, "I meant to leave—
I meant to just forget the things I knew.
The pills, the blade, the bath that took me in…
I meant to go. I didn't think it through."

The hands withdrew. A silence held its breath.
Then from the depths, the woman reappeared—
Not ours, but hers, the ghost she used to be—
She smiled, and that was somehow what we feared.

She reached for her, their fingers just apart.
The room went still, the tiles began to crack.
The woman fell—but we were faster now.
The dog leapt in and dragged her body back.

The spirit screamed, a wail too wet to bear.
The pool erupted in a burst of teeth.
The hands all tore at one another's arms—
Then vanished in the mist that lived beneath.

The steam collapsed. The water turned to glass.
The pool went dry, revealing things we'd fled:
A comb, a shoe, a blade, a ragged dress,
All things she left the moment she was dead.

We fled. The tiles behind us hissed and sighed.
The room exhaled and folded in its grief.
The woman wept but said no single word—
Her truth now aired, her guilt now touched and brief.

The hallway felt no pity in its walls.
The air returned, though every breath was cracked.
A door appeared, too narrow and too low.
The number twenty-two was sharp and black.

The Twenty-Second Room

The twenty-second door was squat and mean,
Its wood too tight, its grain too deeply bruised.
The number gouged as though by splintered teeth,
A crude attempt—like something once abused.

The handle loose, it spun beneath the hand.
The dog gave two short barks, then backed away.
We forced the frame, which moaned as if in shame,
And found a room too cold for night or day.

It reeked of chalk and ink and rotting books,
Of paper damp with sweat and nervous hands.
The walls were lined with desks in jagged rows,
Each carved with names, each tagged with reprimands.

A blackboard loomed, too tall for sight to scale,
Its words all smeared but never truly gone.
A cane lay snapped across the teacher's desk,
And silence deeper than a tomb drew on.

A child sat slumped beneath a crooked lamp,
Its cord frayed thin, its bulb a twitching eye.
He wore a uniform of dust and thread,
His fingers bound with tape too thick and dry.

His head was bowed, his knuckles scraped and red.
He did not move, nor flinch, nor breathe a name.
We stepped too close. He stirred with sudden weight—
And raised a slate that bore one word: "The Same."

The dog began to bark, then whine, then back.
The man stepped in, his face a growing white.
The woman froze and turned toward every desk—
And found in each a child erased from light.

One bore a wound across her open palm.
Another drooled into a page of math.
A third had pins set in his lips like stars—
Their eyes were dark, and stared along our path.

A voice began, not shouted, but decreed.
"We taught them pain," it said, "and called it worth.
We punished every joy that didn't match.
We taught them fear and promised them rebirth."

The child now stood. He faced the board with shame.
His back bore marks too raw for time to hide.
He raised a stick and scrawled across the chalk:
"They said my name, then taught me not to pride."

We stepped away, but every desk now shook.
Each one gave rise to ghosts in childish frames.
Their mouths were stitched with pencils, tongues with ink—
Their ears still bruised from all the shouted names.

The cane began to twitch across the desk.
It rose, then cracked the air with thundered spite.
The child turned once, his face now split with tears,
And pointed us to where we'd failed to fight.

The man collapsed. He sobbed into the floor.
"I laughed at him," he said. "I told them too.
He didn't cry until the last note rang.
I watched them beat him—I knew what to do."

The ghosts drew close. The room began to bend.
The desks collapsed, their wood too warped to bear.
The child now stood with slate against his chest—
And shattered it with hands still thin with care.

The pieces flew. The chalk ignited bright.
The blackboard cracked and bled a line of flame.
The desks fell back into the gnashing dark.
The children moaned, but never said a name.

We found the door just as it pulled away.
We crashed back out into the waiting hall.
Behind, the cane still wrote upon the floor—
Its final word was just: "You let me fall."

We helped the man to rise, his face gone grey.
The woman's hand shook faintly at her side.
The dog lay down, exhausted, burned with smoke.
The House grew still, but never satisfied.

Another door began to stretch and groan.
Its number twenty-three glared pale as glass.
The hallway yawned, and somewhere down its throat—
We felt the voice of what we could not pass.

The Twenty-Third Room

The twenty-third door bled a subtle glow,
Its seams outlined in gold, though chipped and cracked.
The number shimmered faintly, hard to hold,
As if it moved when no one's gaze looked back.

The wood was warm, too warm for human craft.
The air around it buzzed like bees in jars.
The dog stood up, but would not meet our eyes.
We passed the frame like thieves beneath the stars.

The room was filled with portraits, side by side—
A gallery of faces bound in dust.
They lined the walls from floor to vaulted arch,
Their frames ornate with bone and flaking rust.

No nameplates marked the subjects as we passed,
But still we knew each one was once alive.
Their painted eyes would follow as we stepped,
And in their gaze, the room began to thrive.

A velvet carpet stretched beneath our feet,
Its fibres curled like fingers from the floor.
And everywhere we looked, the air was thick
With something sweet and spoiled behind each door.

A man's face loomed above a shattered frame.
His smile was wide, though teeth were far too few.
A voice called out—not loud, but far too near—
"You came to look. Now let me look at you."

The canvas shook, and from it stepped a form,
A man-shaped smear of pigment, flesh, and soot.
His suit was oil, his hands were painter's knives,
And each long step left footprints black as root.

He lifted up a brush of human hair,
Its bristles soaked in blood or something black.
He said, "I framed them all, one stroke at time—
Each sin, each shame, each name you failed to back."

He pointed to a woman near the door.
Her portrait bore her wounds with poised regret.
She stared, her dress aflame, her hands raised high—
Her smile the mask of someone who'd forget.

The woman with us gasped, then fell to knees.
She said, "My sister. No—it can't be—no…"
The figure smiled. "You left her in that room.
She lit the match. You said, 'I didn't know.'"

Another canvas flickered into flame.
A child's face screamed, though no sound could escape.
The man among us backed into the wall—
His portrait formed with bruises in its shape.

A thousand paintings blinked as if alive.
The gallery began to stretch and warp.
Each frame expanded, opened, reached like mouths—
To swallow us into the painted corpse.

We ran—but frames grew arms to drag us back.
The dog bit hard, and broke a reaching wrist.
We pulled the woman from her sister's shade.
The portrait cracked but still the flames persist.

The painter screamed, his brushes spinning fast.
The oil poured and smeared across the room.
But through the storm, a door revealed itself—
A tear in canvas shaped like rising doom.

We dove through paint and fire, out to air.
The hallway spun, now streaked with crimson tones.
The wall behind still bore our painted shapes—
Trapped, screaming in a frame that rattled bones.

The House had kept our stories on display.
It hung us by the guilt we dare not name.
Another door began to hum and peel—
Its number twenty-four, now sharp with flame.

The Twenty-Fourth Room

The twenty-fourth door flickered like a flame,
Its surface scorched, its number burned to bone.
The frame was blackened, still it breathed out heat—
A pulse of ash that shivered through the stone.

The dog stood firm, though quivering with fear.
The man now limped, his face too tight with dread.
The woman watched the smoke that slipped beneath,
And whispered, "Something here already bled."

We stepped inside, and fire met our gaze—
Not flame that danced, but fire locked in stone.
The walls were blackened steel, the ceiling gone.
Above, the smoke revealed the night alone.

A furnace roared at centre, mouth agape,
Its door wide open, glowing fierce with breath.
A table stood with tools of tongs and blades,
And scattered all around, the smell of death.

Then from the forge, a figure crawled and stood—
A woman forged from cinder, soot, and steel.
Her apron hung with rivets, burned with names,
Her hands two brands that seared the air they feel.

Her face was veiled in iron, cracked with rust.
Her voice, when born, was hammer striking glass.
"They gave me ash," she said, "and called it gold.
They told me, 'Build. Endure. And let it pass.'"

She raised her arm and summoned from the coals
A glowing mold that shimmered like a chain.
"Each life," she said, "becomes its shape in heat.
You press the soul. You mold the mind through pain.

They gave me children. Broken. Bent. Unmourned.
They said, 'Refine. Restore. Repair. Remake.'
But iron screams when forced against its will.
And not all shapes survive the fire's stake."

She thrust the mold into the open flames.
The fire shrieked, and out it came anew—
A figure, small, with limbs not yet complete,
Still glowing red with torment bursting through.

It crawled along the floor and reached for her.
She turned away and raised a hammer high.
The dog began to bark in helpless grief.
We stepped between them, shouting "Let it die?"

The figure paused, its shell now cracked with light.
The woman stared, then let her hammer fall.
"This is the truth of all who tried to fix—
We break the broken, thinking we know all."

The furnace hissed, the ceiling started moan.
The floor grew hot enough to burn the boots.
The tiny forged creation fled from sight—
And where it stepped, the iron left its roots.

We ran, the dog ahead to seek the door.
The woman's foot was scorched, her skin now split.
The man now held her tight and dragged her free—
While in the forge, the child began to sit.

The smith looked down and laid her hammer bare.
She whispered, "Let the broken shape their own."
Then shut the furnace door and sealed her fate.
The flames rose high. The forge was left alone.

The hallway met us, blistered at the touch.
The air was thick with metal, salt, and screams.
Behind the door, the pounding would not stop—
As though the House had sparked a thousand dreams.

A newer door slid up with shrieking pins.
Its number twenty-five, carved deep in ice.
We did not rest. The House gave no reprieve—
Its lessons sharp, its mercy never twice.

The Twenty-Fifth Room

The twenty-fifth door rose on frozen tracks,
Its hinges lined with frost too thick to scrape.
The number hung in icicles and thread,
As if the House had let the chill reshape.

The wood was white, but humming deep with blue—
A throb like breath exhaled in long regret.
The woman trembled, though she said no word.
The dog drew close and whimpered near her step.

We opened it, and all the heat withdrew.
A cold too deep for flesh to bear poured in.
The room was tiled in bone-white, gleaming bright,
With frost that spidered high along the skin.

A bed of iron sat at centre stark,
Its frame too clean, its sheets too stiff with cold.
Beside it stood a tray of gleaming tools—
And walls of drawers where nothing ever grows.

It was a morgue, though wrong in size and sound—
No buzz, no hum, no sigh of filtered breath.
The silence rang as loud as any scream,
A sterile hush in love with ordered death.

A figure moved in shadows near the wall—
A doctor, or the shadow of one once.
He wore a coat that trailed behind his steps,
And gloves that squeaked like leather soaked in months.

"The body lies," he said, "but truth remains.
The flesh forgets, but I am paid to know.
You brought this corpse," he whispered, facing us,
"And now we see what you have failed to show."

He beckoned to the slab, and with a nod,
The drawers slid out with bodies pale and bent.
Each one a version of ourselves in sleep,
Each one a lie we told, a choice unspent.

"You said you didn't mean to go that far.
You claimed you didn't see the final fall.
But every act must rot beneath the skin.
And now the House will show you all of all."

He pulled the sheet from one still-shaking form.
It was the man—his eyes wide shut with glue.
His chest was scarred, his lips sewn with a truth:
"I knew she screamed. I closed the door. I knew."

The woman gasped, her fingers at her mouth.
Her drawer slid out, revealing someone small—
A younger her, with wrists too wrapped in gauze,
And eyes that stared straight through the hallway's wall.

"I told them it was nothing, just a bruise.
I told them not to worry, not to stay.
I begged them not to call it what it was.
I walked away. I let it rot away."

The dog now barked, a sound of deep despair.
Its drawer slid next, revealing—nothing there.
Just bones wrapped in a collar torn and red,
A leash that reached for hands that never cared.

The doctor raised a scalpel made of glass.
"The cut is quick, but knowing takes much more.
The House demands you carry what you find.
It gives no peace. It only keeps the score."

The corpses screamed—not out, but inward deep.
Their voices came like sobs across the tile.
We turned and ran, though nowhere was escape.
The slab split wide and birthed a final file—

Our names atop, with space for time of death.
We slammed the door and left the chill behind.
The hallway hissed, then sealed the morgue with ice,
And in our ears, the scalpel still aligned.

The woman shook. The man could barely speak.
The dog now walked with limping haunted pace.
The House had shown what lay beneath the flesh—
And carved our griefs into the hallway's face.

The next door peeled from plaster pale as skin.
Its number twenty-six too faint to trace.
But we moved on. For nothing we had seen
Could rival what the House had yet to place.

The Twenty-Sixth Room

The twenty-sixth door rose like stitched-up skin,
Its leather creased, its seams pulled taut and sore.
The number carved in pale, half-faded flesh,
As if the House had borrowed it from more.

A smell of iodine and something sweet
Hung thick around the frame like breath gone bad.
The dog lay down and growled but did not bark.
We crossed the threshold slowly, tense and sad.

Inside, the room was dim and dressed in white—
A ward, or something meant to look like one.
Each wall was padded, though not clean or soft—
But bulging where the fabric came undone.

A single bed was strapped against the floor.
Its mattress stained with sweat and darker things.
Above, a light swung slowly side to side,
And from the walls came low, unearthly rings.

A chair sat in the corner, face to wall.
A figure slouched within, bound wrist to arm.
Its head was hooded, though it turned to us—
And when it spoke, the syllables could harm.

"They said I wasn't sick enough to stay.
They said I didn't scream the proper screams.
They locked the door and told me I was free—
Then fed me pills to cauterise my dreams."

Its voice was dry, like chalk scraped on a stone.
It laughed, then coughed, and laughed again through dust.
"They visit now, of course. To take the notes.
To prove I lied. To paint me down with trust.

I showed them what the House had done to me.
I showed them where it whispered in the tile.
They told me I was sick for telling truth—
But never checked the hallway for the file."

The room began to close around our steps.
The padded walls grew tighter as we breathed.
The chair stood up, though no one broke the ropes.
The figure swayed, a marionette beneath.

"You come to see the patient? Sit, then, please.
You brought your symptoms with you down the hall.
Your grief, your guilt, your silence and your shame—
They're chronic now. The House will treat them all."

The bed began to creak, though none lay there.
The lights swung harder, brighter, sharper still.
The corners hissed with whispers none had taught—
And something sang from deep beyond our will.

The man began to stammer, words unfit.
The woman scratched her arm until it bled.
The dog now whimpered, backed into the door,
And barked as if to say: "Not in your head."

We staggered through, but not before we saw
Our names appear upon the padded wall.
Each etched in thread that glistened like a worm,
Each spelling truths we'd tried to not recall.

The chair collapsed, the hood fell loose, revealed—
The figure wore no face, just mirrored glass.
We saw ourselves reflected in its frame—
Then slammed the door and let the moment pass.

The hallway flexed with fever in its breath.
The dog stood still and growled into the air.
The House had pressed a finger to our minds—
And showed us madness hiding soft and fair.

A door slid next from out the hallway's spine.
Its number twenty-seven scratched with bone.
And we moved on, not out of strength or hope—
But knowing we would never leave alone.

The Twenty-Seventh Room

The twenty-seventh door was tall and thin,
Its shape too narrow for a human frame.
The number scrawled in soot and greasy ash,
As though a chimney coughed it out in shame.

The air around it swirled with choking heat—
But underneath, a colder scent prevailed:
Of cellar stone and mildew thick with mold,
Of pages damp, and parchment curled and pale.

We ducked to pass beneath the crooked arch.
The room beyond was dim and full of dust.
Its floor was stacked with books from wall to wall,
Their spines all rotted, silvered deep with crust.

Some lay in piles, their ink dissolved in grief.
Some screamed in silence—open, gasping wide.
And in the centre sat a wooden desk,
Where someone scribbled fast, as if to hide.

The figure wore a cloak of parchment skin.
Its fingers cracked like quills with every twitch.
Its face was buried deep in curling scrolls—
Its tongue split down the middle like a stitch.

It turned to us, but did not meet our eyes.
Instead it said, "What will you write today?
Confession? History? Or just excuse?
The House records, no matter what you say."

Its hands began to move across a book—
Not pages, but a slab of open bone.
The words appeared in blood or ink or both,
Each letter groaned, as if it walked alone.

"I wrote the stories no one else would keep.
The memories you hide are stored with me.
Each one becomes a chapter in the House.
Each one ensures the ghosts remain set free."

The man stepped back and knocked a stack aside.
It burst apart, and shrieked a single word:
"Liar." Then the parchment caught to flame,
Though none had touched it, and no match was heard.

The woman turned, and saw a page with hers—
A diary she'd burned when she was twelve.
It opened up, and there her secrets crawled—
A thousand truths she never meant to shelve.

"You write your life in whispers," said the scribe.
"You edit guilt and trim the sharpest edge.
You tear out pages others tried to read.
But every story ends with you on ledge."

It offered her a pen with pointed teeth.
The nib was dipped in something dark and red.
She would not take it. Still, her name was penned—
It wrote itself with thoughts she left for dead.

The dog now barked, but softly, low with fear.
The books began to fold themselves like hands.
They opened wide and roared without a tongue—
A thousand volumes of abandoned lands.

We tore away and found the hallway gone—
Replaced with shelves that stretched in writhing loops.
And from above, a tome the size of death
Fell hard enough to crack the wooden roots.

We forced a door from splinters in the wall.
We fled into the hall with lungs afire.
Behind, the scribe still whispered as it wrote—
Our names now marked in House's thickest choir.

The man collapsed and spat a string of words—
A tale too short to ever find relief.
The woman clutched the dog and kissed its head.
Her eyes were full of paper cuts and grief.

Another door began to uncoil next—
Its number twenty-eight engraved in flame.
The House had read our stories in its ink—
And every word would bleed us just the same.

The Twenty-Eighth Room

The twenty-eighth door pulsed with rhythmic beats,
As if a heart behind it pressed and swelled.
Its surface black, and soft like bruising fruit,
Its grain like veins beneath where warmth was held.

The number throbbed in threads of living skin—
Not carved, but grown, like scarred and stitched regret.
The dog began to whimper, backpedal.
But still we pressed—though none had spoken yet.

Inside, the room was pulsing, red and vast,
A chamber made of meat and bone and breath.
The walls contracted slightly with each step,
Alive, aware, and steeped in stench of death.

No ceiling overhead, just throbbing dark,
No floor, just tissue thick with pulsing lines.
And in the centre, something hung from cords—
A sack of flesh that blinked between its spines.

It shivered as we stepped beneath its gaze,
Its mouth unfolding wide across its chest.
It bore no teeth, just rows of breathing pores
That whispered in a tongue too dark to guess.

Then came a voice, from nowhere we could see:
"You are the hunger carved into the House.
You bring the feast. You bring the open skin.
You let me in, and I will never douse."

The sack began to pulse, then split apart—
Revealing limbs too thin to hold a name.
Its hands were claws, but gentle in their twitch.
Its body slick with guilt and growing flame.

The woman froze and gripped her tattered coat.
"I've dreamt this thing," she gasped. "I drew it once.
I saw it when I was too young to speak—
It smiled at me, and whispered, 'We are months.'"

The thing unfurled itself into a shape—
Not man, not beast, not ghost or god or worm.
It stepped on feet too flat, too wrong, too wet.
Its breath a furnace fed by every term.

It turned to us and laid its palm to floor.
The muscle hissed and split to show our sin:
A scene from childhood, bathed in savage glee—
Where we had laughed when cruelty crept in.

The man fell back and screamed into his hands.
"That wasn't me!" he wailed, though none believed.
The thing just stared with eyes it did not own—
And from its mouth, a second face was weaved.

A woman's face, stitched into living flesh,
Her mouth sewn shut, her eyelids torn away.
"You watched me break," she said without a voice.
"You watched, and turned, and hoped I'd fade to grey."

The dog now barked and snapped its teeth at air.
The floor recoiled and tried to bite us whole.
We ran through cords that whipped like grieving vines,
The hallway reappearing as our goal.

We flung the door shut just as meat pursued—
The sound of breathing followed through the crack.
We dropped, and gasped, and tried to purge the stench—
But still it clung like shadow on our back.

The House grew still, but never less alive.
The walls now throbbed with something deep and grim.
The woman cried, her voice a hollow drum.
The man just stared with vision going dim.

Another door rose thick with coiling thread.
Its number twenty-nine, red-etched with spite.
The dog began to howl without a tone.
The hallway moaned. The House had more to write.

The Twenty-Ninth Room

The twenty-ninth door glistened, slick with oil,
Its surface pulsed with shifting, rainbow sheen.
The number danced like mercury on stone,
Elusive, sharp, and far too cold to glean.

No frame held fast—just flowing, warped design,
As if the House had melted in this part.
The dog refused to step, its teeth now bare.
We entered slow, our hands upon our hearts.

The room was made of mirrors—none the same.
Each pane distorted, twisted, stretched, or crushed.
The air was hushed, yet thick with quiet clicks—
As if the walls themselves could think and blush.

No sound save that. And something else: a tune—
A waltz we'd heard before, but not in time.
It echoed through the mirrors, wrong and right,
A music box rebuilt to punish rhyme.

The first reflection smiled, then broke apart.
My face dissolved into a stranger's grin.
The man gasped loud—his image laughed at him,
Then reached out from the glass and pulled him in.

The woman screamed and struck the pane with fists.
Her mirrored twin just tilted back its head,
And opened up her chest with ghostly claws—
Then whispered something none of us had said.

"This is the self the House remembers most,"
A voice proclaimed, though none could find its mouth.
"Not how you see, but how you're seen and shaped—
The eyes you loathe, the ones that faced your south.

You wore the mask so long it learned your skin.
You smiled through teeth that dreamed of sharper ends.
You lied so well you birthed a second you—
And that is who the House now calls its friend."

A mirror cracked, and from it stepped a child.
Not innocent—but perfect in its sin.
Its eyes were black with knowing, calm and clear.
It spoke, though not from lips, but from within.

"You're not afraid of monsters. You're afraid
They know the parts you keep beneath the floor.
And in this room, the ones you used to be
Return in glass, and knock upon the door."

The mirrors rippled. One by one they bled.
The dog barked loud and shattered one with force.
We saw the woman trapped inside a maze—
A thousand selves, each worse than the divorce.

The man now stood before a wall of him—
Each version made of rage, of grief, of spite.
They watched him with a hatred he had earned—
And opened mouths that swallowed every light.

We fled into the hall, through breaking glass.
The mirrors screamed in voices not our own.
They called us cowards, sinners, every truth
We buried deep and dared not set in stone.

The House had peeled another skin away.
We saw ourselves, and found no place to hide.
The woman shook, her mouth repeating prayers.
The man just whispered names and barely cried.

A door grew next with iron bar and brace.
Its number thirty, scarred into the steel.
The hallway groaned with echoes made of doubt—
And deeper still, the House would make us kneel.

The Thirtieth Room

The thirtieth door was chained in loops of rust,
Each link like ribs pulled tight across the frame.
The number stencilled faint in flaking black,
As if it feared the burden of its name.

The dog lay down and whined beneath its breath.
The woman held her chest, too scared to knock.
But still we pried the chain loose one by one—
And stepped into a room too still to mock.

Inside, a courtroom cracked with age and mold,
Its pews decayed, its benches split with rot.
A gavel sat upon a crooked stand,
The judge's seat long empty, long forgot.

But all around, the air was stiff with weight—
With judgment passed by voices we had heard.
And every shadow lining wall and beam
Was shaped like someone silenced by our word.

The witness box was filled with broken glass.
The gallery was packed with vacant stares.
And in the dock, a mirror in a cage—
Reflecting us through scratches, smoke, and prayers.

A figure cloaked in robes of stitched-up mouths
Rose from behind the pulpit of the damned.
Its face was blank, save for a blood-red brand—
A symbol none of us could understand.

It raised one hand. The dog began to bark.
The woman gasped, the man fell to his knees.
The figure spoke, in tones like grinding stone:
"The court now hears the evidence of pleas."

From somewhere deep, the silence took on form—
It throbbed with footsteps we had once denied.
And then the shadows stood and faced the light—
And spoke with all the wounds that never lied.

"You let me fall and laughed behind the glass."
"You watched me drown and left before I screamed."
"You passed me on the stairs, and saw the bruise."
"You knew. You always knew. You only dreamed."

Each voice was one we thought we'd left behind.
Each tone too clear, too close, too sharp to miss.
The room began to shrink with every claim—
And echoed back our silence as abyss.

"How do you plead?" the robed thing finally asked.
But none of us could speak, could bear the choice.
The man just wept and shook his broken head.
The woman could not match her inner voice.

The dog stood firm, as if to shield our shame.
But in the mirror, we were all alone.
No judge, no jury—only us to blame.
Our guilt was carved in marrow, breath, and bone.

The gavel dropped without a hand or sound.
The floor gave way, a trapdoor into void.
We leapt as walls collapsed with roaring weight,
Our verdicts sealed, our innocence destroyed.

The hallway caught us like a dying breath.
The dog now limped, its eyes like fading glass.
The House had passed its sentence with no words—
And still, we had a hundred doors to pass.

The next door rose with hinges made of locks.
Its number thirty-one was etched in lead.
The wall behind it pulsed with coiling roots—
And somewhere, far below, we heard the dead.

The Thirty-First Room

The thirty-first door hummed a metal hymn,
Its hinges creaked in slow, mechanical groans.
The number stamped in lead was bent and cracked,
As if the House had crushed it into bones.

The dog stepped close, but halted at the seam.
It whined, then turned and scratched the hallway's tile.
The woman wiped her brow and met our eyes.
We stepped inside and held our breath awhile.

The room was filled with wires, tubes, and screens—
A humming chamber lit by ghostly green.
Each wall was lined with buttons, knobs, and glass,
And screens that showed us things we hadn't seen.

At first, just static—shifting, shapeless grey.
Then slowly, images began to form:
Our lives, replayed in fractured, silent loops—
But twisted, bent, and eerily transformed.

One screen showed me alone at age of ten,
A stranger's shadow looming at my back.
Another showed the woman lost in snow,
Calling a name the hallway still held black.

The man stepped close and touched a flickering face—
A version of himself that held a knife.
He whispered, "This... I never... I would not..."
But none of us could swear it wasn't life.

The air grew thick with circuitry and buzz.
A screen went red, and then another blinked.
They now revealed the things we nearly did—
The choices caught in breath and never inked.

"This is the Room of Possibility,"
A voice intoned from somewhere in the wall.
"These are the lives you shaped, then left behind.
Each spark ignored. Each time you did not fall."

The dog began to bark at looping scenes—
A girl alone who reached and found no hand.
A brother drowned because no help had come.
A crash, a fire, a name too late to stand.

The screens began to spin and flash with speed.
The room grew loud with every life we passed.
And then the central monitor turned black—
Before it bled one image made to last.

It showed us here, within this very House.
The doors behind. The ones ahead still sealed.
And on the screen, a version of ourselves
Still walking, though no longer quite concealed.

Their eyes were hollowed out. Their mouths sewn tight.
The man was dragging something on a chain.
The woman held a portrait made of skin.
The dog was still, but staring through the pane.

"These are the selves the House has almost made,"
The voice explained, with tones like iron sleep.
"Keep walking and you join them soon enough.
You are the things you bury and don't keep."

The man collapsed and screamed at every screen.
He struck one down; it shattered with a wail.
The woman turned and grabbed him by the coat.
The hallway called. The images grew pale.

We ran. The monitors began to melt.
The wires sparked and hissed and reached like snakes.
The House had let us see the almost-truth—
And all the lives we broke with quiet fakes.

We shut the door before the sparks could bite.
We gasped and wept and clawed the hallway floor.
Another door had started bleeding light—
Its number thirty-two, a shifting sore.

The Thirty-Second Room

The thirty-second door was soft to touch,
Its surface lined in velvet, deep and red.
But stitched across it ran a thousand threads,
Each one a strand from dreams the House had fed.

The number floated high in golden thread,
But tarnished where the fingers tried to pull.
The dog let out a low and trembling growl—
Its eyes were locked on something dark and dull.

We stepped inside and met the scent of wine—
Of rose and rot, of candlewax and skin.
The room was round, its corners dressed in veils,
Its air perfumed with pleasure soaked in sin.

A ballroom, though no dancers filled the floor.
Just mannequins in masks of sculpted grief.
Each posed mid-step, mid-bow, mid-fainting fall—
A crowd of silence, gorgeous in their brief.

At centre stage there stood a twisted throne,
Its arms made up of hands both carved and real.
Upon it sat a woman draped in silk—
Her body still, her gaze too sharp to feel.

Her face was painted thick with waxen bloom.
Her lips were stitched, though curved into a grin.
A crown of thorns adorned her powdered brow.
Her fingers drummed the chair with measured sin.

Behind her stood a curtain steeped in red—
And something breathed behind it slow and deep.
The mannequins began to hum one note,
A tone that swelled and slipped beneath the feet.

The woman rose and pointed to the glass—
A mirror framed in bone and bound in thread.
It shimmered once, then showed a different room—
A bedroom lit with roses, pain, and dread.

"This is the part you never let them see,"
A voice emerged, though not from lips or air.
"The fantasy. The wanting. Not the act—
But thoughts you'd kill before you even dare.

The things you dressed in poetry and shame.
The masks you wore so no one knew the shape.
The hunger clawing under every smile.
The hands you stilled. The ones you let escape."

The mannequins began to twist and dance.
Their masks fell off, revealing stolen eyes.
Their limbs now soft, their motions not quite wrong—
But just too close to truth to pass as lies.

They danced toward us, their hands outstretched and warm.
Their mouths began to open, one by one.
"You dreamed of us," they whispered. "We were there.
You called us dark, but danced before we'd come."

The woman screamed and pulled the man away.
The dog now lunged and bit a reaching limb.
The mirrored room grew bright and pulled us near—
But we broke free before the House could win.

The woman-queen upon the throne now wept.
Her makeup ran, her crown fell down in fire.
And as we fled, the curtain yawned wide—
Revealing nothing... but a deep desire.

We slammed the door and leaned against the wall.
Our breath came fast, our hands too hot to hold.
The hallway pulsed with velvet at our backs—
And somewhere down its throat, the candles rolled.

A door appeared, its knob like melted wax.
Its number thirty-three, in threads of gold.
We looked ahead, not back—not now, not yet.
The House had more, and none of us were whole.

The Thirty-Third Room

The thirty-third door groaned like splintered wood,
Its hinges swollen thick with tar and pitch.
The number etched in soot across the top,
Still glowing faint like coals beneath a witch.

Its frame was bent, too narrow at the base,
As if it bowed beneath some ancient grief.
The dog stayed back and growled without a bark—
Its hackles raised, its breath too short and brief.

We pressed the door and felt it push us in.
It sucked us through as if it breathed us whole.
Inside, a chapel scorched and torn apart—
Where saints had burned and gods had lost control.

The pews were ash, the pulpit split in half.
The ceiling gone, replaced by pulsing dark.
A choir stood, their mouths sewn shut with gold,
Their robes like smoke that barely held a spark.

The altar held no book, no flame, no cross—
Just rusted tools arranged with loving care:
A knife, a crown of pins, a crooked bell,
A mask too smooth to show if it could stare.

Behind the altar knelt a figure thin,
Its spine a cage of ribs too sharp for skin.
It turned, revealing sockets filled with wax—
And whispered, "Blessed are the ones within."

Its voice was made of dust and crumbling leaves.
It beckoned us to kneel, and so we did.
Not out of faith, but something near to that—
A sickness we no longer knew we hid.

"You came to pray when praying had no worth,"
It crooned, "You begged for things that cost no pain.
You whispered names and promised to forget—
But left them in the flood and begged for rain."

It raised the knife and pointed to our hands.
The man looked down—his palms were marked with ash.
The woman wept, and blood welled at her wrists,
Her breath a psalm now sung in broken gasps.

The choir hummed behind their golden threads.
Their muffled hymn became a thundered tide.
We felt the walls begin to bow and close—
And knew the House had sealed us deep inside.

The bell rang once. A silence fell like ice.
The figure reached, and laid the mask down flat.
It said, "Confess not just the acts you own—
But all the times you stood and watched them spat.

You didn't lie, but silence is its twin.
You didn't strike—but you were still the hand.
You didn't bind—but you watched others bleed.
And now the House demands you understand."

The tools all rose—no hands, no cords, no breath.
They circled us like halos dipped in sin.
The knife came close, and laid itself to skin—
But left no mark... not yet, not from within.

We staggered back, and found the door behind.
We pulled it open, fled through holy dust.
The altar cracked, the choir burst to flame—
And in the dark, we left behind our trust.

The hallway now was longer than before.
Its lamps all dimmed, its walls began to tilt.
Another door appeared, this one in stone—
Its number thirty-four, carved deep in guilt.

The Thirty-Fourth Room

The thirty-fourth door bloomed from living rock,
Its surface veined with veins like bruising stone.
The number etched in granite flaked and cracked,
Still pulsing slow with something not its own.

A tremor shook the threshold as we neared.
The dog growled once, but stepped inside with care.
The hallway sighed as if relieved to pass
Us into arms that knew what waited there.

Within, the room was carved into a cave,
Its walls alive with carvings etched by nails.
The torchlight flickered from the ceiling dome—
A hundred eyes had watched our countless trails.

Each wall was marked with images too raw:
A man who struck, a child locked away,
A lover drowned, a mother starved for peace,
A friend who smiled and watched us slip astray.

They danced in lines, each carved with shaking hand,
Each frozen mid-betrayal, wound, or prayer.
Some figures wept, their mouths cut into stone.
Some reached for help and found no comfort there.

A hammer lay against the farthest wall—
Its handle stained with rust, or blood, or both.
Beside it sat a block of granite grey,
Half-shaped into a figure bound by oath.

A voice began, but not from any shape.
It echoed in the stone, behind the eyes.
"You came to shape your legacy in truth.
But all you made were silence, stone, and lies.

This room is yours. These walls are yours to fill.
What did you build? What statues bear your name?
You hid your work behind the acts of others—
But stone remembers. Stone will keep your shame."

The man walked forward, hand upon the wall.
He found a carving shaped like something real—
A younger self who watched his brother fall,
Then turned away before he chose to feel.

The woman found a figure, arms outstretched,
A child she mocked when no one else would speak.
She touched the groove, and blood welled from her thumb—
The stone had teeth, and penance has its cheek.

The dog lay down, its eyes on something far—
A shape emerging slowly from the gloom.
Another carving, moving now with breath,
And dragging with it grief enough to bloom.

It showed a man with many hands and heads—
Each face a mask we wore throughout the years.
It pointed to the wall, then back to us,
And whispered, "Build with guilt, or build with fears."

We grabbed the hammer, struck the wall apart.
Each blow revealed another buried wrong.
Each crack released a sound too sharp for hope—
A scream, a song, a cry too old and long.

The stone collapsed, and light poured through the dust.
We staggered back into the hallway wide.
The walls now bore the echoes of our acts,
Etched deep in veins the House refused to hide.

Another door grew tall with polished bone.
Its number thirty-five was carved with care.
We did not speak. We only breathed and knocked.
The House still waited. It was always there.

The Thirty-Fifth Room

The thirty-fifth door gleamed with lacquered pride,
Its wood too rich, its grain too finely dressed.
The number inlaid deep with gold and pearl—
A surface crafted just to be impressed.

The dog stood tense, its growl a low, dull thrum.
The woman wiped the sweat beneath her eye.
The man, now pale, reached out with trembling hand.
The House was calm—but always with a lie.

Inside, a study grand beyond all means,
With walls of books no hand had ever touched.
A chandelier of ivory and silk,
A globe still spinning though no finger brushed.

The desk was vast, its wood a crimson stain,
Its surface bare but polished to a sheen.
A portrait loomed above the fireplace,
Depicting someone almost like a king.

He wore a suit too perfect to be stitched.
His smile too wide to ever have been true.
His eyes were bright, but dead beneath the glaze—
And every brushstroke shimmered, red and blue.

A phonograph began to creak and play:
A speech, not song, from somewhere in the room.
"You built the myth," it said, "and wore it well.
But myths are tombs disguised as golden wombs."

The man stepped forth, as if the voice was his.
He looked upon the desk and found a pen.
"I used to dream I'd write the world to peace,"

He whispered. "All I ever wrote was when.
When I'd be praised. When others knew my name.
When silence meant I'd won the room again.
I preached of truth, but only wore its coat—

And left the collar high to hide the stain."
The painting shifted subtly in shade.
The man within it smiled, then raised his brow.
He stepped from canvas slowly, proud and poised,

And bowed before the man who'd shaped him now.
"You wrote me," said the figure, calm and crisp.
"You sharpened me with clever, cutting turns.
You dressed me in conviction, fame, and charm—

But never gave me blood that ever burned."
The woman reached and smashed the phonograph.
It shrieked, then fell, and spilled a spool of tape.
The words it held unraveled on the floor:

A thousand praises meant to mask escape.
The painting-man now cracked and turned to ash.
The portrait above burned away in blue.
The desk burst open, spilling sheafs of names—

Each one a voice the man ignored as true.
We fled. The books began to flap and moan.
The globe spun wild and shattered into flame.
The chandelier collapsed like falling bones.

The air turned black and cried the man's own name.
We burst into the hallway full of smoke.
The man fell back, his coat singed at the seams.
The House had shown what pride could never hold—
A gilded mask pulled off by burning dreams.

Another door emerged, its frame askew.
Its number thirty-six was sharp and wide.
We steadied fast, and crossed the threshold thin.
The House had more. It always waits inside.

The Thirty-Sixth Room

The thirty-sixth door leaned against the wall,
As if too tired to stand beneath its weight.
Its frame was warped like wood left out to rot,
Its number scratched as if to challenge fate.

The dog approached and sniffed the splintered edge,
Then backed away, its tail between its legs.
The man stood still, one hand upon the frame.
The woman nodded once. No one begged.

Inside, a hallway stretched in looping turns,
A hallway in a room, or so it seemed.
Its walls were lined with clocks that had no hands,
And every light above them buzzed and beamed.

A thousand doors, all bolted shut and still,
Each bearing names—none known, yet strangely near.
The hallway circled round itself again,
And time was lost, replaced with something clear.

A ticking came, though none of us wore clocks.
The sound was not from brass or gear or chain.
It came from underfoot and overhead—
It came from somewhere buried in the brain.

The woman paused and touched one nearby door.
Her name was etched in silver near the lock.
She gasped. The door swung open by itself—
And there she stood within, too young to talk.

A version of herself, no more than five,
Sat drawing pictures with a crayon red.
She looked up once, then smiled, then turned away,
And kept on sketching ghosts that begged and bled.

The walls were lined with paintings, rough and crude,
Each one a scene the woman had forgot.
A house on fire. A body in the snow.
A hand she'd drawn, but labeled it: "do not."

The woman fell to knees and cried aloud.
The child stood up and looked her in the eyes.
She whispered once, but we could barely hear—
Just syllables too soft to carry lies.

Then silence. She walked back into the wall,
And vanished through a paper-thin divide.
The door slammed shut. The nameplate turned to ash.
The hallway spun again from side to side.

"Each door is yours," a voice began to say.
"Each choice you made, each time you looked away.
The hallway loops because your steps were false—
You changed your face, but never learned to stay."

The man now found his name on distant wood.
He stared, then shook, and tried to step aside.
But still the door swung wide and showed the room—
A hospital, a scream, a girl who died.

He backed away and fell against the wall.
The door closed slow, as if it mourned the sight.
And everywhere around us, ticking grew—
A thousand doors began to blink with light.

Each one for every moment passed in shame.
Each one a record, waiting to be weighed.
We fled the hall that looped within a room—
Its truth too vast, its sorrows too well laid.

The hallway we emerged in felt less real.
The air was thick with time we could not spend.
The dog was limp. The man was nearly gone.
The woman's face had aged around its end.

Another door appeared, this one of brass.
Its number thirty-seven, slick with steam.
We touched the knob and stepped into the dark—
Where rooms were realer still than any dream.

The Thirty-Seventh Room

The thirty-seventh door hissed low with steam,
Its hinges wet, its bolts too hot to hold.
The number glowed like iron fresh from flame,
Yet pulsed beneath with something cracked and cold.

The dog growled once, then backed against the wall.
Its ears pressed flat, its tail curled tight with dread.
The woman whispered, "Don't," but still we moved—
The House had learned to walk us where we bled.

The room was vast and filled with rusted pipes,
Like arteries beneath a wounded skin.
Each valve exhaled a groan too soft for words.
Each piston pumped regret we kept within.

A catwalk stretched across a gaping void,
And far below, some engine churned and cried.
Its rhythm beat like fists upon a door,
And echoed all the names we'd left to die.

Along the path, machines were bolted down—
But not for use, and not for any grace.
Each one preserved a moment far too real:
A child alone, a hand across a face.

A lever here replayed a mother's plea.
A switch lit up a hospital at night.
A gauge marked how a scream was never heard.
A valve released the scent of blinding light.

A figure stood atop the farthest beam,
Its body grafted into wires and brass.
Its arms were spliced with tubes and grinding cogs,
Its chest a furnace masked with fogged-up glass.

It turned, and sparks fell curling from its jaw.
Its mouth moved slow, as if it had to try.
"This is the place where futures once began,"
It said. "Now only consequence can fly."

It raised a hand, and all the lights went dim.
The machines began to echo back our steps.
Each time we failed became a burst of steam.
Each time we lied, the pistons flexed and wept.

The woman slipped, the dog began to bark.
The man stood still, his breath too rough to speak.
The figure on the beam looked straight at him—
"You pressed the switch. You didn't wait to seek."

The man collapsed and screamed into the steel.
His voice was drowned by pulleys grinding low.
The dog pulled hard, the woman raised her arms—
"We didn't know! We didn't want to know!"

The figure stepped, and every footfall hissed.
Its eyes were bulbs, and flickered dim with grief.
"Desire is the engine of the House.
But guilt, my friends—guilt is its bright motif."

The path began to split and bend and fall.
The catwalk moaned, its joints too worn to last.
We ran beneath the coughing pipes and gears—
And found the door half-melted from the past.

We burst into the hallway smelling smoke.
The air was thick with oil, rust, and flame.
And as we left, the furnace screamed our names—
And whispered all the times we played the game.

The hallway tightened, narrower than skin.
The House grew hot with breath behind the brick.
Another door now hissed from metal lungs—
Its thirty-eight etched deep in steel and sick.

The Thirty-Eighth Room

The thirty-eighth door pulsed like wounded flesh,
Its seams wrapped tight in gauze now soaked with red.
The number etched in bone across the lintel,
Still slick, as if it only just had bled.

A moan came low from somewhere past the frame—
Not pain, not speech, but something near to both.
The dog refused, and whimpered at our heels.
But still we passed. The House had made its oath.

Inside, the room was dim and hung with sheets,
So stained with rust and bile they swung with weight.
The floor was tiled with old infirmary brick,
Still wet in seams that hadn't dried since hate.

Hooks dangled down from chains too thick to sway,
Each one suspended over rusted drains.
A single gurney stood beneath the light—
Its leather straps well-worn with phantom stains.

The walls were shelves of jars in murky glass,
Each held a lump of flesh or shrivelled thing.
An eye. A tongue. A finger scorched to black.
A shriek still lived within a pickled ring.

A shape emerged, dressed in a surgeon's garb—
Though blood had turned the white to dried maroon.
Its mask was flesh, its gloves were stitched from lips.
Its breath was slow, like sleep beneath a moon.

"You're back," it said, with voice too calm, too near.
"The patient's ready. You have brought the chart?"
The man stepped back, and dropped his face to hands.
The woman froze, her pulse a hammer's start.

"You lied when you said pain would make them whole.
You carved them up, then stitched your conscience clean.
You told yourself that silence meant consent.
But I record what happens in between."

It turned and gestured toward the gurney straps.
The dog let out a single, keening cry.
The lights above grew white with sterile fire—
And every jar began to moan and sigh.

"You didn't touch the blade, but you stood near.
You called them mad, then left them for the knives.
You thought that guilt belonged to men in masks—
But guilt is quiet, walks on softer lives."

The man collapsed, his scream a choking flood.
The gurney's straps curled up and reached for skin.
The surgeon did not move, just watched and smiled—
Its mask sagged low, and showed the face within.

It was the man's—though gaunt, distorted, grey.
It blinked with blood, then turned its eyes to me.
The woman shouted, dragged him to the door—
And still the House whispered: "Let it be."

We fled, but not before the jars all cracked.
The moaning rose into a single choir.
The hallway caught us in its tightening throat—
Still damp with smoke, still pulsing low with fire.

The gurney rolled behind, then came to rest.
The surgeon watched us vanish from the light.
And in its hand, it clutched a second chart—
With names we knew, and dates we failed to fight.

Another door grew out like growing bone.
Its number thirty-nine, in dark tattoo.
The House had dressed itself in flesh and scalpel—
And deeper still, it waited to cut through.

The Thirty-Ninth Room

The thirty-ninth door hissed with wheezing breath,
Its hinges smeared with grease and tar-like glue.
The number stung the eyes—bright red, and raw,
As if the House had just carved something new.

The frame was metal, but too thin to touch—
It pulsed with heat, though not from fire or flame.
The dog paced back and forth and whined aloud.
The woman spoke: "This room... it knows my name."

Inside, the floor was lined with tangled cords,
A maze of wires snaking through the gloom.
Screens hung like bats across the concrete walls,
Each flickering with static, fear, and doom.

A central chair stood bolted to the floor—
Its arms were spread, its leather ripped with wear.
A helmet, wired and crowned with rusted screws,
Hung overhead like some electric prayer.

The walls began to light, screen after screen.
Not windows—no, but memories in frame.
Not ours at first, but others lost to time—
Their final thoughts, their guilt, their words of shame.

One showed a man who begged into the dark.
Another wept with wires through his chest.
A third just stared into the endless void,
And whispered lies he never had confessed.

The woman gasped—one screen now changed its scene.
It showed herself, alone and near collapse.
She held a match. Her room was filled with gas.
She cried, then smiled, then vanished in a lapse.

"I tried," she said, her voice now faint and dry.
"I tried to leave the noise, the guilt, the ache.
But when they found me, I had left no note—
And still they blamed me for what I could take."

The screen grew dark. The helmet sparked above.
A figure stirred beside the wired chair.
Its head was bound with cords across the skull,
Its eyes replaced with lenses made to stare.

"You see?" it rasped. "The thoughts you never spoke
Are now your chains, and this your final rite.
The House receives what reason leaves behind—
The raw, the dark, the secrets born at night."

It gestured to the chair, and wires moved.
They slithered out like veins that sought to feed.
The dog now barked and pulled against a cord,
Its teeth drawn back, prepared to bite and bleed.

The man began to scream and back away—
A screen now showed his childhood face in frost.
A fire crackled. Someone banged the door.
He turned it louder. That was what it cost.

The cords lashed out. The lights began to spark.
The screens all screamed with voices out of tune.
We tore our way back through the wires' nest,
As sparks fell down like rain from some dark moon.

The helmet dropped, but missed the woman's head.
The chair cracked open, coughing smoke and sparks.
And from the screens, our names began to scroll—
In languages too old to mark in marks.

We slammed the door and fell upon the floor.
The hallway spun like film stripped off the reel.
Our breath returned, but not with peace or calm—
Just sharp and shallow, stiff and barely real.

Another door began to split the brick.
Its number forty, etched in burning white.
The dog stood first and stared into its glow.
The House was nowhere near the end of night.

The Fortieth Room

The fortieth door was white as driven snow,
But not the snow that warms a quiet hill—
The kind that blinds, that drowns a frozen breath,
That wraps the lost in something pale and still.

Its number shimmered faint like distant stars,
As if the House had etched it with regret.
The wood was smooth, but colder than the grave.
The woman touched it once, then whispered, "Debt."

We stepped inside and found the world turned white.
The room had walls, but none of them could show—
Just blinding fog and frost beneath our feet,
And ceilings humming low with distant snow.

The wind blew soft, but sharp enough to cut.
Each flake that fell had weight beyond its size.
They hit the skin like needles dipped in ice,
And whispered names we never thought to prize.

No furniture. No door behind us now.
Just endless white, and swirling air, and loss.
The dog growled once, then tucked its tail and shivered,
Its prints erased beneath the frost and gloss.

A figure formed within the falling haze,
A silhouette too far to name or track.
But as it walked, the snow beneath it hissed,
And all around us started turning black.

The closer that it came, the more we knew—
Not stranger, no, but something left behind.
It wore our features, changed by time and frost.
It wore our guilt, but never lost its mind.

The woman wept and dropped down to her knees.
She said, "This room... I know it. I was here.
When I was young. When I had done the thing.
This is the place that swallowed me in fear."

The figure stopped and raised a frozen hand.
The storm grew still. The snow hung motionless.
The sky above now opened like a wound,
And showed a night we couldn't help but guess.

It showed a room—this room—but years ago.
A girl stood in it, barefoot, pale, and small.
She whispered names to no one, scratched her arms,
And left them bleeding on the mirrored wall.

The man stepped close and whispered, "It was you..."
The woman sobbed, "I left myself to drift.
No one would look. No one would ever come.
The House was here before. It gave me gift."

The figure nodded, then dissolved in snow.
The room collapsed, the whiteness cracked like ice.
The sky fell in with mirrors by the mile,
Each one reflecting cost, and not the price.

We found the door had reappeared behind—
Its shape now warped by winter's raw demand.
We fled, the dog limping through as we screamed,
And slammed it shut with trembling, bleeding hands.

The hallway sighed, then narrowed into black.
The cold still clung like silence after sin.
Another door appeared from plaster veins—
Its number forty-one etched deep within.

The Forty-First Room

The forty-first door creaked with groaning grief,
Its surface bowed as though it held a weight.
The number carved too deep, the strokes too raw—
A mark made not by craft, but death and hate.

It wept with tar from seams along the edge,
And every drop let out a brittle moan.
The dog lay down and placed its head on paws,
As though it sensed the room would claim alone.

We pressed inside, and dimness met our eyes—
Not darkness, but a haze that dulled the mind.
A study, perhaps once rich, now drowned in dust,
Where clocks were melted, books unread, unlined.

A fireplace smouldered low with choking smoke.
Above it hung a portrait, turned to face
The wall as if ashamed to show its truth—
Its canvas sagged, its colour lost to grace.

A desk was placed at centre, cracked and worn.
Its drawers hung open, spilling out the past:
Old letters, photographs in black and white,
And notes unsigned but trembling from the last.

A single chair, still rocking though untouched,
Faced toward the hearth, as if it watched the flame.
And seated there—a figure old and slack,
Its eyes twin coals, its lips too dry to name.

It stirred as if disturbed from endless thought.
It turned but not by will, more like by rule.
Its skin hung loose like drapes on broken bone.
Its voice was brittle, learned in every school.

"You came at last," it said, though not with pride.
"I knew the House would walk you down to me.
You've kept your ledgers neatly, word by word—
Now write the names of those you failed to see."

It handed us a pen with bloodied stem,
A book with every page already torn.
The woman shook and tried to step away—
But found her feet were planted in the worn.

The man stepped forth and opened to a page—
There was his name, and lists beneath like vines.
Each one a moment left in silence wide.
Each one a voice he'd failed between the lines.

The fire flared, revealing other chairs.
Each one held echoes faint but still intact:
A father lost, a teacher turned to fear,
A stranger weeping on a railroad track.

"You watched," the figure said, "and called it fate.
You measured harm in inches, not in cost.
You told yourself that stillness was a shield,
But in that stillness, how much more was lost?"

The woman stepped, and now her page was bare.
She tried to close the book, but it would scream.
It listed not her crimes, but all her dreams—
And each one crushed beneath her self-esteem.

"I wanted light," she said, "but learned to hide.
I wanted to be loved, not always right.
But every time I neared the place I broke,
I told myself the night was still polite."

The fire surged and nearly reached the desk.
The figure slumped, its purpose now complete.
The portrait turned itself around at last—
And in its eyes, our own defeat did meet.

We fled the room as ashes filled the air.
The dog was first to cross the closing seam.
Behind, the House sighed once and dimmed the flame—
And took from us another fractured dream.

Another door now shivered into view.
Its forty-two was nailed with iron twine.
We breathed but once and let the hallway speak—
The House had yet to show its last design.

The Forty-Second Room

The forty-second door was rimmed in brass,
Its hinges oiled though black with ancient grime.
The number burned behind a pane of glass,
As if preserved against the rot of time.

The knob was warm—not hot, but strangely so,
Like flesh remembered once and never found.
The dog stood still, its ears pinned flat with fear.
We opened slow. The House gave not a sound.

Inside, a parlour dressed in grieving green,
Its walls adorned with clocks that all had stopped.
A single chandelier hung from the dark,
Its chain too tight, its crystals finely cropped.

The room was quiet, but not out of peace—
A hush like one that knows it must remain.
Each step we took sank deep into the rug,
As if we walked through someone else's pain.

A tea set waited, placed for three, not four.
The porcelain was chipped, the sugar grey.
One cup was cracked, and full of something dark—
A liquid not yet still, but in decay.

A metronome sat ticking on the shelf,
Though nothing else around it kept a beat.
A rocking chair moved softly, slow and slight,
As if it bore a guest we could not meet.

The woman stepped, then froze, and shook her head.
"This room," she said, "I dreamed it as a girl.
There was a voice—it whispered through the walls.
It told me I could trade myself for pearl."

The man walked past her, eyes on something near.
A photograph, half-burned and framed in brass.
He touched the glass and flinched—it burned his skin.
It showed his mother, staring through the past.

"You called it fate," a voice began to hiss,
Though not from form, nor mouth, nor cornered shape.
"But fate is just a story told too much—
A blanket pulled across the eyes to drape.

You did not fall. You leaned into the fall.
You weren't deceived. You simply chose not truth.
You poured your tea, then cursed the taste of blood—
And blamed the cup for poisoning your youth."

The rocking chair now groaned as something sat.
A weight took shape though nothing touched the cloth.
A teacup lifted, floated to the lips
Of something not quite here and not quite lost.

The dog began to bark, its fur on end.
The metronome ticked faster, then too fast.
The chandelier gave out a shattering cry—
And shadows spilled from every faded past.

The photograph ignited in the man's hand.
He dropped it as it screamed a mother's song.
The woman ran and pulled us through the dark,
Where curtains wept and every wall felt wrong.

We burst back through the door, then slammed it shut.
The House fell still. The dog began to shake.
We held each other, speaking not a word—
Too tired now to name each fresh heartbreak.

Another door began to rise in rust.
Its number forty-three was split and burned.
The hallway groaned, and somewhere up ahead,
We saw a shape we knew we hadn't learned.

The Forty-Third Room

The forty-third door wept with something thick—
A fluid dark as ink, but slow as oil.
Its number warped, as if it tried to move,
To hide itself beneath the House's soil.

The knob was slick and beat with pulsing heat,
As if a heart had found its resting place.
The woman paused, then whispered through clenched teeth:
"I'll enter first—whatever wears this face."

Inside, the walls were breathing like a lung.
The air was warm, too warm, but not from fire.
The room resembled something once a womb—
A chamber draped in flesh and wired desire.

Red velvet lined the floor with slickened threads,
While bulbs like eyes blinked gently from the walls.
The ceiling hung with tapestries of skin,
And dripped with whispers made of unseen calls.

A figure rose, unclothed and featureless,
Its body shaped like clay before it dries.
Its arms were long, its legs too short to walk,
Its back all spine, its head all open eyes.

"You dreamed me," said the thing. "And still I live.
You conjured me in silence, in disgust.
You shaped me from the parts you couldn't name—
The hunger dressed in shame you would not trust."

It slithered forward, not with rage but grace.
Its voice grew sweet, a lull that pricked the skin.
"You're not afraid of me. You're afraid
You'll see yourself beneath my weeping grin."

It touched the woman's cheek—her eyes went wide.
"When I was twelve, I saw a corpse that smiled.
I told myself it wasn't really dead—
But then I laughed. And I became defiled."

The man stepped back. The dog began to bark.
The walls turned redder, moaning in their folds.
The room was not a place, but something else—
A thought, a need, a secret left too bold.

"This is the part of you you swore you'd burn,"
The thing now said, its voice a rasping prayer.
"But fire fears the body more than guilt.
And here, the heat is shaped like your despair."

We turned to flee, but doorways weren't the same.
The exit split into a dozen mouths.
Each gaping wide with mirrored teeth and tongues—
Each hissing truths that slithered from the south.

The woman screamed and pointed through the dark.
The rightmost door was wet, but real, but torn.
We passed the mouths that sang in coiling verse,
And fled the room of longing, grief, and scorn.

The hallway opened like a gasping chest.
We stumbled through and dropped upon the tile.
The dog lay down and trembled without sound.
The woman wiped her face and forced a smile.

The man could not meet either of our eyes.
The door behind still pulsed like living meat.
A new one stirred, its frame a bruising blue—
Its forty-four hummed low beneath our feet.

The Forty-Fourth Room

The forty-fourth door groaned like grieving wood,
Its edges scarred by fingernails and flame.
The number carved in soot, then smeared by hands
That tried to wipe away a whispered name.

The knob was cold, too cold for skin to bear.
The dog growled once, then backed into the shade.
The man exhaled, his breath like curling thread.
We crossed, though every heartbeat said we'd stayed.

Inside, a staircase spiralled like a shell,
Descending far beyond what depth should hold.
No walls confined it—only open dark,
And ropes that swung like veins grown stiff with mold.

Each step we took creaked low with distant weight,
As though the stairs remembered who had died.
No railing stood to hold us from the fall,
Just air too thick and darkness stretched too wide.

The woman led, her hand along the stone.
The dog followed with ears pinned to its head.
The man walked last and muttered to the dark,
"We're going down into the part we fled."

Around us, shapes began to take their form—
Not solid yet, but hinted in the gloom.
A child in chains. A girl with stitched-up eyes.
A man who dug his own unmarked exhumed.

"This is the fall," a voice began to call.
"Not sin, not fate—just gravity of shame.
You brought your weight, and now it drags you down.
You named the fault, then played another's name."

The woman stumbled, gasping, "That was me—
The time I watched her slip, and did not shout.
I told myself she'd catch herself in time…
But time just stops. It doesn't sort things out."

The man cried out, then dropped upon a stair.
He held his knees and shook beneath the strain.
"He asked me once—just once—for food, for warmth.
I turned away. He died inside the rain."

A sudden flash—then torches lined the stairs.
They burned not light, but memories in bloom.
A thousand sins hung dripping from the walls,
Each named and framed to decorate the tomb.

At last, the staircase ended on a floor—
A cavern made of bones that echoed guilt.
At centre, stood a pit of breathing earth,
Its mouth agape, its edges soft as silt.

The dog barked once, but did not dare to cross.
The pit began to speak with pulsing steam:
"I do not burn. I do not freeze or bite.
I only show the root behind the dream."

The woman stepped and peered into the hole.
Her face went pale. Her fingers touched her chest.
The man drew near and looked but said no word—
His lips had curled too far from all the rest.

I did not look. I couldn't face the depth.
I knew what lived inside that endless fall.
The pit was shaped to mirror all our steps—
The core of House, the reason for its call.

We turned, and somehow stairs had reappeared.
We climbed in silence, limbs like stone and clay.
Behind, the pit still breathed and said one word—
Repeated slow: "Remain." Then slipped away.

The hallway met us colder than before.
Its walls were damp, its ceiling hung with thread.
Another door was waiting in the dark—
Its forty-five engraved in hands long dead.

The Forty-Fifth Room

The forty-fifth door throbbed with muffled sound,
As if a heart beat softly in its grain.
The wood was dark, but glistened like it wept,
And every knot was shaped like hidden pain.

The number scrawled in wax, then smeared by heat,
As though a candle died while naming it.
The dog stood back and growled into the floor—
Its stance was still, its tail a silent writ.

Inside, a room of curtains, red and thick,
Their folds like veils of flesh and silken thread.
No windows shone. No corners met the eye.
Just hanging drapes that whispered what was said.

The scent of powder, blood, and something sweet
Hung in the air like guilt on whispered prayer.
A stage was raised, but draped in shadow cloth.
A dozen chairs sat empty in despair.

A spotlight flared with no clear source of flame,
And from the dark emerged a painted man—
His smile too wide, his suit too sharp, too neat.
He walked with grace, but not of mortal plan.

His eyes were coins, his fingers stiff with rings.
His voice rang out like laughter in a crypt:
"Welcome! Oh, at last, our guests arrive—
To play the roles they wrote but never script."

The dog began to bark, then whimpered low.
The woman froze, her lips too dry to speak.
The man just stared as curtains drew aside—
And there, upon the stage, they saw the weak.

Reflections of themselves began to move:
The woman in a scene she'd sworn was gone—
She mocked a friend in front of leering crowds,
Then smiled and turned away before the dawn.

The man now stood, portrayed in golden light—
He lied with ease, then claimed he meant no harm.
He raised a glass while someone cried behind,
Then shook their hand and smiled with crooked charm.

Each scene performed in pantomime and grace,
Their worst regrets now choreographed in smoke.
The painted host applauded every act,
And bowed with flair as each illusion broke.

"This is your theatre," he said, all teeth.
"You built it every time you chose your part.
You knew your line. You read the room just right—
And left the bleeding act without a heart."

He clapped again, and all the lights went red.
The curtains fell like guillotines of thread.
The floor beneath the stage began to split—
And from it rose a chorus of the dead.

Each wore a mask shaped like a former friend.
Each sang in voices cracked with truth and rot.
"We watched you shine while we were cast aside.
You kept your lines. Our parts you had forgot."

The woman screamed. The man began to beg.
The dog leapt forward, barked and tore a mask.
The stage collapsed in smoke and falling dust—
And all went dark, as though we'd failed the task.

We found the door behind us once again,
Its edges scorched by all the lights before.
We fled. The hallway yawned like curtain calls—
Another room behind another door.

And now another rose from shadow's breath.
Its forty-six scratched deep in scorched maroon.
We braced our backs, but still we stepped ahead—
The House had not yet played its final tune.

The Forty-Sixth Room

The forty-sixth door pulsed with steady thuds,
Like muffled fists against a padded wall.
Its wood was wrapped in bands of iron grey,
As if to cage the pain it had to haul.

The number etched in chalk upon the frame,
Then smeared by sweat or tears long left to dry.
The dog sat down, then whimpered once and howled—
A long, low note that seemed a lullaby.

Inside, the light was low and copper-red,
Like dusk arrested just before it fell.
The walls were draped with chains, all rusted thin,
Each one too short to drag, too long to sell.

The ceiling sagged with beams that bent with weight—
But what they held was hidden out of view.
The floor was slick with wax and scattered nails.
And in the dark, a voice we almost knew.

"You bound me once," it said, "in words and looks.
You named me wrong before I knew my name.
You called me nothing, then you asked for love—
And blamed me when the silence turned to shame."

A shape emerged, shackled from neck to spine,
Its face obscured by veils of braided hair.
It dragged behind it twenty broken locks,
And left behind a trail of thinning air.

"You tried to fix me with your guilt," it hissed.
"You tried to polish chains with Sunday speech.
But all the time, you prayed I'd disappear—
Then preached of freedom just outside my reach."

It raised one arm, and all the chains began
To whisper like a choir out of tune.
Each lock swung slow, a pendulum of guilt—
And tapped the wall in rhythm with a rune.

The dog barked once, then twice, then backed away.
The man stepped forth, his lips too thin to speak.
The woman trembled, fists clenched at her sides—
Then stepped ahead, her voice not small but weak.

"I mocked the way they moved. I said their name
In twisted tones to earn a crueler laugh.
I made the space between their world and mine
A mirror cracked—a twisted second half."

The figure turned, and chains fell to the floor.
Beneath the veils, a face too young to weep.
Its eyes were stitched with thread pulled from a flag—
A country torn, a secret buried deep.

"I didn't want revenge," it whispered low.
"I only wanted silence not to scream.
You brought me here. The House just gave me form.
Now leave. But know—you echo in my dream."

We fled the chains, which writhed and clanged in song.
The doors behind us sealed with braided steel.
The hallway stretched, its bricks now damp with rust—
As though it too had learned at last to feel.

The dog walked first, its tail no longer high.
The man just stared at nothing near or far.
The woman's hands were raw from where she clenched.
Another door emerged, shaped like a scar.

Its forty-seven carved in slant and spite,
As though the House had slashed it in retreat.
We did not rest. The House had more to show—
And every step would strip us incomplete.

The Forty-Seventh Room

The forty-seventh door was barely wood—
A patchwork thing of boards and shattered glass.
Its number etched with charcoal, jagged, thin,
As though some hand had carved it in a pass.

It leaned upon its frame like one in pain,
And every breeze from under smelled like rot.
The dog stayed back and let out just one bark,
Then quieted as if the choice was not.

Inside, a nursery in black and white,
Its toys arranged in order far too neat.
No child had touched these blocks in many years—

Yet every one still bore a name, complete.
The walls were scribbled through with tiny hands—
Crayons snapped, the drawings steeped in dread.
Stick figures burned, and monsters danced in ink.

The sun was crossed out thick and marked as dead.
A cradle rocked although no wind had come.
A mobile turned with teeth instead of stars.
A music box began to slowly wind,

Its tune like weeping trapped behind locked bars.
The woman gasped. The man stepped back in dread.
The dog let out a whimper not its own.
For from the crib arose a tiny shape—

A doll-like form, its face a polished stone.
It stared with sockets blank and smooth and deep.
Its limbs were jointed wrong, yet moved with grace.
It walked with purpose—small but absolute—

And reached toward us with stitched and silken face.
"You left me here," it said, in voices two—
One low and cracked, the other high and sweet.
"You named me monster, problem, curse, or plague.

You turned the lights out softly, then retreat."
The woman shook her head. "You weren't alive—
You weren't—I mean… they said there was no heart!"
The doll just smiled and tapped its little chest.

A thumping came—too slow and far apart.
It beckoned us and pointed to the toys—
Each bore a tag with names we once had known.
A boy who cried too much. A girl who shook.

A friend who couldn't bear to be alone.
The man now found a block that bore his name—
And underneath, the word: "Defect" carved in wax.
He fell to knees. "I locked the closet door.

I told my son that monsters came through cracks."
The doll walked up and laid a hand on his.
It burned like frost, like shame too deep to flee.
"You called me wrong before I learned to walk.

Now look at what your House has made of me."
The toys began to dance in twos and threes.
A jack-in-box screamed loud without a spring.
The crib began to rock with phantom weight.

The mobile spun until it cracked its ring.
The dog barked once and tugged the woman's sleeve.
We stumbled to the door and broke the frame.
Behind, the lullaby played slow and low—

Still whispering our guilt but not our name.
The hallway breathed like lungs too close to burst.
Its walls were scratched with childish, trembling script.
The woman wiped a tear and did not speak.
The man stood still, his lips too faintly gripped.

Another door now rose from shadow's bed.
Its number forty-eight looked worn and grey
The House had turned our children into ghosts—
And had a hundred more still on the way.

The Forty-Eighth Room

The forty-eighth door leaned against the wall,
Its hinges missing, torn from rusted root.
The number scratched by claw or crooked nail—
Still fresh, like something watched its own pursuit.

The frame was bent, the jamb half chewed away,
The gap beneath it wide enough to breathe.
The dog let out a growl, low, slow, and firm,
Then stepped aside—as if to grant us leave.

We crossed beneath the lintel, slow and still,
And met a chamber darker than the grave.
No light, no shape, no sound, no ground to hold—
Just breath, our own, and something breathing brave.

The dark was thick, as if it had been poured.
The air was soft, too soft to truly trust.
We walked on nothing—just the shape of space,
Until our thoughts began to turn to dust.

"You've come at last," a voice began, not near.
It pulsed within our bones, behind our eyes.
"You've walked the House, but left this room untouched—
The place where all your silence builds and dies."

A shape emerged, though not in form or frame.
It was the dark itself, the mind in black.
A human outline made of broken night,
It smiled with teeth the dark had long held back.

"You've spoken truth, and owned your wicked work.
But this is not about what you have done.
This room remembers everything you thought—
The things you hid each time you faced the sun."

The woman shook, her eyes lost in the gloom.
The man stepped back, but had no wall to find.
The dog began to whine, then bark, then howl—
But all the sound was swallowed by the mind.

"This is the room where honesty can rot,"
The shape went on. "You never dared to see
The stranger that you formed behind your ribs—
The soul you fed with dreams of being free.

But here you are. The door is closed behind.
Now tell me: when you cried, was it for them?
Or for the part of you that saw yourself
In every scream, in every condemned stem?"

It reached for us—not fast, but slow with care.
Its hands were voids, its fingers made of doubt.
We felt it touch our foreheads, one by one,
And saw what even nightmares dared leave out.

The woman saw her mother drown alone—
Not real, but feared, and thus, forever true.
The man saw all the truths he'd left unsaid,
And every one of them accused anew.

And I—I saw the things I never dared,
The thoughts I clipped before they formed full face.
The monster made of might-have-been and wish—
The hunger dressed in empathy and grace.

We stumbled back, and found the room had walls.
They closed with books, all blank, but humming deep.
Each held a truth we'd never dared to write—
And one by one, they opened in their sleep.

We fled before the dark could read them all.
The air behind us split in cracking moans.
The shape just smiled and said, "You'll come again—
When all your other ghosts have claimed your bones."

We crashed into the hall, too stunned to speak.
The dog lay down, and whined into the stone.
The House exhaled, content with what it stole—
Another page of secrets not our own.

A door emerged, this one of perfect calm.
Its forty-nine engraved in polished brass.
The handle gleamed, too clean, too gently cool—
As if the House now let the future pass.

The Forty-Ninth Room

The forty-ninth was low and built in dread,
Its frame too wide, its ceiling drooped and bowed.
The hinges moaned as though they knew our names,
And in the grain, a word was half-allowed.

The number carved not once, but scored anew—
Each time more jagged, deeper than before.
The dog stayed back, and whimpered at the crack,
And would not near the threshold of that door.

Inside, a parlour dressed in noble style,
With wine-red drapes and chairs of heavy oak.
A fire roared, though no logs lined the grate,
Its light too white, its heat a breathless choke.

The floor was clean—too clean for age or time—
And on the walls, portraits of wealth and pride.
But none had names, and every painted face
Was turned away, as if it longed to hide.

A butler stood, or rather, something posed—
A waxen man in suit too finely cut.
His eyes were glass, his hands clasped at his chest,
His skin too smooth, his mouth a seamless rut.

He turned to us without a single twitch,
And somehow bowed, though nothing in him moved.
He did not speak, but pointed with a hand,
And led us to a seat he had not proved.

The chairs were velvet, but they writhed with mold.
The table bore a feast, untouched by flies.
Each dish was plated silver, high with meat—
But all was raw, and breathing through disguise.

A guest sat waiting, slumped but still alive,
Her hands in gloves, her face beneath a veil.
And when we neared, she raised a broken fork,
And whispered, "Every comfort hides a nail."

The man stepped back; the woman held her breath.
"We know you," said the guest. "You've tasted well.
You've lived on debt and guilt wrapped in delight,
And learned to call the copper sweet as spell.

You walked past hunger. You ignored the cold.
You passed the shelters lit by blood and wine.
And every time you claimed the feast was clean,
You gave this House another inch of spine."

The waxen servant served the plates with grace.
Each course a story fed to mask the pain.
One dish was shaped like folded, begging hands.
Another steamed with steam from someone slain.

We did not eat. We could not make a move.
The guest just laughed and poured us cups of red.
"No guilt," she said, "unless you knew the cost.
But look how well you've feasted on the dead."

The dog began to snarl and bark again.
The chairs began to sink beneath our weight.
The table cracked, the silver bled from light—
And every face in portrait turned to hate.

We burst into the hall, our limbs ice-cold.
The walls were breathing like a sleeping beast.
The House had fed on what we would not name—
And dressed our mercy like a wedding feast.

We stumbled on, the dog now trotting wide,
Its head turned back, unwilling to proceed.
The corridor grew narrow, close, and warm,
Like lungs exhaling smoke we couldn't read.

The floor beneath us pulsed with every step,
The ceiling bowed as though to hear us speak.
Another door emerged without a name—
Its wood still damp, its frame too soft, too weak.

It wasn't built—it grew from House and breath,
A mouth of passage, neither shut nor wide.
The dog lay down and would not cross its line,
But stared at us with sorrow in its hide.

We looked ahead and knew we had no choice.
The House was growing closer to its truth.
And when we stepped beyond that breathing wall,
It felt like entering the House's womb.

The fiftieth room

The fiftieth door was shaped from older wood,
The kind that splinters thought as well as skin.
Its scent was sweet, like flowers sealed in rot,
And grief too ripe to know where to begin.

The number was not written, but inferred—
Its knots aligned in shapes the soul could feel.
The dog stayed back and paced in slow, tight arcs,
Its tail low, its whine a warning real.

Inside, a chamber not unlike a womb—
Too round, too warm, too close, too faintly red.
The walls were stitched in velvet thick with dust,
And ceilingless, as though it mourned its head.

A cradle sat, not new, but carved with care—
Its rock a rhythm matched to pulse and breath.
And from within, a whisper faintly called,
"You found the seed. The House was built from death."

A figure sat beside the cradle's edge—
No face to see, no name to recognise.
It held a book, but not one meant to read—
A tome of breath, of gesture, tear, and cries.

"This room's not mine," it said, "and yet I stay.
For I am what the House has used to grow.
The grief you bore, the cut you wouldn't close—
I fed them roots, and let their shadow show."

The woman stepped and reached into the crib—
But found no child, no doll, no voice or ghost.
Just soil still warm from something newly gone—
A pit that held what memory loved most.

"I lost her," she confessed, "but never wept.
I kept her name beneath my tongue for years.
I planted gardens, told myself she sleeps—
But never once allowed the weight of tears."

The man stepped close and touched the cradle's side.
Its carvings pulsed beneath his trembling hand.
"I told myself the bullet missed the truth.
That she just broke—too frail to understand.

But I had carved the path she walked alone.
I lit the room and left the match to burn.
And now I see this room was always hers—
A wound that grew the House with every turn."

The cradle rocked, though no one stood nearby.
The book swung open, pages dark as coal.
And every line was etched in looping names—
The ones we lost to silence, rage, or role.

The velvet walls began to drip with sound—
A lullaby in minor, sung in gasps.
We ran before the breath could name us too—
Before the House could wrap us in its clasp.

The dog began to bark, and led us through.
The door behind us sealed without a seam.
The hallway flared with red too dark for flame—
The House alive and closer to its dream.

Another door arose with blood beneath.
Its fifty-one already wept its frame.
We passed along, unsure what path remained—
But knowing now we helped to build its name.

The Fifty-First Room

The fifty-first door trembled as it swung,
Though no wind stirred, no draft disturbed the hall.
Its number stitched in threads of mourning black,
Still damp, as if sewn recently by call.

The frame was bowed, not broken, just fatigued—
Like something built too long to bear the weight.
The dog stood still, its head pressed to the ground,
And whined a note too soft to navigate.

Inside, the air was silent, sharp, and bare.
The room was long, with beds aligned in rows.
Each mattress thin, each blanket tucked with care,
Each pillow carved with names no ledger knows.

The walls were lined with cupboards, locked and sealed.
A lantern hung but offered little light.
And from the farthest bed, a whisper came—
A voice that had not spoken out of fright.

"They came here last," it said, "when no one would.
They begged in breath, and begged without a sound.
The House received them not for who they were,
But for the way they filled the waiting ground."

We stepped along the aisle, past each cot.
Some bore a dent, a stain, a ragged sheet.
Some had a note still folded in a fist—
Each note began with "Please," but non-complete.

A nurse appeared, her form as pale as thread,
Her cap askew, her apron marked with names.
She did not speak at first, but bowed her head,
And turned to us through gestures old as flames.

"This is the ward of those not mourned," she said.
"The ones who vanished with no rite or prayer.
Not just the dead—but those you let slip through.
They lived, they cried, and you were never there."

She walked us to a bed near to the door.
Upon its frame was carved the woman's name.
She gasped and touched the sheet with shaking hands,
Then whispered, "I remember her. The same."

A girl from school, so quiet none would speak.
She reached, then paused, then left the girl alone.
The next week, gone. The teachers barely flinched.
And now, her bed was here, her room, her stone.

The man stepped next, his cot adorned with thread.
The name upon it stitched in slanted line.
A cousin—yes. One lost to drugs and frost.
He'd mocked him once, then said, "He'll be just fine."

The nurse just stood, her hands behind her back,
Then nodded once and stepped into the shade.
Her form dissolved like cloth released by time—
And in her place, a single lantern laid.

We took it up, and light returned in part.
The cots now shone with dignity and pain.
A hundred beds, a hundred names we passed—
And not one cried for vengeance. Not one chain.

We left the room in silence, not in dread.
The hallway met us cooler, dim, and wide.
The dog now walked between us, slow but sure.
Another door had formed, not far aside.

Its fifty-two was written in relief—
A carving soft, like breath beneath a prayer.
The House had given peace, but not release—
The ones we left behind were waiting there.

The Fifty-Second Room

The fifty-second door was pale as dusk,
Its paint flaked off in curls like shedding skin.
The number carved in chalk, then half erased,
Still lingered like a sigh too weak to win.

The knob turned smooth, as though it knew our grip.
No screech, no snap, no sudden break of seal.
The dog sniffed once, then pressed against my thigh.
We stepped inside and felt the world unheal.

The room was filled with mirrors, none alike—
Some tall and warped, some cracked along the edge.
They hung from ceiling, floor, and broken beams,
Suspended in a tangled iron hedge.

Each one reflected not what stood before,
But something slightly wrong, askew, displaced.
I waved my hand—but in the glass, it clawed.
The woman smiled, but in the pane, she braced.

"You see yourself, but not as you believe,"
A voice emerged from every mirrored face.
"These are the selves you sculpted out of need—
The masks you wore to win, to run, to chase."

In one, I stood as judge, too clean with power.
In one, I wept but knew I wasn't true.
In one, I struck before the hand could land—
In all, a shadow stretched behind the view.

The man approached a mirror tall and wide.
It showed him old, alone, and cloaked in spite.
He whispered, "That is me, if I don't change—
But change from what? I've never lived it right."

The woman touched a shard that showed her youth.
She saw herself alone beside a tree.
A mirror next to it showed hands in chains—
She whispered, "I was cruel to set her free."

The mirrors started speaking all at once,
A riot of regret and false acclaim.
They called us brave, then called us cowards too.
They mirrored nothing—only blame by name.

The dog began to bark and crack the sound.
Its breath appeared upon the silver haze.
One mirror split, and through it stepped a form—
A version of myself with hollow gaze.

It stared at me, then reached into its chest,
And pulled a knot of mirrors, tight and raw.
It said, "This is the part you've never faced—
The lie you told that never found its flaw.

You said you hurt to save, you bled for good.
You made your guilt a badge and not a plea.
You wore your sorrow like a velvet coat—
But always left the needle in the sea."

I stepped away, and shattered it with stone.
The shards dissolved to dust upon the tile.
The mirrors screamed and vanished one by one—
Until the room was bare and free of guile.

We found the door behind us whole once more.
The hallway breathed, and bent like softened steel.
We stepped into its hush with trembling steps—
Too numb to grasp what mirrors truly feel.

Another door rose slowly from the wall.
Its fifty-three carved deep into the wood.
The House had shown not what we were alone—
But every time we lied and called it good.

The Fifty-Third Room

The fifty-third door bloomed from knotted rope,
Its frame entwined in strands of hemp and vine.
The number etched in looping, fraying twine,
Hung loose, as if to mock the strict design.

It smelled of salt, of sweat, of distant sea—
And something deeper: mildew, mold, and rope.
The dog let out a snarl it could not stop,
Then shrank behind, its stance bereft of hope.

Inside, the walls were planked with swollen wood,
Their grain long warped by water, time, and cries.
A ship, or something built to seem the same,
But held in place by breath and blackened ties.

The floorboards groaned, not under weight, but guilt.
The air was damp and moved with tidal dread.
And from the farthest bulkhead came a voice—
"There's always one who leaves the rest for dead."

A lantern swayed in rhythm with the creaks,
Its light too dim to chase away the gloom.
Around it, hung from hooks that split the beams,
Were coats, and hats, and ropes that spelled out doom.

A figure sat within the captain's chair—
Not flesh, but cloth and buttons dressed in shape.
Its face was stitched, its lips were drawn and sewn,
Its fingers black with mold it could not scrape.

"You ran," it said. "The boat was meant to sink.
But still you found a place to let it rot.
You told them all the storm would pass by dawn,
But knew the signal flare was never shot."

The woman stared and slowly shook her head.
"I was a girl. I saw him drown. I froze.
I told them I was sleeping when he slipped.
I told myself the ocean only knows."

The captain laughed—a brittle, burlap sound.
It tapped its boot against the hull of guilt.
"They say the sea forgives, but not the ship.
And in this room, your silence is rebuilt.

Each word you failed to shout becomes a knot.
Each cry ignored becomes a swollen board.
Each empty vest becomes a name you dropped—
And every wave becomes the oar you hoard."

The man stepped back, the dog began to whine.
The room began to sway without a breeze.
The captain stood, its arms now lined with rope—
And let it slither down like hungry pleas.

"One knot to bind, another just to blame.
A third to hang the story from the mast.
But none for those who drowned without a name—
Just rope for ghosts who died for coming last."

We turned and found the door was hung with sails.
They cracked like whips, though nothing stirred the air.
The hull began to splinter at the base,
And through the cracks, we saw no sea—just stare.

We bolted out, the ship collapsing whole,
The lantern bursting dark instead of flame.
The hallway heaved beneath our stumbling steps,
Still echoing the captain's last, dry name.

Another door was swelling up with breath.
Its fifty-four was soaked and bruised with tide.
The House had shown what sinks within the self—
And left the ropes we'd tied ourselves to hide.

The Fifty-Fourth Room

The fifty-fourth door rose on spines and nails,
Its hinges forged from forks and rusted blades.
The number gouged into the wooden face,
As if by claws in fits of fearsome shades.

Its knob was bent, as though once torn away—
Then forced back in with tools too dull to hold.
The dog stood still, its body stiff with dread.
We opened slow, the air already cold.

Inside, the room was narrow, bleak, and bare,
Its floor a slab of stone both wet and worn.
The walls were smeared with charcoal-coloured marks—
Some names, some pleas, and many scratched with scorn.

Hooks dangled from the beams above like teeth.
A single chair sat bolted to the floor.
Its back was high, its seat engraved with nails,
Its arms still stained from those who came before.

A figure sat upon it, barely real—
A man-shaped shell of leather stretched too thin.
Its mouth was stitched in circles, edge to edge,
Its hands were nails, its ribs exposed within.

It turned its head, though creaking was the sound,
Not bone nor breath, just tension in the frame.
Its voice came not from throat, but from the wall—

A dozen whispers breathed into one name:
"Torturer."
It echoed once, then died.

The man stepped back, his lips too numb to part.
"I never—" but the silence struck him down.
The room replied with heat that pierced the heart.
"You didn't act, no. That much might be true.

But you observed. You watched, and let it play.
And though you didn't hold the whip or chain,
You laughed. You left. You simply walked away."

The woman whispered, "This… this isn't fair.
We cannot pay for sins that weren't our hands."
The figure stirred, and on the wall appeared
Their names, their scenes, their long-forgotten stands.

A boy bound down, a class who looked and laughed.
A girl made sport, then left behind the school.
A silence held by fear of speaking out—
A dozen times we learned to be the cruel.

The man sank down and held his shaking face.
"I didn't know," he murmured, "didn't see.
I never wanted anyone to break—
But no one broke as perfectly as me."

The figure cracked, then stood, its spine like bark.
It held a mirror carved from shards of pain.
"You need not swing to bend another's shape.
You need not stab to leave a lasting stain."

We fled the chair, the shackles, and the hooks.
The hallway breathed, its walls now lined with scars.
The dog ran on ahead, but looked behind,
Its eyes like stars extinguished behind bars.

Another door rose hard against the brick.
Its fifty-five was forged in rusted chain.
The House had named what hides in passive hearts—
And showed how silence, too, can foster pain.

The Fifty-Fifth Room

The fifty-fifth door shrieked with unseen wind,
Its frame bowed out, as if from pressure deep.
The number scratched with nails into the wood,
Each stroke a cut too shallow yet to keep.

The handle wrapped in vines of dying thorns,
Their tips still wet, though no fresh bloom had grown.
The dog let out a bark that died mid-breath,
Then crept behind as if to stay alone.

Inside, a courtyard paved with shattered glass—
But overhead, no sky, no sun, no moon.
Just walls that climbed too high for any end,
And air that hummed like blood beneath a tune.

Around the yard, great statues watched in stone,
Their faces draped with veils of rusted lace.
Each one held tools: a blade, a mask, a bell—
But none dared turn to show their weathered face.

A well stood at the centre, black and wide.
Its mouth was rimmed with broken teeth of brick.
The wind that cried within it sang in grief—
A song both low and oddly rhythmic, sick.

The woman stepped, and shards beneath her cracked.
She paused, then whispered, "I remember this."
The man said nothing—only stared ahead.
The dog refused to move past shadow's kiss.

Then from the well arose a form of smoke—
No legs, no face, no shape that stayed the same.
It hovered, shifting like a thought not caught,
Then spoke each of us by our hidden name.

"You come to pour your guilt into the dark,
To toss it down and say, 'Be gone, be past.'
But every drop returns, drawn back in need—
For all your griefs were built to ever last."

It offered us a bucket made of bone.
Within, a liquid shimmered, dark and red.
"One drop for every time you passed the weight.
One drop for every word you left unsaid."

The woman reached, then let her hand withdraw.
"If I let go, what part of me remains?"
The man stepped forth, but paused above the well.
"Will this bring peace—or just more silent chains?"

"There is no peace," the thing replied at once.
"But there is truth. The well keeps nothing hid.
You came to pour your poison in its mouth—
But now you drink what others never did."

The statues stirred and turned to face our forms.
Their veils were gone—their faces were our own.
Each one a version shaped by coward's hands—
Each one a moment we had not atoned.

We fled. The glass beneath us sliced our feet.
The well roared once, a howl of wanting loss.
The wind returned, and with it came the cold
Of guilt no longer buried in the moss.

We slammed the door and gasped against the wall.
The hallway narrowed tighter than before.
The dog lay down, its tongue out, limp and cracked—
Another wound to lay before the door.

Another rose, with quiet made of stone.
Its fifty-six engraved with even breath.
The House had asked us once to pour regret—
But found us thirsting just as much for death.

The Fifty-Sixth Room

The fifty-sixth door bore no name at all,
No number marked its surface, frame, or face.
Just smooth, pale wood that breathed like steady sleep,
And pulsed with warmth too dead to still embrace.

The grain ran upward, wrong against the weight,
As if the door were growing toward the sky.
The dog stood frozen, hackles stiff with fear.
The woman whispered, "This is where they lie."

Inside, a crypt, but not of stone or tomb—
No coffins lined the walls, no names engraved.
Instead, great drawers like morgue trays filled the dark,
All numbered, locked, and none of them behaved.

Some rattled soft, some thumped with muffled hands.
Some cried in gasps like lungs without the air.
A few were open—just an inch or two—
Enough to glimpse the flesh once buried there.

The scent was sweet at first, then sharp with rot.
Not death alone, but death that had been moved.
A table stood, its cloth still damp with brine,
A single scalpel gleaming, not yet proved.

And from the rear, a figure rose in white—
A surgeon, coroner, or priest of bone.
Its face was blank, a mask without a mouth,
Its eyes two holes that echoed like a moan.

"You catalog the deaths you think are yours,"
It spoke without a breath, a sound, or strain.
"But never once did you remember them.
You grieved in symbols, never named the pain.

They passed, and you performed the rites of loss—
But in your heart, you left them undefined.
You buried blame and called it time or fate.
But I exhume the griefs you left behind."

It opened one long drawer without sound.
Inside, a girl with ribbons on her wrist.
The woman gasped and dropped onto her knees.
"Anna," she said. "I kissed her cheek. I missed…

I missed the signs. I told myself she lied.
I thought she'd find the strength to breathe again.
She asked me, 'Would you still love me if…'
I laughed. And walked. And left her in that den."

The next tray pulled revealed a man unknown—
But in his eyes, the man we traveled with
Saw something that collapsed his spine with grief.
"My father. Not in blood, but in the myth.

He taught me how to fight, then disappeared.
I called him weak, then drank to chase the gap.
I told myself that love had to be earned.
He died. And I was not there for the wrap."

The thing in white now placed a hand on me.
A tray slid out with cloth across the frame.
I reached and lifted just the edge to see—
And found no face, but silence dressed in name.

"This is the one you let fade without mark.
You held no hand. You wrote no final word.
You mourned them not, but used their death to rise—
And every speech you gave left them unheard."

We fled. The drawers all opened, one by one.
The air grew thick with names we'd never said.
And as we passed the door, we heard behind
A hundred whispers longing to be dead.

The hallway coughed and flexed beneath our feet.
The dog now limped with blood upon one pad.
Another door grew quiet in the stone—
Its fifty-seven carved not bold, but sad.

The House had shown what loss, when left unnamed,
Becomes: not grief, but hunger dressed as shame.

The Fifty-Seventh Room

The fifty-seventh door was rimmed in smoke,
Though nothing burned, no ember lit its frame.
Its number carved in ash upon the grain,
Then smeared by wind or some regretful flame.

The wood was warped, as though it once had drowned,
Then dried and bent by sorrow's longest sun.
The dog growled low, but did not try to flee.
The man said, "This is where the lies begun."

Inside, a study lit by flickering screens—
Each one played loops of silent, sleepless nights.
Desks cluttered high with pens that never wrote,
And journals full of pages torn from fights.

The walls were cork, with strings that crossed like webs,
Connecting headlines, photos, scraps of thought.
A thousand stories hung from rusty pins,
Each claiming truth—each purchased, sold, then caught.

A single figure sat among the mess—
Its face obscured by masks too thin to bind.
Each time it spoke, a different voice came out:
One soft, one proud, one trembling, one unkind.

"You told the tales the way they ought to feel,"
It said, "Not how they truly came to be.
You chose your facts with care and polished lies,
Then wept when they came back to disagree."

The woman hissed, "We tried to tell it right.
We shared the wounds. We framed the pain with care!"
The figure turned and pointed to the board,
Where her own words were pinned in thinning air:

"She ruined him."
"He must have known."
"It's not abuse, it's just a phase."
Each quote in red, with threads drawn to her name—
Each lie she let go viral, phrase by phrase.

The man stepped back. One screen showed him alone,
Recording late at night his earnest face.
He called out those who'd harmed him, raw and fierce—
But left out names when power took their place.

"I told the truth," he murmured, "just enough."
"You told the part that bought you grace," it said.
"You left the ones without a voice to drown.
You sold your scars, then bled them when they bled."

The dog now barked and knocked a monitor,
Which burst in static shaped like reaching hands.
The walls ignited—not with fire, but light—
Each lie replayed in digital demands.

A screen showed me in silence on a stage,
Accepting praise for stories not quite mine.
I took the bow, then smiled and named no names—
And let the truth be something I'd refine.

We ran before the footage found new frames.
The figure watched, then whispered as we fled:
"To bend a truth is still to shape a noose—
And every voice you borrow must be fed."

We closed the door and caught our breath in heat.
The hallway throbbed with words we'd never said.
The dog lay down, too tired now to warn.
Another door emerged, its edge blood-red.

Its fifty-eight in dripping black was drawn—
As if the House now bled its own deceit.
The path ahead grew darker in its heart—
And we had yet to reach its hungriest seat.

The Fifty-Eighth Room

The fifty-eighth door pulsed with whispering,
Its surface damp, like breath too close to skin.
The number smeared in ink that wouldn't dry,
Still wet with words too scared to stay within.

The wood was soft, like leather long decayed,
And curled at edges where the mold had fed.
The dog stood back and whined but did not bark—
A single thread of drool hung from its head.

Inside, a chamber choked in paper scraps.
They fell like leaves from rafters made of books.
Each page half-torn, each sentence left unformed,
Each journal shredded more than one soul looks.

The floor was buried deep in scrawls and drafts—
Confessions penned then quickly torn apart.
A dozen desks stood rotting in the gloom,
Each one still warm with some abandoned start.

The air was thick with murmured, half-said things—
A rustle not of wind, but failed intent.
A shadow stirred, not walking, just a pulse,
A living blot made out of words unmeant.

It formed a face, then lost it mid-reveal.
It whispered names, then choked on every one.
It said, "You left me halfway through the truth—
And called the lie a kindness when you'd run."

The woman stepped, her fingers in her coat.
"I wrote the letter—yes—but didn't send.
I told myself that silence was a shield,
That some truths only wound, they never mend."

The figure coiled around her trembling words.
"Then who did you protect?" it softly hissed.
"Yourself? The one who harmed? The one betrayed?
You built a wall, not bandage—still, you missed."

The man now found a page that bore his hand—
A letter to a man who'd gone too soon.
He'd scrawled, "I'm sorry. I was scared to help."
Then scratched it out beneath a weeping moon.

"I should've called," he murmured, eyes now wet.
"I should've said a single goddamned word."
The paper in his hand began to burn—
Then whispered back, "Too late is still unheard."

A wind began to tear the pages free—
Each one a thought we swallowed in the dark.
A poem penned, then never passed along.
A warning stopped before it hit its mark.

The shadow grew, not huge, but vast in weight—
A gravity of words we left unsaid.
It breathed, then screamed—not loud, but low and close,
And every scrap replied with what we fled.

We ran. The paper hissed beneath our feet.
The letters lashed like ribbons through the air.
We found the door as one last page took shape—
And bore my name, then burned it with a stare.

The hallway swallowed us with quiet gloom.
The dog lay down, its eyes now red with tears.
Another door rose slowly from the mist—
Its fifty-nine carved deep by inner fears.

The House had read what we refused to send—
And kept the ink alive to write the end.

The Fifty-Ninth Room

The fifty-ninth door rattled in its frame,
As though it breathed, but not through lungs or throat.
Its number etched in trembling, jagged cuts,
Like someone carved it mid a panicked note.

The wood was grey and splintered into scales,
A shifting surface hard to touch or trust.
The dog approached, then turned its face away,
And whimpered once, then laid its snout in dust.

Inside, a bedroom soaked in twilight blue,
Where every lamp was lit, but none gave light.
The bed was made, the pillows sharp and clean,
But sheets were stained with sweat from nameless night.

The walls were padded, not with care but shame—
Each square sewn shut with threads of grieving years.
And in the corner, facing from the world,
A figure sat, constructed out of fears.
Its body wrapped in robes of folded cloth,

Like hospital gowns soaked long in dread and dusk.
Its head was bound with scarves of moth-eaten black,
Its breath a rattling thread of air and musk.
"You came to talk," it said, though not aloud.

Its voice arrived inside us, sharp and numb.
"You always spoke, but never let me speak.
You wondered why the rest would never come."
The woman stepped, then stopped beneath the bulb.

Her fingers brushed a scrap of cloth and flinched.
"I told them I was fine. I smiled. I ate.
I drank enough to keep my edges pinched.
But still, I locked the bathroom every night.

I stared. I shook. I whispered into glass.
And no one ever knocked to ask again.
They thought I'd healed. I let the silence pass."
The man looked up, his face already ash.

"They said, 'You're strong. You've made it through the worst.'
So I performed. I laughed when I should cry.
I bit my tongue and made the pain rehearsed."
The figure rose and opened wide its coat—

Inside, no organs, only shapes of grey.
A thousand selves that almost took a step,
But never found the words they dared to say.
"This is the room of almost-reaching hands,"

It whispered, now in voices old and raw.
"Where people waited for a sign, a word,
But found no breach, no bridge, no basic flaw.
You were not cruel—you simply were not near.

You made no wound, but never found the balm.
And every time you said 'They seem alright,'
A scream went unheard, folded into calm."
The dog began to howl, then stopped mid-note.

The air was thick, but not with grief—regret.
We turned, but every wall had grown too soft,
Too padded to recall what we'd forget.
We fled. The bed collapsed into the floor.

The lights blinked twice, then buzzed and burned away.
Behind us, something gently wept and said:
"You were the reason someone lived a day."
The hallway found us barely standing now.

The woman sobbed, but nothing left her mouth.
The man just stared ahead without a sound.
The dog walked slow, its breathing pointed south.
A new door stirred, its knob like fractured bone.

Its sixty carved with stillness, long and wide.
The House had found the quiet none confessed—
And turned it into grief we could not hide.

The Sixtieth Room

The sixtieth door was vast, but low and bowed,
A frame designed to make us stoop and crawl.
Its number stitched into a funeral shroud,
Then nailed atop the arch like death's own scrawl.

The wood was warped by moisture, age, and grief—
A door that had been closed too long to breathe.
The dog let out a slow and stifled snarl,
Then pressed against our legs and bared its teeth.

Inside, a dining hall of endless length,
With chairs that twisted upward into claws.
A table stretched so far it met itself—
A loop of hunger stitched by broken laws.

Each plate was set with knives and shattered cups.
No food, no drink—just name cards placed with care.
And on each card, a phrase that curled and bit:
"You took too much."
"You left them nothing there."

The chandelier hung low with candle stubs.
Their flames were blue, and hissed like boiling fat.
Each one burned names we tried not to recall,
And smoked with scents of guilt we never sat.

The woman stopped and found her seat alone—
It bore her name, engraved in bone and gold.
She read the card: "You starved them just enough."
She closed her eyes, her body going cold.

"I fed myself when they could barely eat,"
She said. "I said the pantry shelf was bare.
I blamed the rain, the bills, the time, the pain—
And ate in secret, just to not be there."

The man found his, a goblet filled with ash.
His card read: "You devoured what was meant."
He whispered, "I took care, but not for them.
I fed my dreams, then claimed I paid the rent."

The head of table stirred—a bloated thing
With limbs too soft, its mouth a ring of knives.
Its apron stitched from napkins soaked in red,
Its eyes two coins from debt unpaid in lives.

"You always took," it said, "and dressed it fine.
You called it earned, or justified, or fair.
You told yourselves you needed more than most—
Then praised the poor for learning how to bear."

It reached, and plates began to fill with bones.
Each one too small—each gnawed to nothing whole.
The candles flared, the silverware took shape—
And knives began to scrape across the soul.

The woman screamed and pushed her chair away.
The man collapsed beneath a feast of ash.
The dog leapt forth and barked into the dark,
Its voice like flint that sparked against the lash.

We fled, the chairs now snapping at our heels,
The plates all clanging loud like mourning bells.
The chandelier let loose a flood of wax—
It chased us out with boiling, bitter smells.

We slammed the door behind and dropped to floor.
Our breath came fast, our guilt poured out in sweat.
The hallway dimmed and stretched toward one more frame—
A door of hunger none would soon forget.

Its sixty-one was carved in fork and blade,
Its hinges greased with gluttony and dust.
The House had served the things we chose to hoard—
And dared us now to reckon with our trust.

The Sixty-First Room

The sixty-first door gleamed like polished glass,
Too perfect for a place so choked in dread.
Its number etched in silver near the latch—
A mirror more than script, more seen than read.

The knob was cold, not metal, but like stone,
A monument to things we dared not name.
The dog refused to bark or growl or whine.
It simply stared. The hallway did the same.

Inside, a chamber clean and sterile-bright,
Its walls a shine of chrome and pristine tile.
No dust, no cracks, no scent to pierce the calm—
Just silence pressed in symmetry and style.

A desk was placed exactly in the centre.
Upon it: papers, pens, a plastic cup.
Behind it sat a man in mirrored clothes,
Who smiled, then slowly gestured: "Please, speak up."

His face was mine, though neater, younger, calm.
His hands were clean. His teeth were straight and white.
He said, "We've read the record of your sins—
But tell us what you think you did just right."

The woman frowned. The man stood back in doubt.
But I stepped forth. I wanted to believe.
"I listened. Once, I stopped someone from pain.
I didn't act, and maybe that's reprieve."

The mirror-man just laughed—a pleasant sound.
"And what did that inaction truly fix?
You think that not being cruel earns a prize?
That merely not destroying makes you mix?"

He tapped a screen. It blinked with acts I praised.
Good deeds, small gifts, the kindnesses I gave.
But next to each, a scene I'd never named—
The cost, the pride, the back I turned to save.

"You give to be the one who gives, not serve.
You help, but only when they call you saint.
You feed a hunger dressed in noble lines—
But never wipe the table where they faint."

The woman cried, "We did the best we could!"
The mirrored man stood slowly from his seat.
"And isn't that the softest kind of lie?
The kind that lets you sleep while others bleed."

The lights above grew harsh, then sharp, then thin.
The walls became a thousand mirrored frames.
Each one showed us as heroes in disguise—
And then the scene beyond, scorched into flames.

We turned, but found the door now rimmed with light—
Not gold, not white, but blinding, clinical.
A voice rang out: "You tried, but not enough.
You loved—but kept your hands too cynical."

We ran, though nothing chased us through that place.
No monster screamed, no blood boiled through the floor.
Yet still we fled, because we'd seen ourselves—
Not worse than real, but truer than before.

The hallway dimmed, then split to either side.
We paused, but in the wall ahead it grew—
A door of mirrored steel and sterile black,
With sixty-two gleamed freshly through the dew.

The House had judged our kindness, not with wrath—
But something colder: praise dissected clean,
Until we saw the virtue we had worn
Was just a costume stitched by want unseen.

The Sixty-Second Room

The sixty-second door was tall and thin,
Its height unnerving, stretched beyond the norm.
Its number etched in charcoal running down,
As though it wept its form from some past storm.

The wood was dry, but hummed beneath our hands—
Not sound, but tension, thick as breath withheld.
The dog growled once, then paced in looping steps.
The man stood pale, his shoulders sharp and shelled.

Inside, a courtroom shaped like ancient guilt,
Where pews of splintered oak stood row by row.
A pulpit loomed, but bore no cross nor law—
Just scales that tipped before the gavel's blow.

The walls were carved with faces, not alive,
But somehow watching, waiting to accuse.
And every bench had names carved deep in grain—
Not just of crimes, but those who let them loose.

A judge sat high in robes of woven dusk,
Its face a mask made out of stone and glass.
Its eyes were dark but flickered once with red,
Its gavel gripped like futures yet to pass.

"You've come to argue innocence," it said.
"To claim that what you did, you did from need.
But need is just a word you learned to wear—
And now the House will test what it can bleed."

The man stepped forth and raised a trembling hand.
"I hurt her once. I didn't mean to strike.
I told myself I'd never do it twice.
I said, 'It's stress. She knows I'm not the type.'"

The judge struck down the gavel, once and slow.
A bell rang out behind the chamber wall.
A door slid wide, revealing her alone—
Her bruises fresh, her breath too faint to call.

She looked at him, then vanished in the dark.
The man collapsed, his fists against his chest.
"I said I changed. I swore I'd never be—"
"But still you were," the judge said. "You confessed

Not for her pain, but just to clear your name.
You dressed your guilt in tears and therapy.
But never once did you remove the knife—
You just agreed to never let it see."

The woman stood, her jaw set tight with rage.
"Then judge me too. I let him stay too long.
I told myself he needed one more chance—
I told myself his hurt could right his wrong."

The judge leaned back and weighed her words with care.
"And so you did. And in that grace, he fed.
You were no villain—no. But silence sings
When justice shivers, whispering instead."

The gallery began to breathe and moan.
The carved faces now wept or bared their teeth.
The scales began to tip from side to side,
And dust fell down like ash from grief's beneath.

The dog barked once, its voice a sound of end.
We turned and fled beneath the screaming eyes.
Behind, the judge declared with final toll:
"The sentence is to carry what you prize."

The hallway reappeared with cracks and moss.
The floor now sloped, as though it mourned our steps.
Another door grew silent in the wall,
Its sixty-three still wet from verdict's depths.

The House had tried us not with iron bars—
But made our guilt the gavel and the scars.

The Sixty-Third Room

The sixty-third door yawned with breathless dark,
Its hinges lost beneath a velvet drape.
The number carved in dust upon the wall,
Then wiped away as if to aid escape.

The knob was brass, but smudged with prints and ash—
A thousand hands had touched it, none held firm.
The dog crept low, then laid upon the ground,
As though it knew the House would make us squirm.

Inside, a theatre drenched in blood-red light,
Its seats all cracked, their cushions long devoured.
The velvet curtains hung like torn-out tongues,
And cobwebs wrapped the lights that once had powered.

A stage stood bare except a single chair,
Where shadows danced in place of flesh and bone.
A spotlight swayed without a source or shape—
Its beam revealing truths not told, but shown.

A film began to play upon the wall.
It flickered, blurred, then sharpened into pain.
No actors came, no music rose to swell—
Just silence cut by sobs we'd tried to feign.

A scene appeared: a woman in a room,
Her hands clenched tight around a letter torn.
She read, then wept, then folded in on air.
No answers came. No calls. No soft return.

The woman gasped. "That's me," she said. "That day—
I waited for a voice I told to go.
I said I needed time—but took too long.
He died before I answered, and I know."

The film cut sharp to footage full of noise:
A man beneath a bridge, alone, unshaved.
He held a phone, but didn't press the keys.
He stared until the signal left unsaved.

"I should have called him back," the man now said.
"I said I would. I swore it on my pride.
But I was scared. He cried too much. Too fast.
And in that pause, he chose a longer slide."

The reel broke down, then burst into a blaze.
The flames took shape and staggered to the edge.
A figure stepped, its body made of film—
Its eyes two reels that rolled beneath a pledge.

"This is the show you never dared to write,"
It said, "The one where truth outlives the plot.
Where endings don't resolve, but only stop—
And heroes fail to say the line they sought.

You wrote your life like fiction, safe and clean.
But here, the edits bleed beneath the prose.
You cropped the pain to fit your monologue,
And left the wounds to rot between your pose."

The stage collapsed with smoke and stuttering light.
The chairs began to creak with unseen guests.
The curtains rose, revealing empty scenes—
A thousand lives we'd touched but left unblessed.

We fled before the audience could rise.
The dog looked back and whimpered, then moved on.
The hallway welcomed us with heavy hush—
Its walls more red than when we'd first begun.

Another door emerged, no longer shy.
Its sixty-four engraved in stage-light gold.
The House had shown the stories we perform—
And those unwritten lines that still take hold.

The Sixty-Fourth Room

The sixty-fourth door pulsed with patient calm,
Its wood too still, too smooth, too finely grained.
The number not engraved, but simply there—
As if the House itself had just explained.

No handle marked its face, no key, no hinge.
It opened at our breath, not at our hand.
The dog looked up, then pressed against my leg,
Its body stiff, its paws sunk in the sand.

For sand there was—the room was dry and bare,
A desert held in walls that had no edge.
The wind blew low, but carried not with sound—
Just heat, and thirst, and silence near a pledge.

Bones half-buried rose like broken teeth,
Their ivory stained pink beneath the sun.
A tree stood far, its branches hung with stones,
Each tied with strings that never came undone.

The woman stepped and felt the sand give way.
"This place... I've dreamt it, though I don't know why.
I wake with grit between my teeth and nails.
And always there, a shape behind the sky."

The man walked on and picked up one small stone.
It bore a name, a date, a word: regret.
"I think I buried people here in thought.
They died for things I never did... and yet."

The tree began to stir, though had no leaves.
Its trunk was marked with prayers and final lines.
One read, "Forgive me for the door I closed."
Another, "I was young. I missed the signs."

A third, still wet with ink, began to form:
"She needed more than I could ever give."
The wind returned and spun the stones like bells—
Their chimes like sighs that never learned to live.

A figure sat beneath the hanging weights—
No eyes, no face, just skin the colour sand.
Its back was bent, its fingers curled and cracked,
Its body buried deep, but not unmanned.

"I am the one you let grow small," it said.
"The friend you told to quiet, sit, and smile.
The one who held your secrets like a tomb—
Then vanished when I wasn't worth your trial."

The woman knelt and reached toward one small string.
"I told her not to make things worse. To hush.
I said it kindly, but I said it still—
And watched her shame collapse beneath the crush."

The man let fall the stone he'd dared to lift.
"I said I couldn't be what he would need.
I let him drown beneath his softest ask.
And told myself it wasn't out of greed."

The sky above grew darker, red with ash.
The sand began to swirl with whispered weight.
We ran, though no one chased, no hands arose—
Just all the things we let deteriorate.

Behind, the tree grew taller in the dusk.
Its roots had names, its branches new and wide.
The House had let us see the ones we shrunk—
And built this desert graveyard for our pride.

The hallway cooled, as if the storm had passed.
But none of us felt clean, or safe, or whole.
Another door grew gently from the stone,
Its sixty-five a scar too deep to scroll.

The Sixty-Fifth Room

The sixty-fifth door leaned against the wall,
Detached, yet bound by something more than nails.
Its number carved with trembling, crooked lines,
As though some child had scratched it out through wails.

No knob to turn, no latch to guide the hand—
It opened with a sigh too thin to hear.
The dog stepped back and growled into the dark.
The woman whispered, "Something's waiting near."

Inside, a nursery, but wrong, askew.
Its cradle swayed though still, its mobile spun.
The wallpaper peeled back in curling strips,
Revealing script that moved when watched by none.

A rocking horse stood broken at the base.
Its mane was thread, its body stitched with teeth.
And in the corner, dressed in soot-stained silk,
A doll sat smiling, hollowed out beneath.

The man stood still, his fingers at his lips.
"I had a sister. Lost before she grew.
She cried too much, they said, she made things hard.
They left her in a place too cold, too new."

The woman neared and touched the broken crib.
It moaned beneath her hand like haunted air.
She found a note tied to the cradle's leg:
"Return when you have learned to truly care."

The doll began to blink with button eyes.
Its voice was stitched from childhood lullabies.
"You never let me be," it said. "You watched.
You told them, 'She's too weird. She never tries.'

They took me where the walls were soft and pale.
They fed me silence, needles, prayer, and thread.
And when they asked if I was missed at all…
You said you thought perhaps that I was dead."

The dog began to bark, but not at her—
At all the toys that now began to move.
A puppet danced, its strings pulled by no hand.
A jack-in-box spun slow to mournful groove.

A music box began to play in gasps,
Its chimes too soft to carry any tune.
And through it all, the doll just calmly rocked,
Then sang a song we once knew by a moon.

"She's just a phase, she'll grow out clean.
She bites her tongue, she won't be seen.
She cries too loud, she stares too long—
But soon her quiet proves you wrong."

The cradle cracked and spilled its empty sheet.
The wallpaper now wept with ink and ash.
We ran before the song began again,
Our heels struck chords in every broken crash.

The doll just waved as gently as the dead.
Its smile too wide to form another plea.
And on the wall, the scribbles left a phrase:
"You are the ones who silenced more than me."

The hallway swayed as if it, too, had cried.
The air was sharp with talc and thinning fear.
A door grew next, its hinges soft with rust—
Its sixty-six engraved in mother's tear.

The House had shown the ones we left behind—
The lost, unheard, dismissed, denied, maligned.

The Sixty-Sixth Room

The sixty-sixth door breathed a mother's breath,
Too warm, too slow, too filled with something known.
Its number inked in milk upon the wood,
Then smeared by time until it stood alone.

The grain beneath was split with quiet knocks—
Like tiny fists had tapped it through the years.
The dog refused to move or even whine.
The woman murmured, "This is made of tears."

Inside, a bedroom steeped in borrowed calm,
Its shelves arranged with bottles, cloths, and toys.
But nothing moved—not air nor sound nor light.
Just stillness shaped by absence, not by poise.

A crib sat full of blankets, never stirred.
A chair beside it rocked with hollow pace.
And on the walls were photographs unlived—
Each child posed in a life they'd never face.

The man stepped forth and found a rattle near.
He picked it up, but it refused to shake.
"I told her not to keep the child at all.
I said, 'You're broke. You'll only grieve. You'll break.'

I said it kindly. Gave her half a fare.
She left without a word that final day.
I still don't know if she gave birth or not.
But sometimes, I can't sleep unless I pray."

A shadow stirred beside the rocking chair—
Not mother, not the child, but something else.
A cradle-shape, but made of fabric torn,
Its face a blur like dust upon a shelf.

It hummed, then whispered, soft and sharp as bone:
"You told yourself you couldn't change her fate.
You offered reason, budget, logic, law—
And wrapped your fear of love inside debate."

The woman touched a blanket near the crib.
"I worked in clinics. Sat with girls alone.
I told them what the state would never give.
I thought I helped—but left them skin and bone.

I walked away when one looked back and said,
'Do you have kids?' I smiled and said, 'Not yet.'
But I remember what her silence meant.
She needed more than lectures and regret."

The room grew thick with powdered air and cries—
Not newborns, no, but griefs that never grew.
A lullaby began to echo slow:
"You didn't hold me, but I still knew you."

The walls peeled back and showed more cribs below—
A thousand rows of cloth with names unseen.
We turned and ran, the hallway pulling near,
The cries now quiet, distant, soft, and clean.

The dog walked slow, as if it, too, had known
The ache of lives that never came to be.
Another door was forming in the gloom—
Its sixty-seven carved with reverie.

The House had held the ones we let unborn—
And mourned them not with rage, but quiet scorn.

The Sixty-Seventh Room

The sixty-seventh door was made of glass,
But warped and stained, too thick to truly see.
Its number etched from underneath the pane,
A frost-like scrawl that seemed to plea or flee.

The surface hummed with every breath we took,
Reflections trembled though we did not move.
The dog let out a low and quiet whine—
And pawed the floor, unsure of what to prove.

Inside, a hall of mirrors stretched and curled,
Each one too tall, too thin, too near to crack.
The glass did not reflect us as we were—
But warped us into versions bent and black.

The man stepped first and saw himself in youth,
A child with bruises no one thought to see.
His mouth was sewn, but tears still streamed down cheeks.
His fists were clenched around a broken plea.

"I locked him out," he whispered, voice gone pale.
"He begged to sleep inside. I shut the door.
I told myself I had to teach him strength...
But really, I just couldn't take much more."

The glass began to drip with fluid thick,
As though his guilt could liquefy and run.
Another mirror showed him older still—
His son now turned, his punishment begun.

The woman stared into a bending pane—
It showed her wedding, every step rehearsed.
But in the corner stood a figure faint,
A sister never asked, a heart reversed.

"She said she couldn't come. She felt ashamed.
I knew the truth. She hadn't eaten well.
I didn't call. I thought she'd ruin things...
I smiled and danced while knowing she was hell."

The mirrors laughed, not loud, but like a cough—
A sound of rot that dresses up as grace.
"You didn't act with malice," came the voice,
"You simply let indifference take her place.

Each moment not of cruelty, but hush—
Each 'not my fault,' each 'wasn't really mine'—
Those built the walls, and in their fine, smooth gloss,
You watched the worst and said the view was fine."

I saw myself then—blurred and badly lit.
A friend I left unread. A text I dodged.
A funeral I skipped, too scared to cry.
A joke I let them tell while others lodged

A quiet scream behind their growing smile.
I nodded, laughed, then turned and played along.
And in the glass, I watched them age and die—
And knew I'd known the silence all was wrong.

We ran, though no one chased, no glass had cracked.
But all around, the walls began to weep.
Our faces faded out from every pane—
Replaced with those we'd promised we would keep.

The dog moved first, its paws unsure in pace.
We followed close, our chests too full to speak.
Another door stood waiting at the bend—
Its sixty-eight still damp and soft and weak.

The House had held the mirrors to our will—
And made us watch the ways we chose to still.

The Sixty-Eighth Room

The sixty-eighth door leaned like broken bone,
Its hinges straining from a load long held.
The number scratched in soot and smeared with wax,
Like something burned and never fully quelled.

The frame was bowed as if the House itself
Had tried to keep this chamber from the rest.
The dog stood stiff, its hackles rising slow—
It barked once low, then laid down to protest.

Inside, a chapel sunk in shadow's grip,
Its pews collapsed, their cushions rotted black.
The altar split and warped with rising mold,
The stained glass shattered inward from attack.

But at the front, a pulpit still stood firm,
And seated there—a priest with hollowed eyes.
No mouth remained, just stitches drawn with thread,
Its hands outstretched like someone selling lies.

The walls were lined with verses torn and scorched,
Their ink dissolved in sweat or weeping oil.
A thousand bibles bound in human skin
Lay chained along the aisles like cursed soil.

The woman stepped and read a faded sign:
"Forgive and you shall be forgotten too."
She whispered, "That's not how I learned the word."
The priest just bowed, as if it knew what's true.

"You called it faith," the voice rang in the dome,
"But meant obedience, masked well with shame.
You prayed not for the truth, but peace through fear,
Then blamed the ones who dared to speak a name."

The man stepped forth, his face both clenched and pale.
"I taught in schools where prayer could keep you safe.
I told a girl, 'Don't talk. You'll only burn.'
She swallowed fire. I walked away in faith."

The priest now rose, its robes revealing chains.
Each link a name. Each link a gasped decree.
"You knelt and wept and asked for storms to end—
Then cast out those who bled for being free.

You said, 'Forgive them, Father,' then you ran.
You called their pain a trial for the soul.
But penance is not healing, only weight—
And every cross you gave became a role."

The altar split, revealing pits beneath.
From them arose a choir built from ash.
No song they sang—just breathless, beating chants
Of names erased when mercy clashed with lash.

The woman backed away, then dropped to knees.
"I said their sins were sicknesses to treat.
I meant to help—I really did, I swear.
But all I did was wash their blood with heat."

The chapel cracked and dripped with salted wax.
The stained glass howled in tongues we once had praised.
We fled beneath the arms of broken saints,
Our lungs too tight, our pasts too loudly raised.

The dog ran hard, then stopped and whimpered low.
We followed close and left the chapel dim.
The hallway found us shaking in its grip,
And birthed another door with muted hymn.

Its sixty-nine was etched in scorched refrain,
A psalm rewritten by the ones we spurned.
The House had asked if mercy still could stand—
Then showed how easily that grace was turned.

The Sixty-Ninth Room

The sixty-ninth door breathed a bitter hymn,
Its frame warped inwards like a lung collapsed.
The number stitched with thorns in rotting thread,
Still pulsing faintly where the wood had lapsed.

A symbol marked the grain—a crooked cross
Bent downward, smeared with wax and moss-stained ash.
The dog stood trembling, tail curled tight beneath,
Its body tense, prepared for shriek or crash.

Inside, a schoolroom frozen deep in dusk,
Its desks all skewed, the chalkboard cracked in two.
The ceiling sagged with mildew and old prayers,
While windows wept with rain that never grew.

Upon the board: an alphabet in blood.
But letters swapped, as if the rules had burned.
The air was thick with shame not spoken loud,
The kind that hides when pages are not turned.

A figure stood with pointer clenched in bone,
Its robes too tight, its collar etched with guilt.
Its face obscured by pages glued in place—
Each one a lie on which the school was built.

"You raised your hand," it said, "but not for them.
You read the rules, then weaponised the test.
You marked their wrongs in ink too dark to clean—
Then praised the few who mimicked you the best."

The man stepped forth and saw a younger self—
His hand held high, his voice loud in its pride.
A child beside him squirmed beneath the gaze,
Then disappeared before the truth could bide.

"I got awards," he said. "I passed each grade.
But I mocked those who couldn't follow fast.
I laughed when they were pulled to special rooms.
I knew it hurt—but let the moment pass."

The woman touched a desk that bore a name—
Half-erased, but still warm to the skin.
"She stuttered once, then twice. I mimicked it.
The class all laughed. I didn't reign it in.

She never came again. They said she moved.
I told myself it wasn't why she left.
But every time I hear that halting sound,
I wonder what I broke with my neglect."

The chalk began to write itself in lines:
"They struggled not because they wished to fail.
You built the stairs, then mocked them when they fell."
The teacher shrieked, then struck the board with flame—

The desks flew back, the room began to melt.
We fled through rows of childhoods we had shaped,
Each one distorted by the way we dealt.
The dog howled once, then bolted for the door.

We followed close, the hallway drawing near.
Behind, the voice still rang across the ash:
"You taught them pain. And told them it was clear."
We crashed into the cold of corridor.

Our breath returned, but none of it was clean.
Another door arose, pale, proud, and wide—
Its seventy engraved with spite unseen.

The House had led us through the place we learned—
And made us face the minds we left unturned.

The Seventieth Room

The seventieth door was carved of something wrong—
Not wood, not stone, not metal, cloth, or glass.
Its surface breathed like skin beneath the grain,
And twitched each time our shadow tried to pass.

The number etched in scars too deep to fade,
Still red, still raw, as if the wound was new.
The dog refused to near the oozing frame—
It backed away, its instincts cold and true.

Inside, a chamber shaped like no true room,
Its corners bent where geometry had failed.
The floor was soft, a carpet made of hair,
And walls were veined like marble, cracked and veiled.

The ceiling hung with pictures made of mouths,
Each one repeating words we once had said.
And at the centre, nailed to shifting air,
A figure writhed—half-living, half long-dead.

It wore our clothes, but none of them quite fit.
It spoke our names in voices twice removed.
It bore our thoughts, but twisted them in turn—
Each one a truth we'd buried, then approved.

"You made me," said the thing, "from half-formed wants.
You fed me dreams you never dared to speak.
You told the world, 'I never wished for harm,'
Then watched me grow where conscience once was weak."

The man stepped forward, sweat across his brow.
"I joked about her weight. Just once. I swear.
She laughed at first… then vanished from my life.
I meant no harm, but harm was waiting there."

The woman stared at something in the walls—
A thousand eyes, each shaped like someone known.
"I posted things. Just quotes. But meant for her.
Then told myself the pain was all her own."

The thing unhooked itself and moved with cracks—
Each joint reversed, each motion drawn by thread.
It smiled with every face we'd once believed,
Then said, "You tried to kill me. I played dead.

But shame can only sleep if left unfed—
You fed me daily, sweetly, just enough.
You wore a mask and called it who you are.
But underneath, I was your skin made rough."

It lunged, but not to strike—just to embrace.
Its arms too long, its body made of "might."
We turned and ran, the hallway breathing back.
The thing dissolved into the edge of night.

The mouths screamed once and swallowed all the light.
The carpet writhed, the walls began to grin.
We tore away and crashed into the hall,
Still stained by what we'd almost let begin.

Another door was waiting, tall and sleek.
Its seventy-one engraved in subtle curves.
The House had shaped the monster we denied—
And fed it every time we bent our nerves.

The Seventy-First Room

The seventy-first door was thin as paper,
Its hinges barely fastened to the frame.
The number inked in hurried, shaking strokes,
Then crossed out thrice—as if to hide the name.

It fluttered once before it came ajar,
No breeze, no pull—just guilt that begged release.
The dog stood stiff, its breath caught in its throat.
The woman muttered, "There will be no peace."

Inside, a library without a spine—
No books, no shelves, no system, no archive.
Just loose-leaf pages pinned along the walls,
Each screaming from a life we let survive.

The words were inked in hurried, stammered lines—
Apologies, confessions, threats and pleas.
And in the centre, bound in chains of thought,
A child knelt down amidst a swarm of keys.

Not flesh, not ghost, but something made of ink,
With veins of quills and feathers for its hair.
Its eyes were shut with parchment glued in place,
Its ribs exposed, its breathing thin as air.

"You wrote me," said the child, "but left me here.
You started me with care, then let me spoil.
You built a world I never got to live—
Then shelved me where the silence starts to boil."

The man stepped forth, his hands now smeared with lines.
"I wrote about a boy I barely knew.
I turned his pain into a clever tale.
I told myself I helped—but that's not true."

The woman touched a page that bore her mark—
A letter to a lover left unread.
"I wrote him out before he had a chance.
I made his grief poetic when he bled."

The child now stood, its skin unraveling.
From every tear, a sentence slithered free.
"You took the truth, and shaped it for applause.
You gave me trauma, then denied the fee.

You penned the pain and called it empathy—
But never stayed to clean the ink you spilled.
You wrote me in your voice and named me real,
Then walked away when real was not fulfilled."

The pages swirled, a storm of shredded thoughts.
They sliced the air, then turned on us with force.
Each one a line we once had left half-true,
Each one a mouth that shouted with remorse.

We ran, the paper clawing at our clothes,
The dog leapt high to shield us from the storm.
The child dissolved into a stream of script,
Its final words: "You only wrote to warm."

We burst into the hall with ink-stained hands.
The woman sobbed and shook the lines away.
The man collapsed against the bending wall.
The House had read our truths and let them fray.

Another door grew gently from the grain,
Its seventy-two as faint as distant bells.
The House had asked what stories we had shaped—
And found our words were just unwritten spells.

The Seventy-Second Room

The seventy-second door was made of smoke—
Or something close, too fleeting to be grasped.
Its number shimmered like a ghost in oil,
Then vanished when the hallway's breath unclasped.

We reached, but every hand passed through the frame.
It opened not with touch, but by consent.
The dog growled low, then tucked its tail again—
And we stepped in where nothing truly went.

Inside, a void, but not of black or space—
A dreamless place, a womb of want and dread.
The walls were thought, the ceiling built of doubt,
The floor a sea of things we'd never said.

No form remained, no shape retained its place.
Just fragments—chairs that never had a room,
A ring that floated, heavy with a vow,
A mother's laugh that vanished with the gloom.

And then a voice, not cruel, not kind, just there—
A whisper formed of every failed escape.
"You left so much behind and called it done.
But memory, my child, is never drape.

It folds, it hides, it thickens in the dark.
It waits until your steps grow slow with weight.
And then it sings in rooms you once ignored,
And gives your final kindness back as hate."

The man now saw a door that bore no name.
He opened it and found his wedding ring—
Still warm, still bright, still humming with goodbye.
"I told her I'd come home. I never did.

I said, 'Just one more night,' and left the sky."
The woman wandered through a fog-shaped crib.
"I said I didn't want to be a mom.
I left the test unopened in a drawer.

Sometimes I hear a child in dreams, then wake—
And find the drawer is gone, the breath is sore."
The void began to shape our past in full—
Not ghosts, not wounds, but choices once ignored.

Each floated up, then sank into the floor,
Each whispered: "This was never quite restored."
And from the dark, a thousand hands took form.
Not grabbing—no, just waiting to be held.

Some shook with fear. Some trembled in goodbye.
Some bled from lines we never really spelled.
The dog barked once, and light began to shift—
A seam appeared, a fold across the air.

We stepped toward it, heavy with the things
We couldn't fix, but couldn't not repair.
The House had found the parts we left behind—
Not people, no, but promises decayed.

The hallway met us like a lung too full,
And closed the room where none of us had stayed.
Another door was rising, firm and thin.
Its seventy-three was carved with quiet hands.

The House had let us walk inside the void—
And showed what grief unmourned still understands.

The Seventy-Third Room

The seventy-third door bled a subtle heat,
Its grain too smooth, too polished for this place.
The number carved with patient, practiced strokes,
As if composed by some familiar face.

The wood was dark, the colour of old wine,
And smelled of lavender and something sweet.
The dog refused to sniff or make a sound,
But pressed its body low beneath our feet.

Inside, a parlour warm with candlelight—
But every flame was blue, not gold or red.
The chairs were plush, the carpet soft with thread,
And everywhere: the perfume of the dead.

The walls were lined with shelves of untouched things—
A gift, a photo, toys still wrapped in foil.
A thousand tokens marked with names we knew—
But never gave, or gave then left to spoil.

A figure stirred beside a windowed wall,
Its back to us, its posture calm and thin.
It held a cup that steamed with something dark—
And sipped as though no one could look within.

"You came too late," it said, its voice my own.
But softer, gentler—aged without relief.
"You brought your best, when best was not enough.
You gave what you could spare, not what brought grief."

The man stepped near a box still wrapped in gold—
The tag read For your father, Christmas, nine.
He choked and said, "I left it in my car.
He died that night. I said I'd find the time."

The woman knelt beside a dusty case—
Inside, a violin, still full with song.
"I promised I would visit once she played.
She called. I sighed. I told her, 'Not for long.'"

The figure turned—its face a collage made
Of everyone who waited to be loved.
Each time we said, "Not now, I'm far too tired,"
Each silent cry we said we'd rise above.

"You meant it," said the figure, not in spite.
"But meaning fades when action leaves it dry.
You told yourself that kindness had no time—
And then you watched them disappear and die."

The gifts began to rattle on the shelves.
The photos peeled, the ribbons came undone.
A teddy bear collapsed into the floor,
Its thread unraveling one stitch by one.

We turned to flee, but all the doors were locked—
Until we each picked up the thing we'd left.
We held it close, then placed it at the door,
And only then did silence grant us cleft.

We passed into the hall with lowered heads.
The dog looked back and whimpered once, then stood.
Another door grew slowly through the wall—
Its seventy-four was carved in faded wood.

The House had made us open all our hands—
And count the gifts we never let them land.

The Seventy-Fourth Room

The seventy-fourth door leaned without support,
Its hinges held by rust and whispered threads.
The number scratched in soot along the grain,
Then blurred by weeping hands and fevered dreads.

The dog let out a sound like swallowed bark,
Its body trembling though no threat was near.
We reached and pushed—the door swung slow, unsure,
As though it feared what we might see or hear.

Inside, a ward of ancient hospital,
The tiles cracked beneath fluorescent hum.
Each bed was veiled with gauze and breathing sheets,
Yet none gave sign of voice or step to come.

Machines were blinking lights of red and blue,
Their wires trailing into unseen limbs.
The scent was bleach, but deeper, death and dust—
And in the vents, a hum replaced all hymns.

A nurse stood still, her face a paper mask,
Her hands too clean, her apron lined in names.
Each tag a patient filed and left to rot,
Each one still breathing under care that maims.

"You left us here," she said. "Not cruelly, no—
Just by degrees. You walked. You checked. You sighed.
You said, 'They'll call if something goes too wrong,'
Then lived your life, while every one of us died."

The man approached a bed with trembling steps.
A figure lay there, mouth held shut with tape.
"My brother," said the man, "he wasn't strong.
He tried to quit, I laughed and said, 'Escape.'

He overdosed three times. I called it weak.
I told the nurse, 'He's always playing ill.'
He stayed a month... I never once came in.
The night he passed, I think I blamed the pill."

The woman paused before a wheezing frame.
A girl inside, her arms still bruised and bare.
"She asked for help. I told her, 'Not today.'
She said she'd try again. I wasn't there.

I thought I'd fix it when I had more time.
I thought her tears were just a kind of play.
She slipped into a coma I mistook
For silence I could simply walk away."

The nurse walked past and opened every file.
Each one a note that simply read: Too late.
The lights grew dim, replaced by blinking words—
Each spelling names we'd lost beneath our weight.

The dog began to pull, its leash now taut,
Though none of us had held or tied it tight.
We followed fast, the hallway drawing near,
The stretch behind now swallowing all light.

We reached the hall with breath too dry to spend.
The House around us cooled, but not with ease.
Another door arose with stiff, pale blue—

Its seventy-five engraved with fading pleas.
The House had shown the rooms where waiting kills—
And asked us if neglect was less than wills.

The Seventy-Fifth Room

The seventy-fifth door breathed in pulses slow,
As if it feared the moment we would knock.
Its number etched in chalk that smeared with touch,
Then vanished like a secret under rock.

The grain was raw, unfinished, lined with nail—
As if someone began, but never stayed.
The dog let out a whimper soft and short,
Then paced in circles, trembling, yet obeyed.

Inside, a stairway spiralled into dusk,
Its steps too wide, too worn, too soft to trust.
Each tread was carved from failed beginnings, dulled—
Ideas buried under quiet dust.

Along the walls, unfinished art took shape:
A song half-sung, a canvas left in grey.
A novel stopped mid-sentence, ink gone dry.
A letter never sent, nor burned away.

A figure sat mid-stair, with brush in hand.
Its body made of pages, paint, and thread.
Its head a broken mask of shattered pens,
Its limbs were sculpted words it left unsaid.

"You dreamt of me," it said, "but let me fade.
You planned and promised, swore that I would grow.
But each time real life knocked, you dropped the frame—
And left me in the limbo you now know."

The man stepped forward, face now drawn and pale.
"I wrote a play, but let it turn to dust.
I told myself, 'It's not the time to try.'
I buried it beneath the bills and rust."

The woman paused beside a half-sewn dress.
"I drew a child. I dreamed a house, a light.
But said, 'I'll start when things are less unsure.'
The things I loved... I turned them off at night."

The figure stood and raised a ruined score.
It sang a note that cracked like splitting glass.
"You thought of me as luxury or game—
But I was always what could help you pass.

You mourned your time but never made me real.
You praised the art of others with a smile.
But when I knocked, you answered, 'Not today.'
You built this stair with every lost exile."

The spiral stretched with memories unfurled—
The starts, the sparks, the notebooks left behind.
A thousand sketches folded into ash.
A thousand dreams that begged to be defined.
We turned and ran, the stairs collapsing fast.

The wind behind us full of songs unsung.
The House had made us climb the things we quit—
And asked why all our grief still felt so young.
The hallway met us stiff with aching steps.

The dog now moved with slower, limping tread.
Another door rose gently from the wall—
Its seventy-six in lines of failing thread.

The House had shown what never reached the page—
And asked if we had let it out of rage.

The Seventy-Sixth Room

The seventy-sixth door was wide and warped,
Its frame too tall for any human height.
The number smeared in tar across the beam,
Still dripping, fresh and glossy in the light.

The knob was gone, replaced with just a hole—
A wound torn through, as though by rage or beast.
The dog began to pace and moan and scratch,
Its eyes fixed tight as if it sensed a feast.

Inside, a ballroom stretched in rotting gold,
Its chandeliers now hung with brittle bones.
The floor was polished not with wax, but tears,
Collected in the cracks like buried moans.

The walls were mirrors, angled to deceive,
Each one reflecting joy we did not feel.
And in the centre, guests in formal dress—
But none of them were dancing. None were real.

They stood like mannequins with smiles sewn on,
Their limbs too long, their posture poised to prey.
Each clutched a glass, though none had lips to sip.
Each faced the door as if to block the way.

"Welcome," said a man in blood-red tails.
"We toast tonight the lies that wear a grin.
You wore your kindness like a fashion pin—
So drink, and let the masquerade begin."

The woman shook. "This room, it knows my face.
I dressed in hope to hide my hollow frame.
I laughed at jokes I knew would scorch the weak.
I clapped when cruelty won the game."

The man stepped back. A mirror caught his grin—
Too wide, too sharp, not his but something worse.
"I praised a man who mocked the way they spoke.
I said, 'He's harsh, but clever with his verse.'"

The dancers twitched, then stepped in unison.
Their music not of notes, but coughs and cuts.
Each moved like shame pretending it was pride.
Each dragged behind a train of ifs and buts.

"You masked your hearts," the master of the room said.
"You dressed your hate in charm and clever turns.
You smiled, you bowed, you held your glass aloft—
And warmed your hands by fires others burned."

The dog now barked, its voice a rupture sharp.
The dancers turned and moved with broken grace.
They circled us in rings of powdered silk,
Their grins too wide for any living face.

We ran, our heels on glass and fractured bones.
The music chased us like a cruel encore.
The master bowed, then raised a final toast:
"To those who cheered the beast outside the door."

We reached the hall, the echo still behind.
The woman wept, her laughter now destroyed.
The man walked on but left his tie behind—
A ribbon cut from silence once enjoyed.

Another door grew firm beneath the strain.
Its seventy-seven carved in crimson gleam.
The House had dressed us in our finest selves—
Then stripped the silk and left the rusted seam.

The Seventy-Seventh Room

The seventy-seventh door was made of brass,
Its surface dented, scorched, and smeared with ash.
The number hammered hard with tools long dulled,
Then scratched again as though to make it clash.

It smelled of smoke and something rich with fear—
A banquet left to rot upon the floor.
The dog let out a growl too deep to fake,
Then backed away and faced the hallway door.

Inside, a kitchen swallowed by its fire—
The walls were black with soot from ancient meals.
The pots were rusted, stacked in crooked towers,
Their bottoms caked with long-forgotten peels.

A spit still turned though nothing filled its grip.
The hearth had bled but never fully died.
The room was hot, but not with working heat—
A heat that stank of hunger deep and wide.

A cook stood tall in garments scorched and torn,
His apron stitched with names that bled and smoked.
His hands were knives, his eyes two boiling pots.
His lips were sealed, but every word he spoke
Was heard inside—not heard, but known too well.

"You fed yourselves with stories cooked in pain.
You used our lives to sweeten every course,
Then wiped your mouths and said it was humane."
The man stepped forward, face already flushed.

"I wrote a memoir. Used my father's rage.
I dressed it up in prose and metaphors—
Then toured it proud across a speaking stage.
I told myself it helped survivors too.

But really, I just plated trauma clean.
I made his fists a symbol, not a truth—
I never said the parts that felt obscene."
The woman bowed before a shattered tray.

"I filmed her once, when grief had left her numb.
I asked her questions, let her tears run wild.
Then clipped her silence to a touching hum—
And sold the piece as healing for the mild.

She never saw the edit. Never asked.
She vanished soon. I thought she'd understand.
But now I wonder if I bled her dry—
And left her story cold in someone's hand."

The cook began to stir a pot of screams.
They thickened into faces, faint but near.
The scent became unbearable to breathe—
A flavour steeped in decades, shame, and fear.

"You seasoned grief and baked it into fame.
You stole our rage, then served it mild and bland.
You called it art. You called it brave and true—
Then charged admission, passed it hand to hand."

The oven roared. The kitchen walls grew thin.
The knives began to leap from every drawer.
The boiling broth sang names we never knew,
And begged us, "Tell the truth, or leave no more."

We fled, the flames still carving through the door.
The cook just stood, his knives set on the line.
The dog howled once, and leapt into the hall—
Its back now streaked with something raw and fine.

Another door arose, as pale as bone.
Its seventy-eight was stitched in strips of hide.
The House had served the meals we thought were ours—
Then made us taste the pain that lived inside.

The Seventy-Eighth Room

The seventy-eighth door was damp with breath,
Its hinges curled like lips about to speak.
The number painted on in crimson loops,
Each stroke too soft, too careful, yet too bleak.

The frame was wrapped in ribbons torn from sheets—
The kind that once belonged to hospital beds.
The dog refused to move or make a sound.
Its gaze was fixed upon the door like dread.

Inside, a corridor of bedroom doors,
Each slightly ajar, each humming low and deep.
No lights, no lamps—just flickers from within,
As though the rooms themselves refused to sleep.

The walls were lined with handprints faint and small.
Some smeared in ink, some darker, stiff with red.
And from the farthest door, a whisper rose:
"You found me once. Then left me when I bled."

A hallway child emerged with dragging steps.
Its face was blank, its jaw hung loose and wide.
Its limbs too thin, as if they'd never grown,
Its voice a hush too frail to be denied.

"You saw the bruises. Heard me through the wall.
You told yourself, 'It isn't really that.'
You whispered, 'Not my place,' and changed the song.
You let me sleep beneath a shattered mat."

The woman stepped, her breath now slow and thin.
"There was a boy. I babysat. He cried.
He said his dad was 'sick' and sometimes screamed.
He showed me marks. I told him, 'Keep inside.'

I left before his mom came home that day.
I said, 'Be brave,' then ran back to my life.
I never told a soul. I never checked.
I prayed my silence softened all his strife."

The man stood still before another door.
He opened it and gasped with stifled sound.
A girl sat rocking, arms around her knees—
Her eyes two moons too wide to scan the ground.

"She was my neighbour. Twelve, or maybe more.
She told me someone touched her. Said it twice.
I told her, 'Go to school. They'll know what's best.'
I didn't write. I didn't speak it… thrice."

The child stepped closer, mouth still slightly torn.
"We lived behind your ears, your second glance.
You heard, you guessed, you hoped it wasn't true—
Then handed us to time, to chance, to chance."

Behind us, all the bedroom doors flew wide.
And in each one, a child-shaped void took form.
They didn't move. They didn't weep or point.
They simply watched—and stared us through the storm.

The dog began to whine and turned to leave.
We followed fast, our hands against our ears.
The doors slammed shut, one by one by one,
Each whisper fading deeper into years.

The hallway met us cooler than before.
Another door emerged without a sound.
Its seventy-nine was faint as scattered ash—
As if the House had burned the loss it found.

The House had made us look through every crack—
And face the cries we failed to echo back.

The Seventy-Ninth Room

The seventy-ninth door was black with oil,
Its surface slick and dripping down the frame.
The number etched with fingernails or claws,
Half-buried in the sludge of guilt and flame.

A stench came pouring through before we moved—
Of chemicals and metal scorched to ash.
The dog began to shake and scratch the wall,
Its growls now broken, sounding more like gasps.

Inside, a factory without a name,
Where gears still turned though nothing fed their spin.
The air was thick with soot and ghostly steam,
And echoes cried like steel from deep within.

The belts rolled on, still stained with faded prints—
Of hands too small to grip or pull away.
And in the dark, a row of workers stood,
With hollow cheeks that never saw the day.

Their eyes were gone, replaced with ticking dials.
Their mouths were stitched to smile while they bled.
Their hands moved fast, then faster, then too fast,
And shredded cloth that read: "We worked. We pled."

A foreman loomed, his body built from clocks.
His voice was brass, his spine a row of screws.
He did not speak, but turned a massive key—
And all the workers jerked in time to cues.

"You bought from us," the ticking foreman hissed.
"You saw the tag and knew what we endured.
You said, 'It's just a job. They need the work.'
You praised the price. You said you were assured.

You never asked what hands had cut the seam,
Or what child sobbed beneath the factory light.
You wore our pain in colours soft and sleek—
And told yourself you fought for what was right."

The man looked down and tore his coat away.
"This brand—I praised it once for being bold.
I said it fought injustice with its name—
But every stitch was sewn by fingers cold.

I read the truth. I looked the other way.
I clicked 'accept' and waited for the deal.
I called it distant, far beyond my reach—
But wore the thread that proved the pain was real."

The woman stared into a seamstress' face.
A girl no older than a child at play.
Her hands were bandaged, burned and red with dye.
She whispered, "They will learn if they obey."

The belts began to move with iron speed.
The steam turned black, the lights began to dim.
We ran as every cog began to wail—
And stitched upon our backs: "You lived through him."

The foreman rang a bell we couldn't hear.
The workers bowed but never ceased their pace.
The hallway breathed like lungs too thick with smoke.
We stumbled back, ashamed to show our face.

Another door emerged with tarnished bolts.
Its eighty carved with grief inside a chain.
The House had dressed us in our cleanest clothes—
Then showed the blood still soaked into the grain.

The Eightieth Room

The eightieth door was tall and deathly thin,
Its surface wrapped in gauze like binding skin.
The number stitched in thread too red to fade—
A thread that pulsed, as if it lived within.

It hissed when touched, not loud, but full of heat,
As though it hid a fever underneath.
The dog growled once, then lay with head down low,
Its tail curled tight as if to shield its grief.

Inside, a ward with beds of tangled vines,
Their stems like veins, their thorns like stitched regret.
Each bed bore names—so many, etched in wax,
Their edges blurred by hands that hadn't yet
Let go of hope, or guilt, or shame, or both.

IVs hung limp from branches wrapped in thread.
And at the farthest end, a man knelt still,
His face pressed gently to an empty bed.
The air was thick with prayers no one received.

A song half-sung, repeated to no end.
And on the walls, the words began to bloom—
Each one a time we could have helped a friend.
"She called," one read, "but I had plans that night."

"He cried too much. I didn't know the signs."
"They asked for help, but I was out of reach."
"I thought they'd wait. I missed between the lines."
The kneeling man looked up—his face was ours.

But thinner, haunted, drained by every "when."
He whispered, "Do you know how much it takes
To call someone, and hear 'I'm tired' again?
Do you know how it feels to hold the rope—

Not tied to neck, but tied to hope too thin—
And wonder if the person on the line
Will understand you're not just checking in?"
The woman wept, her hands upon her eyes.

"She sent a note. I saw it far too late.
It read, 'I'm tired. Not gone. But close, I think.'
I typed 'You've got this,' then just shut the gate.

She didn't jump that night. Not then, not yet.
But after weeks, I read her name in black.
And every word I meant to say was gone.
And now I dream of pulling both us back."

The man just stood and watched the flowers bloom—
Each one a message never sent in time.
"I thought a smile could stop a flood of grief.
I gave advice instead of warning signs.

He told me, 'Something's wrong.' I cracked a joke.
I said, 'We all get dark.' Then turned away.
He never sent another word again.
His mother called me sobbing the next day."

The vines began to twist around our shoes.
The air grew tight, like lungs too scared to fill.
The walls began to pulse with beating hearts—
A thousand friends whose time stood frozen still.

We turned and fled, the names stuck to our clothes,
Their letters red and stitched across our backs.
The dog howled once, then charged into the dark,
Its voice a plea to pull the silence back.

Another door emerged with solemn breath.
Its eighty-one carved deep in folded hands.
The House had named the times we missed the edge—
And showed the fall we could have made withstand.

The Eighty-First Room

The eighty-first door leaned like grief mid-prayer,
Its hinges wept with rust too thick to clean.
The number carved as though by broken nails,
Then smeared, as if ashamed of what had been.

The wood was scorched, but not by fire or flame—
By memory that pulsed too long beneath.
The dog stood still, its body coiled and tense,
And whined as though it sensed a deeper wreath.

Inside, a hallway stretched with endless doors,
But none would open—none would even shake.
The walls were padded not with cloth or foam,
But pages torn from books we didn't make.

Each one bore names of people we forgot,
Each story trimmed to suit a softer end.
The paint peeled back in shapes that looked like words—
Redacted lines that used to spell a friend.

Atop a desk, a ledger stained and thick,
Its spine still warm from hands that didn't write.
Beside it sat a quill made out of bone,
And ink that breathed like breath denied the light.

A figure hunched, its back a mass of script,
Its skin a page still bruised with every stain.
"You cut me out," it whispered through its teeth.
"You called me wrong. You didn't spell my name."

The woman flinched, her mouth too dry to speak.
"I wrote a book," she said. "I told a tale.
She begged to be included—just a note—
But I was told her story wouldn't sell.

She was too much, they said. Too raw. Too grim.
They asked me, 'Could she die offscreen, perhaps?'
I nodded once, then cut her from the page.
And now I feel her fingers in the gaps."

The man approached a wall of missing names.
"I taught the class. I skipped the lesson once.
The part where people bled for being true.
I said, 'That history just starts a fight.'

I wrote the test and left the question out.
I knew that someone died to carve that page—
But comfort pays the rent more than the facts.
And all the truth I trimmed became a cage."

The figure rose and tore away its mask—
Beneath, no face, just type too blurred to read.
"You call it care when you erase our bones.
You say, 'It's hard to teach the ones who bleed.'

But every silence echoes past the room.
And every child you save from pain too soon
Will grow and ask why no one bore the weight—
And curse the gentle lies you gave as boon."

The pages swirled and struck the padded walls.
The books began to burn without a flame.
We ran while letters clawed into our skin,
Each one a plea to write them back by name.

The dog howled once, then galloped through the door.
We followed, bruised by knowledge we had maimed.
The hall returned, its shadows darker now—
As though the House itself had grown ashamed.

Another door was rising, slick with ink.
Its eighty-two scrawled low in crooked line.
The House had made us read the truths we cut—
And whispered, "Every erasure is design."

The Eighty-Second Room

The eighty-second door was made of glass—
But not the kind that breaks; the kind that sees.
Its number etched in backward-floating script,
Like fogged-up breath, or old apologies.
We touched the pane, and it grew cold with thought.

The surface trembled once, then fell away.
The dog began to whine and paw the ground,
Its ears pressed flat as though it meant to pray.
Inside, a gallery of moving frames,
Each portrait shifting slowly, wrong, and deep.

No oils, no pastels, only living scenes—
Their subjects cursed to move but never sleep.
One showed a man, alone, beside a phone.
He stared and stared but didn't lift the line.

Another showed a girl inside a room—
Her walls collapsing while her friends drank wine.
Each frame was titled: "What They Remembered."
Each plaque engraved in tones of flesh and bone.

A whisper rose: "This is the House of Thought—
Where all your impact breathes beyond your own.
You meant no harm, and yet they still recall.
You were a moment. They replayed it whole.

You shaped the room and never knew it bent.
You left a word that cracked another soul."

The woman reached a canvas rimmed in frost.
Inside, her younger self ignored a cry.

A classmate sobbed, but she just turned away—
Afraid to lose her place, or make the lie.
"I didn't think," she whispered, "didn't mean...
I only wanted not to look too weak.

But now I see she never came again.
And still I hear that silence when I speak."
The man stood frozen by a growing frame.
It showed a crowd, all laughing but one boy.

"That's him," he said. "He tripped. I joined the laugh.
I barely thought. It felt like just a ploy.
He never spoke to me again, not once.
He moved away that year. I never knew.

But now I dream of him with widened eyes—
As if he's asking why I let it through."
The paintings pulsed and pulled us through their light.
We saw ourselves in eyes not shaped by love.

A woman who we brushed with cruel debate.
A child we cut to build our words above.
"You think you're just a footnote in their book,"
The voice returned, "but you were full-blown text.

You haunted dreams. You shaped the voice they took.
You moved along, but they were left perplexed."
The dog began to bark, and light grew thick.
The frames all wept with memories too loud.

We turned and ran as every canvas screamed—
Their silence shattered by the wrong we'd vowed.

The hall embraced us coldly in return.
Another door now bloomed from marble grey.

Its eighty-three engraved with aching truth—
A quote beneath: "We are the things they say."
The House had made us walk through memory's glass—
And taught us how reflections never pass.

The Eighty-Third Room

The eighty-third door shone like tarnished brass,
Its edges dulled by time and oily hands.
The number etched with care, then carved again,
As if by one who couldn't understand.

The handle spun, not once but round and round,
Like someone lost had turned it to escape.
The dog refused to sniff the frame or air—
It crouched and shivered, tail tucked out of shape.

Inside, a room with clocks from floor to vault,
Each ticking not in time, but out of key.
Some rang in hours that never could exist,
While others spun in loops of memory.

The walls were covered not in stone or paint,
But calendars from years we tried to skip.
Each date was marked with something crossed or gone—
Each day a knot we'd left too loose to grip.

A man sat hunched beside a shattered watch,
Its hands removed, its face no longer glass.
He turned a dial that bled a sound like sleep,
Then said, "You thought that time was meant to pass.

But time is not a river, no—not smooth.
It catches. Snags. It folds where pain was made.
You cannot move beyond what holds you here.
You cannot heal until the debt is paid."

The woman stepped and found a clock she knew—
The hour stopped the night her mother died.
"I told her I would visit that same week.
I worked instead. I said the train could slide.

She passed alone, I missed the final ring.
And though I've mourned, and though I've lit the flame,
The hands still grip me just before the hour—
And whisper through the ticking of my name."

The man stared at a wall of wasted days,
Each circled date a promise left unmet.
"I missed his game. I missed her play. I said,
'Next time,' and now I carry that regret.

I marked my planner full of dreams and plans—
But missed the time when they just wanted me.
Now every calendar becomes a grave,
Each square a tomb that used to hold a plea."

The clocks began to ring in painful tones—
Some with a scream, some just with fading breath.
One struck the hour a child once slipped away.
Another tolled the second breath met death.

The dog began to bark, then turned and ran.
We chased it through the time-worn air and dread.
Behind us, all the hours howled in grief—
Each moment not remembered but misread.

We burst into the hall, our legs like stone.
The woman wept and clutched a broken watch.
The man just stared, his gaze too far to reach.
Time doesn't slip—it stays and waits and watches.

Another door rose slow from hallway's heart.
Its eighty-four engraved with stopped clock hands.
The House had shown that time is never gone—
It waits in rooms and ticks through buried lands.

The Eighty-Fourth Room

The eighty-fourth door swayed before it stood,
As if it dreamed or barely held its ground.
Its number written not with ink or blade,
But scratched by fingernails in loops around.

The frame was damp with something like a sigh,
And smelled of wood too long denied the sun.
The dog gave out a quiet, throaty yelp,
Then pressed against my leg and would not run.

Inside, a bedroom built from layered dust,
Its furniture collapsed beneath its weight.
The bed was made, but sagging in the middle—
A valley carved by sorrow, sleep, and fate.

The walls were papered with forgotten plans—
A marriage license, letters, charts, and schemes.
And by the window, looking out through none,
A woman sat, unraveling her dreams.

She turned but didn't blink or speak at first.
Her eyes were full of lists and wedding bands.
Her hands were raw from years of wringing air,
And at her feet: a thousand rubber bands.

"I waited," came the whisper, sharp and soft.
"I waited for the promises you made.
You said you'd come back once the world was right—
But years grew roots, and I began to fade."

The man stepped forth, ashamed to meet her gaze.
"I left her once. Said, 'Only for a while.'
I chased a job. A dream. A future bright.
I told her, 'Write me. Think of me and smile.'

She wrote me once a week until she stopped.
I never asked. I thought she found her place.
But here she is, still frozen in that chair,
A ghost who never learned to be erased."

The woman walked along a dresser cracked—
Its mirror fogged with memories too sharp.
A child's drawing torn and taped again,
A ring left boxed, untouched, beside a harp.

"He asked me if we'd grow into a 'we.'
I told him, 'Later, love. Just not right now.'
He took my maybe, held it like a vow.
And died before I learned to show him how."

The woman near the window bowed her head.
"We don't get stuck because we want to stay.
We anchor to the words you never kept,
And wait to see if one will find its way.

You said, 'I'll write. I'll visit. I'll return.'
And then you didn't—but you didn't kill.
You left us warm enough to still believe—
And hope, like hunger, keeps the body still."

The ceiling cracked, and all the pages fell.
Each one a note we promised we would send.
Each one a truth we said we'd give tomorrow—
And left to spoil before the bitter end.

We fled the room, the woman still and calm,
The dog ahead, its body tense and lean.
We reached the hall and breathed the dust we made—
Still scented faint with everything between.

Another door grew out with faded blue.
Its eighty-five was written in "not yet."
The House had taught us that delay can kill—
And promises can bind like cold regret.

The Eighty-Fifth Room

The eighty-fifth door swelled against the wall,
Its frame too thick, as if it feared the squeeze.
Its number carved in layers, gouged then patched—
A wound reopened just enough to tease.

The wood was damp, its grain like twisted rope,
As though the door itself had tried to flee.
The dog let out a low, reluctant growl,
Then sat, unmoving, trembling at the knee.

Inside, a closet vast beyond all sense—
Its shelves collapsed, its hangers hung with thread.
Old jackets sagged like skins of lives unused,
Their sleeves still shaped by arms of those long dead.

The floor was soft with fabric, stacked in mounds—
Abandoned scarves and coats with stitched regret.
And in the corner, hunched between the racks,
A man sat counting every unpaid debt.

Not money, no, but kindnesses withheld—
A ride refused, a couch not offered twice.
A call unanswered late one winter night.
A jacket never lent in fear of lice.

"You kept yourself," the whisper coiled around.
"You locked your warmth in closets lined with gold.
You told yourself you'd give it when you could—
But giving late is often giving cold."

The woman knelt and touched a woollen coat—
A name tag stitched with someone she once knew.
"She asked to stay. I told her, 'Not this week.'
She slept outside. That night the frost cut through.

She lost three toes. I sent a note. She smiled—
But never walked the same, and left my life.
I told myself I hadn't meant her harm.

But harm that waits still cuts as deep as knives."
The man unwrapped a scarf still stiff with blood.
"He fell. He called. I said I'd call him back.
I heard the fear and muted it with noise.

He died an hour later, cold and cracked.
I told his mom I never got the text—
And now I lie to him each time I sleep.
I wrap myself in warmth I should have shared.

And wonder why that night still cuts so deep."
The coats began to rise and walk alone—
Their sleeves outstretched, their collars turned with spite.

Each one a shape we chose to keep away,
Each one a plea we buried out of sight.
We turned to run, but all the racks had grown—
The walls now pressed with fabric soaked in grief.

The only path was crawling through the weight
Of all the warmth we hoarded underneath.
We gasped into the hall, the air too hot.
The dog limped through, its fur now streaked with thread.

We lay beneath the pressure of the room—
A guilt not shouted, only softly said.
Another door grew slow with quilted trim.
Its eighty-six was stitched in silver seams.

The House had named the help we chose to keep—
And showed how mercy dies in selfish dreams.

The Eighty-Sixth Room

The eighty-sixth door breathed a bitter draft,
Its grain like splinters caught in frozen flesh.
The number scored in chalk, then carved beneath,
As though the first attempt had failed the test.

The hinges creaked before our fingers touched—
Not rust, but nerves—like something tensed to scream.
The dog stood guard but didn't cross the line,
Its eyes fixed wide, as if it watched a dream.

Inside, a room of trophies, tall and thin,
Their bases cracked, their plaques all black with rot.
Awards for things no soul should celebrate—
"Most Trusted Liar." "Best Forgotten Thought."

The shelves were bowed beneath invisible weight.
The carpet worn by pacing feet alone.
And in the midst: a figure dressed in crowns,
Each one a title built on someone's bone.

It turned to us and smiled with practiced ease—
A grin rehearsed from boardrooms, pews, and courts.
"You spoke so well," it said, "and earned such praise.
You turned their pain to well-appointed ports.

You led the crowd with perfect symmetry—
Each phrase well-placed, each silence tuned with care.
You told the truth that wouldn't bruise your skin—
And carved a throne from all you didn't share."

The man stepped back and stared at one gold cup.
It bore the words: "For Silence During Doubt."
"I had a chance to call the man a thief.
I knew the facts. I could have thrown him out.

But he was kind to me. He gave me work.
I told myself it wasn't mine to say.
So others fell. I climbed. And when they asked,
I said, 'I didn't know. I looked away.'"

The woman stood before a plaque in glass:
"Best Dressed at the Hearing No One Won."
"I testified," she whispered, "but I lied.
I softened him. I said he seemed 'undone.'

They begged me not to speak at all, but still—
I took the stage and smiled through his excuse.
They clapped. I wept. I said I told the truth.
But left the part where silence meant abuse."

The figure bowed and placed a sash on me.
Its threads were spun from compliments and guilt.
"You led them well. You told the tale they liked.
You left the ugly parts outside the quilt.

You let the wolves remain because they smiled.
You passed the torch and said, 'The room is clean.'
But legacy is made not by applause—
It's made by who you left behind the screen."

The trophies tipped and shattered into dust.
The walls turned red with words we didn't speak.
Each "not my fight" ignited into flame.
Each "I don't know" now wailed like something weak.

The dog began to bark, its voice too raw.
We fled before the crowns began to weep.
The hallway swelled with shame we couldn't wear—
A stage too soft to ever truly keep.

Another door emerged with brassy glare.
Its eighty-seven carved in crumbling stone.
The House had judged the justice we withheld—
And crowned us kings of silence cast in bone.

The Eighty-Seventh Room

The eighty-seventh door was cold to touch,
Its surface lined with frost too thick to scrape.
The number barely showed beneath the ice,
As if regret had formed a frozen cape.

The knob was smooth, but trembled as we turned—
A pulse of something buried, locked, and still.
The dog let out a muffled cough of fear,
Then took one step and whimpered near the sill.

Inside, a bedroom hollowed out by time,
Its bed unmade, its corners full of dust.
The windows sealed with yellowed curtain threads,
And air too stale to ever earn our trust.

Along one wall, a wardrobe hung ajar—
Its doors revealing nothing but the past.
A mirror faced away, turned to the wall,
As if it feared the questions we might ask.

A figure sat upon a wooden chair—
Their back so still it hardly seemed they breathed.
No face, no limbs, just shadows clothed in grief,
And on their lap, a book they hadn't sheathed.

"You've come," it whispered, not in joy, but fact.
"You finally arrived to read me through.
I've waited while you tried to live and smile—
But I am made of things you wouldn't do."

The woman stepped, then stopped mid-breath, then knelt.
"I kept the letters. Read them once. Then burned.
He begged me to explain, to just be clear.
I blocked his name, then asked why he returned.

I told my friends I'd cut him for my peace—
But truth is, I just feared what he would say.
He wasn't safe—but neither was the past.
And silence seemed the cleaner, cheaper way."

The man now spoke with hands like wilted leaves.
"I knew a man who walked into the fire.
He needed help. He said, 'Don't tell the cops.'
I told him, 'Then you walk your own barbed wire.'

He vanished. Later, headlines made him sin.
I knew the truth—how sick he'd really been.
But I kept still. I let the tale go wrong.
And every night, I hear his scream again."

The figure stood and handed us the book.
Its cover bore no name, no date, no word.
Just silence shaped in leather pulled too tight—
A breath held in where none had yet occurred.

"These are the truths you buried in a cave.
The things you thought you'd carry to your grave.
The lovers scorned, the friends you used and dropped.
The rules you broke, then justified and swapped."

The pages turned with screams we tried to hide.
The ink was blood. The margins full of nails.
Each line began with "Once, I looked away,"
Each paragraph a chain of self-made jails.

We fled, the book too heavy for the flame.
The mirror turned and caught us as we ran.
Our faces cracked and wore the shadow's grin—
The one we hid since long before it began.

Another door emerged in rigid ice.
Its eighty-eight carved deep in frost and pain.
The House had read the things we swore we'd lose—
And filed them where the soul returns again.

The Eighty-Eighth Room

The eighty-eighth door was wide and split with strain,
Its wood like muscle pulled too far to heal.
The number carved in jagged, trembling arcs—
As if each stroke were drawn against a wheel.

The knob was gone, replaced by just a hole,
A socket dark and slick with something red.
The dog began to snarl with quiet breath,
And would not step, though nothing yet had bled.

Inside, a room with chains hung wall to wall—
But none were metal, none were forged or cast.
They were decisions, vows, and weighted words,
Still warm with griefs we thought had long since passed.

Each link was shaped like something once declared:
"I'll always be there." "You can count on me."
"I won't become like him." "I'd never lie."
Each sentence writ in cold calligraphy.

The centre held a post of twisted roots,
Around it wrapped in oaths now dead and torn.
A man stood bound, not by the bark or vines,
But by the words he once gave when he swore.

He turned to us with eyes like blistered glass—
Still wet from tears too long repressed or spilled.
"You spoke with hope, but carried no resolve.
You promised peace, and left it unfulfilled."

The woman paused and held her breath mid-step.
"I told my father, 'You'll be fine with me.'
I made him move. I sold his house for care.
Then dropped him in a ward and paid the fee.

He died before he ever found his chair.
I said, 'They're trained.' I said, 'It's what he needs.'
But really, I just couldn't take the time.
And wrapped my shame in good administrative deeds."

The man stepped forward, nearly losing speech.
"I swore I'd stay with her, through good and worse.
I meant it then. I didn't think I'd leave.
But when she cracked, I said, 'It's just a curse.'

I ghosted. Blocked. I gave her half the rent.
I told my friends she'd begged too much, too loud.
But when I dream, I see her at the door—
Still holding what I left behind, still proud."

The chains began to creak with pulsing weight.
They pulled from walls and wrapped around our wrists.
Each vow we broke returned in phantom grip.
Each one a mouth we'd silenced with our twists.

"A promise made is not a favour given,"
The bound man said. "It's flesh you chose to feed.
And when you starve it, when you walk away—
It learns to bleed, and calls that wound your creed."

The room collapsed beneath the tightening cords.
We fled through nets of every vow we shed.
The dog broke through, its teeth against the strings—
And carved a gap before the hallway spread.

We reached the hall, our arms still marked in red.
The oaths we spoke had etched into our skin.
Another door rose slowly from the dark—
Its eighty-nine engraved in promises thin.

The House had chained us with the words we gave—
And showed that oaths unmet still own the grave.

The Eighty-Ninth Room

The eighty-ninth door leaned with practiced guilt,
Its hinges dulled by use, but strong with weight.
The number carved too shallow to be proud—
A whisper dressed as fact, as law, as fate.

Its surface bore the polish of a mask,
A door once loved for how it looked, not was.
The dog refused to make a sound or move,
As though it knew this room still kept its claws.

Inside, a study walled in heavy books—
But none were whole, and none bore titles true.
The spines were blank, the pages all redacted,
And every shelf leaned slightly out of view.

The desk was wide, its surface lined with names—
Each scratched beneath a stamp that read Dismissed.
And in the chair, a man in scholar's robes,
His face erased, his hands clenched in a fist.

"You learned," he said, "but only what they gave.
You called it truth, though never pulled the thread.
You read the maps and claimed to know the world—
But left unmarked the places where we bled."

The woman stared at walls where faces bloomed—
Portraits formed from stories left untold.
"I wrote about the war," she said. "The facts.
But skipped the girl who died beneath the fold.

I knew her name, I saw her picture fade.
But said, 'Her death might complicate the tone.'
And so I let her vanish from the book—
And made the hero's journey all my own."

The man stepped back from quotes that shook the room.
"I taught the text. I used the state-approved.
I knew that others lived beneath the line—
But thought, 'That chapter isn't really proved.'

I called it balance, called it fair and just.
I told them, 'History is made by men.'
But now I see the names I never spoke—
Still carved in desks and silence once again."

The man in robes stood up and lit a page.
It screamed. It burned. It turned to ash midair.
"You curated the facts to suit your fear.
You loved the myth, but didn't seek the tear.

You made a canon forged from comfort's stone—
And let the stories howl behind the gate.
You said, 'This doesn't fit the arc I want,'
Then wondered why your truth resembled hate."

The shelves began to sway with buried names—
They fell like leaves that never touched the ground.
We ran as voices spilled from every spine,
Each one a tongue that never once was found.

The dog barked sharp, its hackles raised in full.
We passed into the hall with echo's weight.
The books behind us sealed themselves in flame—
A funeral of knowledge come too late.

Another door appeared with stinging air.
Its ninety carved in fonts we'd never learned.
The House had made us read what we ignored—
And showed how every silence must be earned.

The Ninetieth Room

The ninetieth door was smooth, devoid of grain,
Its face too pale to bear the weight of wood.
The number etched in perfect symmetry,
As though it wore its shame the way it should.

The surface whispered truths we couldn't hear,
A breath against the knuckles, faint and slight.
The dog approached, then growled and turned away—
Its fur rose high as if it sensed the blight.

Inside, a gallery of whispered acts,
A hall where no one shouted but all knew.
The walls were draped in veils of gauzy silk,
Each stained by hands that thought they'd passed on through.

The lights were dim, but each concealed a scene:
A woman groped at work, and told to smile.
A boy whose bruises brought him only blame.
A girl laughed off when silence lasted miles.

Each shadow on the silk began to speak—
Not loud, not clear, but with a grinding hiss.
"You knew," they said. "You saw. You heard. You left.
You called it small, or fleeting, just a miss.

You said, 'They wouldn't want me to step in.'
You told yourself, 'They'll fix it. It'll pass.'
But still we sat beside you, still we cried—
And still you let the moment darkly last."

The man approached a curtain shaped like shame.
He reached, and found his own reflection there.
"He joked about her lips. I laughed. I did.
I saw her face collapse, but didn't care.

I told myself I didn't say the words—
So why should I be guilty of the break?
But now I see how silence wears a mask—
And how the echo still keeps me awake."

The woman passed a shadow on the floor.
It looked like her, but smaller, bent, and raw.
"I saw him take her keys. I saw her sway.
I told my friend, 'It's not our place, that's law.'

He smiled and said she's done it all before—
And I agreed. I didn't check. I ran.
She never called. I never asked. Just hoped.
But now her name is carved upon my hand."

The veils rose high and showed us every scene—
Each one a time we could have made it stop.
Each one a day we chose to look away.
Each cry we called exaggeration's drop.

The shadows surged and whispered through the dark:
"It isn't yours, you said, and turned aside.
But wrong that's witnessed, known, and left untouched
Becomes a grave in which the good must hide."

The dog began to snarl and bite the air.
We fled through voices begging us to see.
The silk tore down like judgment soft but sharp—
A cloth that once could cover, now set free.

We tumbled out into the choking hall.
The walls closed in as if to press the shame.
Another door rose quiet, grave, and low—
Its ninety-one burned white without a name.

The House had shown the wrongs we watched and weighed—
And asked if truth unspoken still obeyed.

The Ninety-First Room

The ninety-first door sighed beneath its frame,
Its corners bent by pressure from within.
The number carved too deep, as if it tried
To carve the guilt from where the wood had been.

The handle cold—too cold to come from air—
As if it held a silence not yet said.
The dog stood rigid, tail a pointed line,
Its eyes on us, its body filled with dread.

Inside, a courtroom drowned in paper sheets,
Each page a verdict no one ever read.
The benches carved from gavel-shattered wood,
The air still thick with things that went unsaid.

No judge presided here, no bailiff stood.
No jury watched from pews with sharpened eyes.
But in each seat, a mirror took its place—
And every face we'd wronged began to rise.

A voice began—not one, but hundreds more—
A choir built from all the harm we caused.
Not through attack, but things we let decay,
By letting time or comfort give us pause.

"You judged us quietly," the chorus sang,
"You measured us by what we lacked, not gave.
You labeled us with names you thought were kind—
And walked away before the soul was saved."

The man approached a file marked in gold.
Inside, a photo faded, torn, and curled.
"I called him 'just confused,' when he came out.
I told him, 'Maybe don't tell all the world.'

He left the state that year. We never spoke.
I heard he died before his thirtieth day.
And though I never raised a hand or word—
I built the fence that pushed his heart away."

The woman touched a desk with edges bruised,
Its drawers all locked with locks too small to see.
"She came to me, ashamed to share her scars.
I said, 'We all have pain. Just let it be.'

I didn't mean to crush her with my calm—
But she was asking for a hand, not talk.
And when I said, 'You'll heal in time,' she left.
I didn't see her take that final walk."

The mirrors wept, but didn't break or blink.
They showed not monsters, but the masks we wore.
The times we chose to seem more kind than true,
And left them bleeding just outside the door.

"You tried to be the better ones," they said,
"The ones who never screamed, who kept the peace.
But peace that leaves the wounded on the floor
Is cruelty in kindness' thin caprice."

The room grew tight with paper in a flood—
The judgments we had cast, then disavowed.
We ran as sentences began to bite,
Each paragraph a scream no smile allowed.

The dog howled once, then burst into the hall.
We followed fast, the verdicts in our wake.
The corridor grew narrow as a tomb,
Each breath we drew too deep, too sharp to fake.

Another door emerged with solemn weight,
Its ninety-two engraved in scales untrue.
The House had judged the judgment we had passed—
And asked what cruelty hides in what we do.

The Ninety-Second Room

The ninety-second door was built askew,
Its frame too narrow for the width of pain.
The number hung from rusted hooks and twine,
Half torn away, like guilt we can't contain.

The wood was warped, as if beneath its grain
Some secret strained and pressed to break its shell.
The dog stepped back, then lay with ears pinned down,
Its body still, as if it knew too well.

Inside, a house within the House itself—
A mockery of comfort, clean and bare.
Each room a perfect frame of daily life,
Each cupboard stocked with things that weren't
    quite there.

The kitchen gleamed with knives that never cut.
The chairs arranged for guests who never came.
The walls were hung with paintings of a smile—
But every mouth was signed with someone's name.

A man and woman stood beside the stove,
Their clothes too crisp, their skin too tightly pressed.
They smiled and turned—but did not meet our eyes.
Their voices sang, rehearsed and neatly dressed:

"We did our best. We gave you all we could.
We worked, we fed, we clothed, we bought, we drove.
We didn't hit. We only raised our voice.
We never locked the door. We let you rove."

The man who walked with us dropped to his knees.
"This room—this house—it smells like where I grew.
They never touched me wrong or drank or screamed…
But nothing there was ever good or true.

I learned to thank them when they crushed my dreams.
I learned to laugh before they mocked my tears.
They said, 'We love you,' but with distant eyes.
They raised me well—and filled me up with fears."

The woman wept beside a plastic frame—
A family photo scrubbed until it shined.
"My mother said, 'You're lucky to be fed.'
My father said, 'Your sadness isn't mine.'

They praised me when I smiled through my breaks.
They punished when I named the hurt I knew.
I never left with bruises, only ghosts—
The kind that speak in tones too clean, too true."

The couple turned and laid the tablecloth.
"We did our best," they said, "and that must count.
Intent absolves the damage left behind.
And every gift should make the silence mount."

The walls began to crack with hidden noise—
The screams of children told their pain was fake.
We ran through rooms of kitchens, baths, and beds—
Where not a single soul was free to break.

The house within the House dissolved in dust.
The dog stood firm and watched us find the air.
Another door emerged with painted trim—
Its ninety-three inscribed with "We still were there."

The House had dressed abuse in proper rooms—
And asked if comfort sometimes builds the tombs.

The Ninety-Third Room

The ninety-third door glistened like a wound,
Its sheen too slick to come from polish plain.
The number written not in paint or ash,
But something darker, drawn from marrow's vein.

It pulsed once when we neared, as if alive,
Then settled still—a gate that held its breath.
The dog began to pace with cautious steps,
Its shoulders hunched as if to scent out death.

Inside, a gallery of masks on hooks—
Each labeled with a name we used in jest.
The walls were soft, like soundproofed padded rooms,
But pulsed with chuckles barely held in chest.

The air was thick with perfume worn by lies—
Too sweet, too loud, too heavy for the space.
And in the centre, dressed in seven skins,
A jester danced with tears carved in his face.

"You laughed," he sang, "when cruelty was art.
You clapped when pain came wrapped in clever phrase.
You joked, you jested, mocked the ugly parts—
Then sipped your tea and basked in echo's praise.

You wore our accents, dressed our pain in drag.
You mimicked scars you never dared to own.
And when we wept, you called it 'too intense.'
You said, 'We're friends!' and threw another stone."

The man stepped back, his hand against his mouth.
"I called him names. Just jokes. We all laughed loud.
He said it stung. I said, 'Don't be so soft.'
I told myself, 'I'm fun. I'm not the crowd.'

He left the group a week before he died.
I made a meme to mourn. It got two likes.
But now I hear his voice behind my punch,
And taste his silence every time it strikes."

The woman stared at masks with blinking eyes.
Each one wore features twisted into grin.
"She spoke too fast. I mimicked every word.
She cried. I told her, 'Take it on the chin.'

I wasn't cruel—not really, not by law.
But still, she flinched each time I passed her desk.
And when she left, they asked me if I knew—
I said, 'She was just always so grotesque.'"

The jester stopped and shed his final mask—
Beneath, no face, just mirror, smooth and cracked.
"The joke you make becomes the grave we fill.
You say, 'It's fine,' then laugh when others act.

You twist your guilt into a punchline clean.
You wear our wounds like costumes at a ball.
But cruelty with rhythm still is pain—
And humour doesn't soften hate at all."

The walls began to pulse with giggled sobs.
The masks flew free and circled in a swarm.
They grinned with mouths too wide for joy or truth—
Each one a jest that learned to take a form.

We ran, the laughter swelling like a tide.
The dog howled once, then bit through veil and veil.
The hallway wrapped around us like a rope—
Still warm with all the jokes that tipped the scale.

Another door arose, too sharp to touch.
Its ninety-four inscribed in looping jest.
The House had made us hear the things we laughed—
And asked if every joke was just a jest.

The Ninety-Fourth Room

The ninety-fourth door hung on creaking threads,
Its frame too thin to hold the weight it bore.
The number etched in ash, then crossed with chalk—
As though erased, but crawling back once more.

Its centre cracked, yet never split outright,
Like something trapped inside still pressed to speak.
The dog drew close, then stopped and faced the floor,
Its tail limp, its breath restrained and weak.

Inside, a hallway bathed in amber light,
Where every wall was built of whispered names.
The air was thick with incense, sweat, and smoke—
A hush that pulsed beneath a thousand flames.

Each candle stood for someone never found,
Each flicker danced for one we never mourned.
And in the farthest niche, a woman sat,
Her robes of velvet, scorched and gently torn.

She did not move to greet us or to rise,
But spoke in tones like wind through burning leaves:
"You knew us by the numbers on a screen.
You shared our deaths in sympathy and grieves.

But when the noise had passed, you shut your doors.
You let the stories rot beneath your guilt.
You called it loss, but only when it trended—
And never asked what silence you had built."

The man stepped forward, choking on the smoke.
"There was a boy. They found him in a ditch.
I shared his face. I wrote a post. I cried.
But when his sister reached, I dropped the switch.

I said, 'I've done enough. I showed I care.'
She asked for help. I turned away and blinked.
I said, 'I'm tired. I can't fix every wound.'
And let her plea dissolve before I think."

The woman knelt beside a candle dimmed.
Its wick still warm, its wax a pool of dread.
"A march. A name. A woman choked in cuffs.
I shouted once. Then went to sleep instead.

I told myself my platform wasn't big.
I said, 'I'm not informed. It isn't wise.'
But still I wear her story like a pin—
And sell her name in hashtags, likes, and lies."

The seated figure raised her hand to point—
The walls split open, whispering aloud.
"You took our rage and turned it into art.
You took our grief and fed it to your crowd.

You saw injustice, filtered through a lens—
Then filed it down to something smooth and mild.
But we are not your chapters, or your themes.
We are the blood, the mother, and the child."

The candles flared and screamed without a voice.
The walls poured wax that hissed against our feet.
We fled as names began to brand our skin,
Each letter carved in scars that wouldn't beat.

The dog barked once, then burst into the hall.
We followed, stained by truth we'd sold as gloss.
Another door emerged with blackened rim—
Its ninety-five engraved in voice and loss.

The House had made us face the dead we praised—
And asked if memory was truth or phase.

The Ninety-Fifth Room

The ninety-fifth door groaned with every breath,
Its joints like knuckles worn by time and tears.
The number carved in bone, not wood or steel—
Too white, too raw, too marked by buried years.

The grain beneath was splintered, stretched, and thin,
As though the door had tried to crawl away.
The dog sat down and would not lift its eyes—
Its fur pulled tight with dread it could not say.

Inside, a chapel built from splintered pews,
Its altar cracked, its cross turned upside down.
The stained glass wept with shapes too dark to name—
Its saints all frowning, every angel drowned.

No candles burned, yet everything was lit,
A sickly glow that came from prayer denied.
And in the nave, a priest stood all alone,
His robes too clean for what he held inside.

He turned and smiled—a smile too soft, too smooth—
A practiced warmth that chilled the blood beneath.
"You came," he said, "though not to truly kneel.
You came to seek, but never to believe.

You wore your doubt like armour dipped in light.
You called it reason, but it bled like scorn.
You preached your mercy, yet you mocked the need—
And left the lonely crushed beneath your thorn."

The woman stepped across the broken floor,
Her eyes locked on the shadows hung in chains.
"I mocked my mother's faith. I called it weak.
I said, 'No god could care through all these pains.'

But when she died, I wore her rosary.
I said her prayers as if to catch her voice.
I do not know if heaven heard a thing—
But part of me still wants that kind of choice."

The man approached a pulpit torn with nails.
Its words still faint beneath a smear of wine.
"I stood in church and smiled and shook their hands.
I sang the hymns, but thought them all a line.

And when he wept, I told him, 'God's not real.'
He left the room and didn't come again.
I thought I'd freed him from the chains of myth—
But maybe I just left him in the rain."

The priest now wept with tears like boiling milk.
They sizzled as they fell upon the stone.
"You think that doubt absolves you of belief.
But silence grows in faith's abandoned home.

You left the grieving mother to the cold.
You mocked the child who prayed beside their bruise.
You broke the psalms and praised the empty space—
Then wondered why the broken always lose."

The altar cracked and sang in dying tongues.
The rafters shook with choirs out of key.
We ran as incense turned to choking smoke—
A fog of what we swore we didn't see.

The dog broke free and barked into the void.
We stumbled back into the hallway's breath.
Another door arose with subtle heat—
Its ninety-six carved deep in "truth and death."

The House had questioned all we once condemned—
And asked if faith must always break or bend.

The Ninety-Sixth Room

The ninety-sixth door sagged against its frame,
Its hinges groaned as if they bore a soul.
The number scratched in haste, then carved again—
Each stroke more frantic, seeking lost control.

The wood was pale, like skin denied the sun,
Its grain too thin to truly hold a name.
The dog began to tremble at the edge,
And whimpered once, too soft to cast its claim.

Inside, a nursery, or something near—
A place where childhood tried and failed to grow.
The toys were wrong, too sharp, too tall, too bent,
And every mobile spun a tale of woe.

The cradle rocked though no one touched its base.
The walls were stitched with drawings not yet dry.
And in the corner, hunched within a heap,
A child sat sobbing without mouth to cry.

Its hands were stained with colours turned to black,
Crayons melted down to choking tar.
Its eyes were bandaged with old birthday cards,
And on its arm, a bracelet carved with scars.

"You made me," came a voice not quite from it—
"You made me out of things you never said.
You left your fears beneath my growing ribs,
Then turned away and prayed that I'd forget."

The woman knelt and brushed its matted hair.
"I lost a child, but not in blood or scream.
I never named her—not in law or mind.
I let the fear devour every dream.

I could have fought. I told myself I tried.
But comfort won, and silence made me proud.
And though I live, I know what didn't come—
And feel her hand in every quiet crowd."

The man stood still before a shattered block.
A toy still etched with letters: D-A-D.
"I left. I said I couldn't be enough.
I told her, 'He'll be better off not sad.'

But years went by, and all I did was hope
He wouldn't ask, or miss the way I'd sound.
And when I heard he'd taken on my name—
It burned like truth inside forbidden ground."

The child rose, a thing of almost-form.
It wore their guilt like cloth that wouldn't fit.
"You thought that choice could cancel consequence.
You thought that time would make me never knit.

But I was born in shadows, breath, and wish—
In names you whispered only in your sleep.
And though I never learned to walk or speak,
I learned to follow, and I learned to weep."

The room collapsed into a lullaby,
Its notes all flat, like hearts too numb to pound.
We ran through ribbons stitched with broken hopes,
As every toy began to drag the ground.

The dog barked once, then bit through crib and smoke.
We stumbled back into the House's chest.
Another door arose with colours pale—
Its ninety-seven stitched through mother's breast.

The House had named the children never born—
And asked if ghosts can come before we mourn.

The Ninety-Seventh Room

The ninety-seventh door was chained but loose,
Its locks undone, yet clinging all the same.
The number etched in charcoal, thick with ash—
A smudge where fire failed to cleanse its name.

The knob was cracked, like something crushed by grief,
And when we touched it, silence filled the frame.
The dog lay down and whimpered without sound,
Its breath held tight as if it feared the flame.

Inside, a basement steeped in heavy dark,
Its walls lined deep with shelves of buried files.
No light but ours, which flickered with each step,
As if the House itself recalled our trials.

Each cabinet bore names in dusty ink—
Some crossed with red, some marked with gold and wax.
And from the farthest shelf, a figure rose,
Its back bent low beneath a hundred facts.

"You came to look, though never chose to see,"
It said, while dragging folders through the dust.
"You buried truths in archives wrapped with codes,
Then left them there to rot, forgotten, hushed.

You called it policy. You stamped it 'closed.'
You told the world, 'The past is not our fault.'
But while you slept, we woke beneath your feet,
And every record twisted in our vault."

The man stepped close and touched a rusted drawer.
Inside, a note from someone never found.
"I knew this case. I saw the names erased.
They told me, 'Let it go, it's dead and sound.'

I signed the paper. Told myself it's clean.
That nothing I could do would change the weight.
But still I dream of someone screaming once—
And hear the drawer before it shuts too late."

The woman paused beside a box of tags—
Each one a life mislabeled, filed away.
"She came for help. She spoke with broken lines.
I thought, 'Too vague. I'll check another day.'

She died that week. They said it wasn't clear.
I passed her name in memos twice that year.
And now I see her signature in dust—
Still reaching out through everything unclear."

The figure pulled a page from skin and thread.
It bled a truth too old for courts or cure.
"You said, 'It's buried.' You declared it closed.
But we still breathe in margins you endure.

You built your peace from redacted despair—
You paved your cities on our nameless bones.
And now you wonder why the walls still shake
When ghosts arise to call back what they own."

The files burst, their words like moths on fire.
They swarmed with screams from facts left unrevealed.
We ran, our arms wrapped tight in burning guilt—
The names we lost now carved in every shield.

The dog howled low, then barked into the dark.
We broke into the hall with eyes like scars.
Another door arose from coiled rope—
Its ninety-eight engraved with sealed memoirs.

The House had pulled the folders from the shelves—
And asked what truth survives when we erase ourselves.

The Ninety-Eighth Room

The ninety-eighth door breathed cold as open graves,
Its grain engraved with lines that fought to stay.
The number carved so deep it seemed to bleed,
Then patched again, as if to hide away.

It groaned before we touched it, not from wind—
But from the weight of all it meant to hold.
The dog sat down, its head between its paws,
As though it knew this room would not grow old.

Inside, a courtroom twisted out of shape,
The judge's seat too high to ever climb.
The benches lined with faces blurred by hands—
All watching still, as if to mark the time.

No gavel lay upon the crooked desk,
No jury stirred, no bailiff took their post.
Just files spread like roots across the floor,
Each one aglow with one familiar ghost.

A mirror stood where witness box should be,
And in its glass, not us—but what we were.
A child in shame. A teen who told a lie.
A grown-up cloaked in charm too thin to blur.

The voice that filled the chamber wasn't ours,
But sounded close, like something we once said:
"You think you're good because you feel your guilt—
But good is what you do when shame is dead."

The man approached the glass, then looked away.
"I told myself I changed. I grew. I learned.
But all I did was speak with softer words—
While keeping warm the bridges that I burned.

I never fixed the harm, I only named it.
I never paid, just felt and wrote it down.
I traded penance for a softer past—
Then wondered why my nightmares wore a crown."

The woman stood, her breath against her palm.
"I said I was an ally, raised my voice.
But when she begged me, 'Speak,' I said, 'Not now.'
I feared my job, my peace, my house, my choice.

I wear the pin. I share the solemn quote.
But still I ghost when it's my turn to stand.
And though I cry at monuments and grief—
I drop the torch when asked to lend a hand."

The room began to tilt, the mirror cracked.
Our former selves all crawled into the light.
Each one not monstrous, only incomplete—
Each one the cost of every failed respite.

They did not beg. They did not scream or plead.
They simply watched as all the files took flame.
And every paper bore our names engraved—
Not by the hand of others, but our shame.

We ran before the ceiling caved with truth.
The courtroom fell behind in tongues of red.
The dog sprang forth, and barked us down the hall—
Our guilt still pressing words we never said.

Another door was growing from the wall.
Its ninety-nine inscribed in bloodless grey.
The House had judged not what we did, but didn't—
And asked if change without a cost could stay.

The Ninety-Ninth Room

The ninety-ninth door bore a single nail—
No knob, no frame, no way to pull it wide.
The number hung on thread that frayed and snapped,
Then swung like something barely left to hide.

Its wood was dry as bone yet strangely soft,
It breathed, it sighed, it seemed to draw us in.
The dog began to growl with soundless depth,
And backed away as if to guard from sin.

Inside, a hall without a single shape—
Just walls of smoke and voices turned to mist.
No floor to walk, no ceiling to collapse,
Just drifting space where time itself was kissed.

And through the haze, a shape approached at last:
A silhouette that changed with every blink.
One moment mother, then a faceless child,
Then something shaped from iron, rot, and ink.

"I am the sum," it said, "the gathered shape—
Of all the rooms you've dared and left behind.
I carry every name you didn't say,
Each hurt you dimmed, each hunger you declined.

You came for shelter, thought you'd walk away—
But houses built of sin do not forgive.
They teach. They mark. They weigh the soul you guard.
They ask if what you carry dares to live."

The man stepped forth, his shadow not his own—
It lagged behind, then moved to block his path.
"I faced my past," he said, "I named it clear.
But still it walks ahead to draw the wrath.

I changed. I tried. I crawled out from my grave.
But still I hear the breath behind my fall.
The House has kept my secrets all in frame—
And now I wonder if I climbed at all."

The woman turned to where her voice had been—
But now she found it echoed from the walls.
"I thought I'd choose who I would be from here.
But every room has left me full of calls.

I carry them. I wear them in my step.
I ache with things I claimed were not my own.
And now I see—this House was always me.
Its bones, my words. Its floors, the things I've grown."

The shape began to split and scream in light—
A thousand faces all at once, and none.
A thousand truths that clawed from out our skin,
Until the shape was not the thing we'd run.

It was the thread between each breath and lie.
It was the voice we tried to leave unsaid.
It was the name we feared to carve in stone.
It was the self we stitched from what we fled.

The dog stood still and stared into the dark.
Then turned its head and slowly walked away.
And as we followed, walls began to close—
Not fast, not loud, just like the end of day.

Another door arose, so tall, so black—
It bore no number, only marks and stains.
The final one, the truth we came to meet—
The hundredth room that waits behind our chains.

The One Hundredth Room

The hundredth door stood silent, tall, and bare,
Its grain as smooth as skin too cold to mark.
No number carved, no sign of what it held,
Just breathless stillness waiting in the dark.

The wood was warm—not living, but aware—
And when we touched it, it recoiled, then sighed.
The dog drew back and would not cross the gap,
But lay outside, its muzzle turned aside.

We entered. Not a room, but something else—
A hall that spiralled inward like a thought.
No floor to feel, yet every step was firm.
No walls, yet still, we walked where someone wrought.

And then the air grew close, as if with breath—
Not wind, not ghosts, but something held in sleep.
A whisper stirred, not spoken but implied,
That here, at last, the House would choose to speak.

The hall unfolded like a lung exhaled—
And opened to a chamber dressed in red.
No dust. No rot. No ghostly robed remains—
Just velvet drapes, and candles cold and dead.

And at the farthest wall, beneath a cloth,
A frame too large to ever move or lift.
We stepped in silence, hand in trembling hand,
And felt the air around us start to shift.

We pulled the drape. The cloth fell soft and slow—
And underneath: a portrait hung in gloom.
Two figures posed inside a gilded frame,
Surrounded by the splendour of this room.

A man, a woman. Eyes that seemed too near.
A hand that gripped a knife not out of place.
A body curled, one seated by its side—
A mourner bent to kiss a lifeless face.

We stared. We froze. We saw ourselves in them—
But not as mirror, not as metaphor.
It was our hair, our clothes, our very scars.
Our likeness sealed behind a bolted door.

The plaque below was worn, but still it read:
The Owners of the House. Lost Here by Choice.
The Widow and the Dead. The Grieving Blade.
The Memory Made Flesh. The Silenced Voice.

We stepped away, but knew what we had seen.
A coldness pressed behind our ribs, then spread.
Not ghost, not guilt, but something we had been—
A tale once told, then buried with the dead.

A second frame sat covered by the first—
Smaller, hidden, angled into gloom.
We pulled the cloth and saw what lay beneath—
A study of the hallway we'd assumed.

Inside: a couple entering the House.
A rainy night. A dog. A tilted stair.
The paint still fresh. The candle yet unlit.
The door ajar. Our very moment there.

The plaque beneath was blank except for this:
They came again. They always do. They must.
One comes to grieve the wound they made in love,
The other comes to rot beneath the dust.

The truth uncoiled like ivy through our lungs.
This wasn't fate. We chose to come, to see.
One of us mourned and made the House from grief—
The other lay within, too dead to flee.

We turned—but every hall had gone to black.
No doors remained. No dog. No walls. No floor.
Just portraits, countless, staring from the dark—
The guests who walked, then stayed forevermore.

And now the House was closing us inside.
The lights grew dim. The canvas breathed, then set.
We felt our names begin to fade from sound.
We felt our flesh remember and forget.

A chair emerged, already worn to shape.
A knife was waiting, resting in the frame.
A bed below the portraits made from stone.
A silence called us softly by our name.

We knew, at last, the part that we had played—
One took the life, the other took the blame.
But both remained, and always would return,
To paint the walls, to feed the House its name.

And somewhere far behind the velvet veil,
A brush was raised, the oil still faintly wet.
Our eyes now watched from just inside the gold—
Our story hung, and would not let forget.

The Woman in the Mirror

Part I

She pressed her hand against the glassy frame,
A shimmer ran along her fingertips.
No heat, no chill, no name she ever knew—
Yet something pulsed as if the world had flipped.

A breathless tug, a tremble in the floor,
The light behind her dimmed and disappeared.
She stepped—no sound, no echo, and no door.
The mirror stood where once her path was clear.

A room of white: no seams, no shade, no bed,
No ceiling's depth, no corner where to hide.
The walls were clean as cloth not yet been bled,
The floor as blank as skin before it's tried.

The mirror faced her still—a flawless sheet.
She turned and saw her world across the glass:
The hallway where her coat and shoes were neat,
The lamp still on, the ticking seconds pass.

At first she laughed. "How quaint, how strange, how new!
A clever trick—illusion, dream, or prank."
She waved; the mirrored self waved too. It knew
No more than she—but neither drew it blank.

She watched them come and go, her friends, her kin,
They peered into the glass but could not see.
She shouted, struck the pane to reach within,
But silence held her screams in mutiny.

A day? A week? Time dulled her measured trust.
She slept without a night to fold her in.
No food, no thirst—her tongue grew dry with dust.
Her breath grew thin, though not from want or sin.

She danced, she ran, she wept, she raged, she prayed.
The white gave nothing back, nor took her plea.
The glass remained her window and her blade—
It cut her from the world and left her be.

One day she found a trick of subtle tilt—
A shadow formed behind her frantic hand.
She mimed a wound, a fall, a body spilt.
Outside, a child blinked—began to stand.

The girl returned. She looked with sharpened eye.
She watched the woman pantomime her pain.
She saw the hand against the pane and cry—
And mimicked it, as if to break the chain.

The woman mouthed the words: "I'm trapped. I'm here."
The girl drew close. She touched the pane in awe.
Then left—and came again with something near—
A hammer gleamed like justice, bright and raw.

The woman pounded, "No!" against the frame.
She shook her head. The girl misread the plea.
She thought the tears were grateful ones, not shame.
She could not hear, and took no time to see.

The mirror cracked—a single silver thread.
The woman screamed; the walls began to hum.
The white grew whiter, eating up her dread—
And then the world beyond her went all numb.

The girl stepped back. The glass began to shake.
A spiderweb of fractures leapt and danced.
The woman slammed her fists too late, too late—
The mirror burst. And with it, broke her chance.

The light rushed in—a burst, a painful flare.
Then darkness swelled. The glass became a wall.
No image now, just blank and heavy glare.
No exit left. No watchful eyes to call.

Part II

The glass was gone, and in its place a sheet—
A dead and sightless pane, like polished stone.
She pressed her palm; it gave back no deceit.
No breath, no form, no pulse—she was alone.

No longer could she glimpse the moving world.
No longer could she watch the seasons turn.
The space was white, and white around it curled,
A snow that did not melt, a fire that burned.

She tried to count the steps from wall to wall,
But every count dissolved before its end.
She tried to sing, but sound would never fall.
She tried to sleep—but sleep would not descend.

The room had air, but never wind or breeze.
Her hair hung limp, untouched by any drift.
Her thoughts grew loud, then louder, without cease,
Until her mind began to crack and shift.

She saw herself—another form, the same—
Reflected on the sealed and lifeless screen.
She tried to touch it, call it by her name,
But it looked past her, cold and crystalline.

Was it her soul, now fractured and confined?
Was it her shame, cast off and made to live?
Was this what waited after death? A mind
Without a world, and nothing left to give?

She dreamed, though dreams came jagged, torn and blind.
She dreamed of rain that never struck the ground.
She dreamed of mouths that whispered through the rind
Of silence thick and hanging all around.

A vision came: the girl—the one who broke—
Still standing by the shattered mirror's frame.
She stared inside the shards, and softly spoke
The woman's name, though never knew her name.

And others came. They wondered what she'd seen.
They asked what made her cry and point and pale.
She said, "A woman, white and trapped between."
They laughed. She wept. Her story was a tale.

But still she came. She watched the jagged face.
Each shard a slice of what had once been whole.
She saw a twitch, a flicker, then a trace
Of fingers reaching out, without control.

Inside the room, the woman saw her too.
Not clearly now—the glass was cut and gone.
But in one shard, a pupil flashed in view,
And hope returned, like sickness in the dawn.

She knelt. She whispered through the broken pane,
Her voice a breath, a soundless exhalation.
She begged the girl to find the way again,
To tell someone—restore the true relation.

The girl grew up, but kept the sliver still.
She wore it round her neck—a trinket odd.
And every night, it pulsed against her will—
A heat that hummed, a curse, a silent god.

She dreamed the woman's voice inside her skin.
She woke with bruises, weeping in the dark.
A mirror cracked would whisper her within—
Would write in frost the outline of her mark.

And once, she held the shard up to her face,
And saw the white room shimmer through the glass.
The woman, thinner now, and pale as lace,
Reached out—then vanished when the moment passed.

Years passed. The girl forgot the woman's cry.
The shard grew dim, the voice no longer spoke.
The white room stilled, and so did every try
The woman made. Her final hope had broke.

She walked, and walked, though motion left no track.
She scratched the walls until her nails were torn.
She bit her lips and watched them curling back.
She screamed—but now the silence felt like scorn.

One day she sat and folded in herself.
No light, no dark, no hunger now remained.
Her hands lay limp like books upon a shelf.
Her breath was gone—but still her shape remained.

And on the other side, a mirror shone—
A new one, bought to hang inside a hall.
It had no cracks, no flaw, no whisper drawn—
Until a shape appeared behind it all.

A woman pale, too pale for earthly skin.
No eyes, no mouth—just outline faint and slow.
She moved with weightless, soundless steps within.
She did not wave. She did not want to go.

Part III

The mirror hung in place, untouched, unknown.
Its surface smooth, reflective, clear, and bright.
No trace of what it once had held was shown—
A hallway piece, polite beneath the light.

The girl, now grown, walked slowly past the frame.
She paused—without intent, her body still.
The shard she'd worn still hummed with something strange,
And once again, her bones began to chill.

She turned. A flicker passed behind her face.
A second self, too gaunt, too tall, too bare.
It blinked—black hollows carved where once were grace—
And lingered long enough to steal the air.

The woman stood behind the glass once more.
But changed. Her skin was raw and sickly white.
No lips. No hair. No dress, no woundless floor.
Her body thin and scarred by endless night.

Her eyes were pits—no iris, sclera, vein.
Just holes where darkness sank into her skull.
She raised her hand, and pressed it to the pane—
So slow, so firm, so horribly controlled.

The grown girl stepped in close, against her will.
The air grew thick, the hallway dimmed to frost.
The mirror groaned, the floor began to still.
She knew, at once, what years ago she'd lost.

The woman smiled—but not with any mouth.
A twitch, a tilt, a hunger underneath.
Her hands were claws now, long and thin and south
Of human, jointed wrong with bone-like teeth.

She did not speak, but still the girl could hear:
"You brought me back. You kept me. Now you'll see."
She reached through glass as if it wasn't there,
And brushed the girl's cheek oh so tenderly.

The girl recoiled—but feet would not obey.
The mirror's edge began to ripple wide.
The hallway stretched, the air was stripped away,
And white began to pour from side to side.

She screamed, but no one heard her choking sound.
Her nails dug deep into the hallway wall.
The woman gripped her hair and yanked it down—
One tug, one gasp, one desperate failing call.

She vanished in the pane—no crack, no trail.
Just one more soul inside that soulless den.
The white room breathed, then stilled without a tale.
No mark was left of where, or how, or when.

Now two of them, behind the flawless sheet.
One thin, one fresh, both lost in endless gleam.
They stare through glass with horror, hunger, heat—
And wait to pull the next one through the dream.

They do not blink. They do not turn away.
Their faces hover close behind the screen.
And when you walk too near, you hear them say:
"Come closer. Please. You've always lived between."

So mind the glass. Don't watch too long or near.
Reflections sometimes look too deep, too true.
And if you glimpse a face that seems too clear—
It's not your own. It's them. They're watching you.

The Fiddler's Rite

Part I

He came by train, a stranger with a bow,
A violin encased in weathered wood.
The city breathed beneath a veil of snow,
And promised more than silence ever could.

He wandered streets that glowed in candle-glass,
Where windows blinked like eyes from long ago.
A student still, and hungry, none would ask
What dreams he carried beating soft and low.

He played with masters, trained in halls of fame,
But fortune had not followed with the skill.
He lived on crusts and coffee, not on name—
And chased the thrill that only strings could fill.

He found a bar with laughter in its beams,
A place that hummed with wood and amber light.
He sat and ate, and fed on quiet dreams,
And told himself he'd only stay the night.

His case he kept beside him like a pet.
He stroked the worn brass clasps with gentle hand.
The drink was weak, the stew was thick and wet—
He listened to a sluggish cover band.

Then someone came: a man with winter eyes.
He brought a drink, unasked, and tipped his glass.
He smiled like hunger dressed in friendly guise,
And slid into the open chair with class.

They spoke of songs, of cities, lives on wheels,
Of hollow flats and nights spent making do.
The fiddler laughed, then stammered through his meals—
He'd never met a man who listened true.

The stranger asked, "What's locked inside that chest?"
The fiddler said, "My voice, my fire, my bride."
He nodded once, and murmured with a jest,
"Then let us drink to art you will not hide."

The beer kept flowing. Hours lost their tread.
The fiddler spoke of stage lights, hands that bled,
Of days alone, of bowing until fed—
Of wanting more than hunger, fear, or bed.

They walked the streets, the bells were chiming two.
The fog had draped the corners thick with white.
The stranger said, "My place is close. It's true,
I live alone, but not alone tonight."

The fiddler's cheeks were redder than the moon.
He nodded once, and followed through the snow.
The night grew close, the silence played a tune—
A humming low that only dreamers know.

Inside: a loft with velvet on the walls.
A single bed, a glass of water poured.
The fiddler stood, entranced, while music called—
But not from strings. It pulsed beneath the floor.

They touched. They kissed. The fiddler gave his skin.
The stranger's hands were ice and fire combined.
They moved as if a current pulled within—
And tangled breath and bone and blood and mind.

No words were said. No candle had to glow.
The fiddler sank, and let the storm proceed.
The snow hissed down beyond the window's throw.
The city slept. Desire replaced his need.

He slept at last, his arm across a chest
That rose and fell in rhythm to the past.
The wind outside grew loud, then took a rest.
And in his dreams, a masked crowd danced and laughed.

Part II

He woke to cold, the window rimmed with white.
The stranger's coat still hung beside the door.
But of the man—no trace, no step, no sight.
The place was bare, more silent than before.

His bag was gone, his wallet torn and stripped.
The drawers stood open, empty, mute and blank.
He sat in shock, his breath too tight to grip—
A coinless husk upon a stranger's plank.

He tore the room with hands that shook with fire.
He called his name, the one he'd never learned.
He punched the wall, then sagged beneath his ire—
And found the place where all his hunger burned.

The fiddle still lay nestled in its case.
Untouched, unscathed—as if the thief had feared.
He held it close, ashamed to see his face,
A boy who'd danced with ghosts and disappeared.

He wandered back through streets that grinned like thieves.
The tavern lights were dulled by morning's breath.
The snow had turned to slush beneath the eaves,
And everything was touched by little death.

The barman frowned. "You're not the first to cry.
He comes and goes, like weather, sharp and slick.
You're lucky, lad. He left you with your sky.
Most others wake to worse than empty brick."

The fiddler tried to ask the man his name.
The barman shrugged. "He's known by none, my friend.
He's not of here. He drifts from frame to frame.
You shared a night. You won't see him again."

He stumbled out, the city dull and strange.
The colour bled from signs and coats and stone.
His heartbeat faltered, everything had changed—
He longed for home, but knew he was alone.

He found a bench, where pigeons hopped and cooed.
He held the case like something close to death.
His mouth was dry, his fingers black with mood.
He barely dared to waste another breath.

Then came a shape: a woman clothed in wool,
With eyes like smoke and hands like folded wings.
She moved as though her bones were carved from rule,
And sat beside the boy with quiet things.

She said, "You've lost what little you had left."
He nodded once, too tired now to lie.
"Your case is full. Your soul is what is cleft.
But fiddlers bleed before they learn to fly."

Her voice was thin, but underneath it rolled
A tone that curled like music made of years.
"You played with fire. You played as you were told.
Now play for more than vanity and tears."

He wept at last. She placed her hand in his.
It felt like linen soaked in distant time.
She said, "Despair is fair, but never this:
To leave the note unplayed within the crime."

"Tonight," she said, "go here," and pressed a card.
The ink was smudged, the address scraped and brown.
"Go underground. The stage is not so far.
Your strings will know the door beneath this town."

He took the card, and met her quiet eyes.
They held the weight of moons and maddened sleep.
She said, "They pay in coin you won't despise—
But once you play, the night is yours to keep."

Part III

He found the lane at dusk, its mouth a grin,
A crooked smile of brick and dripping moss.
The sky above was bruised with evening's skin,
The clouds were gold, like parchment smeared with loss.

The street grew thin, then vanished in a bend,
Where crumbling signs hung limp on iron rods.
A broken inn stood waiting at the end,
Its doorway carved with symbols, glyphs, and gods.

He knocked, and silence answered like a breath.
Then creaked the wood, and slowly swung the door.
No hand, no face—just emptiness and death,
And stairs that spiralled down beneath the floor.

A scent of oil, of roses long decayed,
Of wine spilled deep in velvet folds of dark.
He paused, then stepped where time itself was frayed,
And vanished down that throat without a mark.

The staircase turned, the air grew thick and still.
Each step a note, each echo like a drum.
The walls were red, like veins that knew his will,
And somewhere far below, he heard it come—

The distant sound of strings, a patient song,
Like breath exhaled through centuries of dust.
It called to him. It called his whole life wrong.
It fed on longing, sorrow, shame, and lust.

At last, he found the room: a vaulted hall,
With arches high and painted with decay.
A hundred masks looked down from every wall,
And candles bled their secrets into clay.

The floor was set with cushions, rugs, and bowls,
And figures sat in silence, gold and still.
They wore the clothes of other times and roles,
Like flappers dressed for some immortal thrill.

Each mask was gold, with lips too wide to smile,
And eyes like slits through which no soul could see.
The fiddler clutched his case, and paused awhile,
Then stepped into the hush reluctantly.

No one looked up. No hand was raised in cheer.
No welcome came. No glass was raised to clink.
He stood alone, the only thing sincere,
And bought a drink that tasted more like ink.

The band performed: a piano deep and slow,
A cello groaning like a mourning beast.
A viol touched the air with threads of woe,
And nothing broke the silence of the feast.

He drank. He watched. He waited to be asked—
But none approached, and none gave him a glance.
They sat with heads like mannequins in masks,
And swayed in rhythm like a fevered dance.

He nearly rose to leave, but then he heard—
A voice not spoken, more a pulse of thought:
"Now stand. Now play. Now give us the unheard."
The drink grew cold. The strings within him caught.

He rose. His knees were weak. His heart was loud.
He took the case and opened it with care.
The silence shifted through the gilded crowd,
And every mask turned slowly toward his chair.

He tuned the strings. They trembled like a breeze.
He raised the bow. His arm began to shake.
Then down it dropped—he played the first slow tease
Of notes that made the very candles quake.

The room did not applaud, nor blink, nor breathe.
They only watched as sound poured from his spine.
He played a waltz of sorrow underneath,
A haunting reel, a twisted lullaby.

The air grew thick. The ground began to swell.
The lights turned red, the arches swayed and sighed.
The masks began to tilt, and some to yell—
But all without a voice, as if inside.

His hands moved fast, no longer in control.
The bow was flesh; the strings were drawn from flame.
He played a song that carved into his soul,
And every note betrayed his very name.

They rose. The masked ones stood in golden rows.
They moved with sinuous and jerking grace.
Their fingers danced on skin and silk and clothes—
Each body found another in its place.

The music changed: more wild, more sharp, more loud.
The pace grew mad, the chords began to scream.
The fiddler played, surrounded by the crowd,
As if entranced within a living dream.

They touched, they moaned, they twined in slow unrest.
The air was thick with heat and oil and breath.
Their movements tangled, chest to heaving chest—
And every kiss gave way to something… death.

The fiddler watched, but could not stop the bow.
He tried to break, but muscle locked in fear.
He tried to cry, but all he felt was woe—
And music growing louder in his ear.

They dropped their robes. Not all were fair of flesh.
Some moved like beasts, with limbs that bent too far.
Their mouths were red. Their bones were wrong and fresh.
Their skin shone pale, like fungus under tar.

The rite began. He felt it through his strings—
A rhythm made of hunger and of fire.
The masked ones cried, and tore at sacred things—
And love was drowned beneath a mad desire.

He screamed inside, but nothing left his throat.
The bow kept sawing through the salted tune.
He felt the air grow thick as if to gloat—
And knew the climax came, and far too soon.

They pulled out knives. Each dancer found a chest.
Each victim smiled, as if they knew their part.
The blades sank slow—one thrust into each breast—
And from the wounds they tore the beating heart.

They bit, and chewed, and passed the blood around.
They drank from bowls where organs bled and steamed.
And when they laughed, it made a humming sound—
Like strings that echoed everything he dreamed.

Then all went still. The final chord was struck.
The music stopped. The bow slid from his hand.
The masks turned toward him, silent, grim, and struck—
And vanished all at once, as if on sand.

He stood alone, the case still at his feet.
His fingers trembled, red with sweat and ache.
The stage was bare. No sign of blood or meat.
But on the walls, the masks began to shake…

And from the floor, a whisper coiled and said:
"The rite is played. But it is not yet fed."

Part IV

He fled the hall, the bow still in his hand.
The streets were void, the clocks no longer struck.
The wind blew dry, like sand across the land,
And every sign he passed was smeared with muck.

The city seemed the same, and yet not quite—
The windows dim, the faces stiff with frost.
He passed a priest who winced beneath the light,
And whispered, "Son, whatever's done is lost."

He reached his room. He locked the door and wept.
He scrubbed his hands until the skin turned red.
The case he kicked beneath the bed and kept
His eyes from it as if it might have bled.

But every time he turned to seek his rest,
A sound would creep from under floor or wall:
The whisper of a string beneath a breast,
A pluck, a hiss, a lull that seemed to call.

He tried to sleep, but dreamed of golden masks.
They danced upon his chest and licked his jaw.
They asked for hearts, and gave him wicked tasks.
He woke each time with blood across his claw.

The case, once still, would slowly change its place.
He'd find it in the kitchen, in the hall.
Its lock would click. Its clasps would half unlatch.
Its bow would hum—a whisper sharp and small.

He tried to leave the town, but lost the way.
The station signs were scrambled, smeared, and wrong.
Each train would vanish moments from the bay,
And leave behind the echo of his song.

He met no friends. His phone refused to work.
The mirror's face grew stranger by the week.
He'd speak to passers-by—they'd grin and jerk,
And touch his shoulder, whispering, "Don't speak."

He found a café—ordered tea with dread.
The woman serving had no eyes at all.
She simply said, "We thought that you were dead."
And placed the cup with hands too long and tall.

He ran again. The city seemed to move.
The streets would shift, their names would change each day.
And every wall had stains shaped like a groove—
As if some bow had carved its sound away.

He tried to burn the fiddle in a fire.
The flames grew tall, but left it cold and whole.
It lay unharmed, though every log expired,
And whispered, "Play. Or pay the unpaid toll."

He broke it once—he smashed it with a stone.
The wood split sharp—but bled a streak of black.
He buried it beneath a twisted bone.
At dawn, it lay again beside his back.

The music rose within him like a curse.
He'd hum in sleep, and cry in silence, mute.
And when he'd scream, the sound would only nurse
Another song, more savage and acute.

He played. He had to—just to stay alive.
Each stroke relieved a little of the ache.
But every tune would bend, and twist, and drive
The air around him into something fake.

The people changed. They gathered at his song.
At first just one, then ten, then dozens more.
They'd come in masks, or cloaks, or dancing wrong—
And afterward, they'd vanish through the floor.

He tried to warn the world, but no one cared.
The words he spoke would die before they flew.
And when he begged, they nodded, simply stared,
And said, "You play. It's all that's left of you."

One night he dreamt the club beneath his feet.
He dreamt the old woman, her voice like silk.
She said, "You fed them well. You played the meat.
Now wear the mask, and drink their sacred milk."

He woke to find a mask upon his face.
A golden thing, now fused into his skin.
He tried to scream, but sound had left no trace—
Just music, pouring endlessly within.

And now he roams, not knowing time or place.
He plays in alleys, cathedrals, empty parks.
Each time he bows, a crowd appears in grace—
And when he ends, they leave behind no marks.

He cannot stop. His arms belong to strings.
His mind is tied to chords he cannot name.
And through him speaks a song that only brings
The ancient rite, and hunger dressed in flame.

And if you hear a fiddler in the dark,
Who plays without a pause, and will not blink—
Do not approach. Do not request a spark.
Just leave. And never ask for what he thinks.

For he is not a man, not now, not whole.
He is the song, the rite, the open tomb.
He walks beneath the moon without a soul,
And makes the strings the herald of your doom.

They say each time he plays, a mask is born.
They say he's one—but soon there shall be more.
For every heart he draws through string and horn
Becomes a note within the rite's dark score.

And you, who read or listen, mark this well:
The world is shaped by music none should know.
If ever down a stair you feel the spell—
Do not go in. Do not descend below.

For if you do, and if you hear that sound—
Of strings that wail like wolves and children lost—
Then close your ears. Or else, the rite is bound.
And you shall play—forever. At what cost?

Part V

He wandered far, through cities etched in dusk,
Through streets that bent where compasses would fail.
Each breath he took grew steeped in iron musk,
Each sky above him dimmer, thin, and pale.

The fiddle clung, though once he'd left it deep
Beneath a bridge, in chains, in frozen sand.
But now it hummed, as if it woke from sleep,
And reached again to feed upon his hand.

He played by force, not will, nor hope, nor dream.
Each night he bowed to crowds with hollow eyes.
They danced like marionettes beneath his scream,
Their limbs grotesque beneath indifferent skies.

He begged for death. He knelt at chapel doors.
He wept into a cracked and tarnished glass.
The mask had grown into his skin and pores—
He did not know the shape he'd come to pass.

And then, one night, while standing in a square,
Where no one watched, and even stars looked down,
A shadow moved—more solid than the air—
And walked with purpose toward the haunted town.

It wore no face. It made no sound nor heat.
It passed through walls, through alleys, void of breath.
The fiddler saw it coming—felt defeat—
For this was not a man. This was his death.

The fiddle screamed. It shrieked and tried to run.
Its strings uncoiled like serpents made of fire.
The bow split clean. The case burst wide undone—
But still the thing came closer, filled with ire.

It reached for him. He fought. He tried to flee.
But arms of ash and ancient rot held tight.
The shadow grinned—or would have, if set free—
And dragged him down into the throat of night.

His scream went up—a sound that split the air.
It shook the birds down from the chapel spires.
And then—a note, so sharp, so pure, so rare—
A fiddle played, uninterrupted, higher.

No crowd remained. The square was bare and mute.
The only trace: a mask, cracked down the brow.
The violin played on, though none would suit
The bow. No hand would ever find it now.

Epilogue

A train pulls in across the morning mist.
Its whistle cuts the fog like razor breath.
The passengers descend through air half-kissed
By winter's hush, and just a hint of death.

Among them walks a boy with case in hand—
Its surface new, its strings not yet unstrung.
He hums a tune he barely understands,
And thinks of all the songs he hasn't sung.

The streets await. The sky is growing pale.
The windows blink. The bars begin to hum.
He doesn't know the shape within the tale.
He only knows he's come. He's truly come.

And somewhere far beneath the city's roots,
Where candles flicker in a temple red,
A chair stands vacant, polished for new boots.
A bow is drawn. The music is not dead.

Beneath the breath

Part I

He lived as though the world had bowed to him,
With golden light that followed where he stepped.
In health he glowed, his skin and voice both trim,
No wound he bore, no debt he ever kept.

At work they watched his shadow as a sign,
His breath could tilt the scale or spark a cheer.
Men offered praise, and women stood in line—
His smile, it seemed, dissolved the need for fear.

He ran at dawn, the park his courtly stage,
Each muscle honed, each motion clean and strong.
His eyes betrayed no sign of stress or age,
And all who met him felt they'd known him long.

He laughed with kings, he dined with shrewd elites,
His touch could sway the coldest boardroom fight.
The world was glass beneath his ordered feet,
His life a dance of ease, composed and bright.

And on the night the shadow wrapped his door,
He lay in bed beneath his woven sheet.
The wind was calm; the house gave off no roar—
No omen stirred the silence of the street.

Yet when his breath returned, it met no air.
He woke in dark, but not the dark of night.
His mouth went dry; his hands began to tear—
No walls were near, no hint of windowed light.

He tried to sit, but hit a ceiling low.
He struck it with his palm—then groaned, then gasped.
He found his legs, but could not stretch or go.
His breath came fast, his chest was tight and clasped.

He clawed around with fingers dulled by shock,
And brushed against the grain of wooden walls.
His boot struck stone, his nails pulled loose the chalk.
A coffin, yes—a box. A grave. The fall.

A scream rose up, but didn't pass his throat.
He pressed his tongue against his teeth and wept.
What joke was this? What dream? What twisted note?
Who'd laid him here while still alive, and slept?

He fought to still the rising in his lungs,
For panic eats the very thing he needs.
He lay unmoved, and let the darkness hum,
And focused on the sense of air, like seeds.

His hands found cloth: his jacket, sleeves, and seams.
He searched his chest, his belt, his upper thigh.
A lighter, coins, a pen—mundane, it seemed.
Then something flat. He pulled it up, and cried.

A phone. Still charged. Its little screen aglow.
He tapped the glass—his thumb a trembling wreck.
The light revealed a space so tight and low
He nearly dropped it in his growing dread.

He squinted through the apps to see the date.
The sixth of June. His breath grew tight again.
Four days had passed since last he locked the gate.
Four days since last he'd been among the men.

He tried to dial, and silence filled his ear.
No signal pierced the soil above his tomb.
He tapped again, and still the bars were clear.
The world beyond was airless, sealed in gloom.

A scream began to form—he bit it back.
He knew that noise would steal his only breath.
He pressed the phone against his chest, pitch-black,
And shook beneath the pressure-point of death.

He sent a text, though knew not if it flew.
He typed in names, in madness, rage, and prayer.
Each message vanished, swallowed by the blue.
No answer came. Just pulsing light and air.

Then in the dark, a whisper stirred the phone.
He swore he heard a sound, though faint and low—
Like static filtered through a broken tone,
A voice, perhaps. Or something more below.

He placed it near his ear and held his breath.
A hum, a hiss, then... syllables unclear.
A woman's voice? A rasping note of death?
He could not say. But still he held it near.

The words were wrong. Too slow, too cracked, too deep.
A laugh? A sob? The scraping of a claw?
Then silence bloomed, and left him cold and weak—
As though the grave had gasped and drawn its maw.

He turned the phone to light the wooden lid.
And scratched at it with keys, with pen, with hand.
No give, no shift, no crack would let him rid
The lid from where it pressed him like a brand.

The battery held. The hours crawled like beasts.
He counted minutes just to stay alive.
He saw again his kitchen, office feasts—
And wondered who had planned this to contrive.

No memory returned to give him cause.
He drank no drink. He knew no bitter foe.
He'd had no seizures, broken none of laws.
So why this box beneath the soil below?

Then came the sound. A knock, or something near.
He froze, then tapped the wood to match the beat.
Another knock. A silence wrapped in fear.
Then breath. Not his. A breath beneath his feet.

He pressed the phone against the grain and shook.
The breath grew louder, wet and gurgling slow.
He shifted back, though nowhere left to look—
Another voice began to speak below.

Part II

It spoke no words a mouth could cleanly form,
But moaned in notes that warped the air with weight.
The voice was thick, malformed beyond the norm—
A crawling sound that hatred might create.

He pressed his ear against the coffin floor.
The breath below was thick with heat and wet.
And in between each groan, there came once more
A drag of nails, like something tried to get—

To get to him, or reach some upper place.
He jerked away, his spine alight with dread.
No corpse should move, no voice should sound in space
So crushed with death and silence overhead.

The phone still glowed. A single bar appeared.
He tapped a call, his thumb a shaking prayer.
It rang. It rang. Then failed. The signal veered.
The dark grew thicker as he gasped for air.

A whisper from beneath him hissed again—
Not word, but mimicry of speech and song.
It croaked, then laughed, like mockery of men
Who thought the grave was quiet, deep, and long.

He cried aloud, and hit the coffin walls.
He kicked and beat the wood until it cracked.
But every strike consumed the air that stalled—
And soon the edge of sight began to black.

He bit his lip to keep from wasting breath.
He counted seconds, held his chest, and rocked.
His mind began to split beneath the death—
The echo of the whisper never stopped.

The phone buzzed once. A message: "Do not fight."
The text appeared, unsigned, no name or mark.
He stared at it beneath the shifting light,
Then typed: "Who are you? Why am I in dark?"

No answer came. But then the voice below
Repeated back the question he had sent.
Its tone was cracked, too slow, too full of woe—
As if the grave itself knew what he meant.

He screamed, and screamed, though no one heard the sound.
The soil drank all syllables of fear.
He wept until his breath was all but drowned,
Then held his chest and wiped away a tear.

The phone began to glitch—the screen would blink.
The date remained the sixth, but time was wrong.
It jumped and flickered, faster than a blink—
Then showed a year ahead. Then dropped. Then gone.

And in its place, a message: "Join us now."
The screen went black, then bloomed a face unknown.
A corpse's face. No skin upon the brow.
Its eyes were his. Its mouth was split and sown.

He threw the phone, then grabbed it back with care.
It's all he had. The light. The hope. The thread.
He knew now what had dragged him under there—
Not man, not war, but something with the dead.

His thoughts turned back to when he'd gone to sleep.
Was there a sound? A hand? A breath? A taste?
He'd locked the door, he always locked it deep.
Had someone come? Or had he been erased?

The face returned. The screen began to shake.
The voice beneath him moaned in frantic pitch.
The light above him flickered like a lake—
And then he felt it: something cold and twitch.

It touched his boot. A finger? Root? Or claw?
It rose through wood as if the box were wax.
He screamed again and shoved against the maw—
But now the thing had gripped him by the slacks.

It yanked with force. His legs began to sink.
The floor gave way, the coffin opened wide.
He clutched the walls, he clawed the edge, the brink—
But through the crack, he saw what lay inside.

A tunnel downward, lined with rotted flesh.
And dozens more of coffins, stacked and split.
And in the dark, a swarm began to thresh—
Of voices whispering where corpses sit.

He heard his name. Then others he had known.
A teacher dead. A lover lost to sea.
A brother buried years before, alone.
They called his name like they could set him free.

But down below, their mouths were full of soil.
Their teeth were black. Their tongues were cracked and thin.
They reached for him as if to end his toil—
But not to save. To drag his living in.

He fought. He kicked. He gripped the splintered top.
The phone beside him blinked and made a sound.
A single word: "I'm here." It would not stop.
The light began to bleed along the ground.

Then silence. And a perfect stillness fell.
No breath below. No twitching in the dark.
He listened close, and heard no cry from hell—
Just shallow peace. And then... the faintest spark.

A light above. A noise. A shifting sound.
A shovel struck. A voice cried, "He's alive!"
He blinked, near death. His heart began to pound.
The wood above began at last to rive.

And then he saw the light. The sky. The air.
A hand reached down. A face he dimly knew.
They pulled him up with care, and urgent prayer—
He coughed, then screamed, then let the terror through.

But as he sat upon the grass and shook,
The phone still glowed with light, and showed a name—
The last to text. The last to call. He looked.
It matched the man who pulled him from the grave.

He stared in horror, saw the smiling face—
But younger. Pale. And rotted near the chin.
The rescuer now frowned, and left no trace
Of breath. He said, "You're late. Come back within."

Part III

He tried to stand, but strength had left his bones.
The hand that gripped him had a weightless feel.
It left no warmth, no pressure in his own—
And all around, the air seemed less than real.

The grass was pale. The trees had stilled their breath.
The birds, if there were any, made no sound.
The sky above looked dim, as if with death,
And he was cold despite the sun unbound.

The man beside him knelt, then gave a nod.
"You lasted longer than the rest," he said.
"You didn't scream as much. The others clawed."
He smiled. "You nearly earned the taste of bread."

"What—who are you?" he gasped, and took a step.
His legs were weak, the ground beneath him wrong.
He blinked again. The sunlight seemed inept—
Too sharp. Too still. Too silent for a song.

The stranger shrugged and reached to touch his brow.
He flinched away, but couldn't help the chill.
The man's hand passed through air—he gasped. Somehow,
It left a mark. A shadow. Something ill.

"You never lived," the stranger whispered near.
"Not really. All the life you thought you had—
The praise, the pride, the lovers, job, the cheer—
Was made for you. A mask to keep you glad."

"No," he replied. "That's wrong. I ran. I breathed.
I touched the world. I knew my mother's voice."
"You dreamed of her," the ghostly figure seethed.
"You were not born. You were... a kind of choice."

The trees now bent. The soil began to groan.
A wind picked up from nowhere, sharp and foul.
The sky above turned dimmer, nearly bone.
The wind took shape. The wind began to howl.

"The ones who dig," the stranger said with glee,
"They made you bright, and perfect, proud, and thin.
But we who sleep, we know what's underneath—
Your shell is clean, but all is rot within."

He backed away, but everywhere he turned
The world grew flat, as if no depth remained.
Each blade of grass was painted on and burned.
Each breath he took just thickened with a stain.

The man advanced. His eyes were milky white.
"I died like you. But they would not let go.
They buried me and left me there to fight,
And in my fight, I dragged down all below."

"You're mad," he said. "This can't be real. I'm free."
"No," said the ghost, "You passed the mark at last.
You lived too well. You lived too perfectly.
That's why you've joined the others from the past."

Then from the woods, a dozen more emerged.
Their suits were torn, their dresses dark with soil.
Their eyes were dead. Their fingers long and purged.
Their mouths still moved, but never free of toil.

Each one had once been known, or so he thought.
A teacher's face. A girl who died in spring.
A man who'd vanished while he stood and fought.
Now all were husks with grave-mud in their grin.

"You're one of us," the stranger hissed again.
"You think the box was end, but it's the start.
You dreamt of joy. Now wake among the men
Who bought their lives and paid them back in parts."

He tried to run, but every step fell short.
The trees now closed. The air began to press.
The world collapsed, as if it had no port—
A maze of skyless horror, thought, and flesh.

He tripped, and in the fall, he dropped the phone.
It shattered on a root, and dimmed to black.
The light went out. He groaned a hollow moan.
And heard again that rasping voice come back.

"Join us," they said. "You were the best of all.
They fed you praise so you would bloom and gleam.
But those above knew even kings must fall—
And wake beneath the gilded, dying dream."

He clawed the earth, now soft like flesh and skin.
It bled beneath his nails. It breathed. It moaned.
The trees were ribs. The wind, a voice within.
The sky was stitched, the stars already gone.

He reached a clearing shaped like burial grounds.
And there he saw a hundred stones, each bare.
No names, no dates, no flowers, none around—
And every one of them, he knew, was there.

They stood beside the graves they once had filled.
Their hands were clasped. Their faces cracked and red.
And in the wind, their silent songs were spilled—
A lullaby that only suits the dead.

And at the end, a stone with his own face.
His name engraved in letters sharp and clean.
The date: June 2nd. Time: eleven, late.
The stone was warm. The dirt beneath it green.

He sank. He dropped his knees before the stone.
His breath now ragged, and his chest unstrung.
The world began to tilt and crack and groan.
He knew: the final bell at last had rung.

The stranger stepped beside him. "Now," he said,
"You understand. The box was not the end.
You lived a lie, until your breath was bled.
Now let the earth take back what you have spent."

He felt his chest collapse with silent force.
His limbs went numb. His eyes were wide with pain.
The soil beneath now pulsed as if a source
Of hearts and mouths that never learned restraint.

The graves all sang. The corpses danced in place.
The world went dark. The stars were sucked away.
And as he sank into the earth's embrace,
A final voice rose up to end the play—

It came from deep within, a mirrored sound.
His own voice, torn by years of rot and strain:
"You dreamed of life, but now the truth is found.
You are the worm. The breath. The box. The name."

And with that voice, the last of light was gone.
The grave shut tight. The flesh became the stone.
No flowers grew, no prayers, no hopeful dawn—
Just silence where his name was once alone.

The House in the Wood

Part I

He walked the wooded path each dawn alone,
A ribbon carved through dark and dripping green.
The mud would cling, the nettles kissed his knees,
The light, a veil that barely split the screen.

The trees bent low like penitents in church.
The hush was deep, disturbed by neither crow
Nor breeze—except the rustle of his boots
And breath, both steady, slow, and soft below.

He liked it there, the stillness, thick and close.
It made the world feel distant, held at bay.
He passed no house, no fence, no sign of life—
But one, which stopped him every single day.

A crooked home, set deep within a bend,
Where thorns grew fat, and moss adorned the gate.
Its roof had sunk. Its chimney leaned with age.
Its windows frowned with slow, decaying weight.

And yet, despite the rot and broken beams,
Despite the doors half-eaten through by mold,
It drew him with a strange magnetic pulse—
A house that whispered "yours," though dark and cold.

He often paused to stare at it and dream.
To see the boards restored, the garden clear.
To watch himself within, beside the hearth—
A home reclaimed from silence, time, and fear.

Some mornings, when the fog was heavy-laced,
He thought he saw a flicker in the pane—
A pulse of orange, like a candle's breath,
Then nothing. Just the ivy, glass, and rain.

One dusk he lingered longer than before.
The woods were still, the shadows not yet drawn.
And there it was—a glow behind the glass,
A steady light that should have long been gone.

And in the window, motion smooth and slow:
A hand arose and wavered in the gloom.
So solemn was the gesture, near divine—
As if she grieved and blessed him from her tomb.

He froze. The forest held its breath and watched.
The birds forgot to chirp. The trees forgot
To sway. Her hand moved once again, and paused—
A whisper carved from everything he's not.

He turned and fled. The path became a snare.
Each root reached up to clutch his stumbling tread.
The darkness thickened like a dying cough.
He reached his home and slammed the door in dread.

He didn't speak of it that night or next.
But something gnawed the corner of his thought.
What woman waved? Why now, after so long?
What did she want—and what had she been taught?

By noon, he broke and wandered to the square.
The villagers, old roots of land and air,
Were gathered on the benches by the inn—
He asked them softly, "Who is living there?"

A silence dropped like dust upon the wood.
An elder leaned, and stroked his beard with care.
"You saw her, then?" he asked. "She waved at you?"
The man just nodded, held beneath his stare.

"She lives," the elder said. "Or what remains.
She's in that house, they say, but not alone.
She's seated always, near a shattered stair.
She cannot walk. She cannot leave the stone."

Another spoke, a woman slick with grief.
"She had a boy. A darling, quiet lad.
He vanished in the woods behind her home—
They found a ribbon. Never found the lad."

"They say she went half-mad," the elder said.
"She stared for weeks, then stopped, and never cried.
Her voice went out. She wouldn't eat or move.
She sat, and stared, until the last dog died."

Another muttered, "That's not all the tale.
She's seen outside—though chair-bound she must be.
She knocks on doors. And if you dare reply,
You'll vanish too, or drown, or cease to be."

A woman crossed herself. "She comes at night.
And when she does, she takes what pain has touched.
A widow once, a boy who'd skinned his knee—
Each saw her eyes, and died within a month."

The man grew pale, but didn't laugh it off.
He knew their myths, their need to make things sharp.
But still, he'd seen her—hand and light and face—
And something in it hummed a broken harp.

He walked again that evening toward the path.
The trees grew darker, rough with bark and wet.
The sky had drained of any shade but black.
And still he went—he couldn't now forget.

He saw the house, its window lit and cold.
The wind had ceased. The forest didn't breathe.
And there—again—a figure in the glass,
Who slowly waved, as if she knew his teeth.

She didn't smile. Her lips were stretched and drawn.
Her hair was thin and white against the gloom.
And when she blinked, the shadows seemed to change—
He turned again and sprinted from her tomb.

The village bells began to ring at dusk.
The square was filled with shouting, smoke, and cries.
The hall—the very heart of local faith—
Had caught, and burned, beneath unnatural skies.

The fire moved like water on a wall.
The bricks collapsed before the beams could groan.
The flames, the priest said later, hissed with speech—
And yet no mortal voice had shaped that tone.

Three died, and others vanished in the ash.
The firemen fled—their hoses turned to steam.
And when the smoke had cleared, the ruin stood—
A gutted mouth too wide for any scream.

That night, the man walked further than before.
He watched the path. The trees looked down and wept.
The house was dark—but darker still the air—
And from the grass, no sound nor insect crept.

And then he saw her—not within the glass—
But outside, slowly wheeled beneath the stars.
A girl, no older than her seventeenth spring,
Pushed her with effort toward the house's scars.

He stepped toward them. The girl turned sharp and fierce.
"Don't speak," she said. "You don't belong. She sleeps."
But still, the woman in the chair looked up—
And blinked again, with eyes that held the deep.

He knelt. He didn't speak. The girl looked on.
The house behind them pulsed with shifting shade.
The woman blinked again. Her mouth began
To twitch, as if a name begged to be made.

But nothing came. The chair gave one sharp creak.
The girl wheeled her inside and shut the gate.
He stood alone, the forest thick with sound—
Of breathing earth, and something just... too late.

He couldn't sleep. His hands were cold and raw.
He saw her face behind his window frame.
Each blink of his became a blink of hers.
Each thought he had now answered to her name.

Next day, he found the girl behind the square.
She ducked into a shop, refused his call.
He begged her just to talk, to say her name—
But she escaped, like shadow from a wall.

He waited. Hours passed. She reappeared.
He pleaded once again. She stood, then sighed.
"You want to know? Then listen close," she said.
"She cannot hurt her blood—but you can die."

"I'm hers," she said. "But only in the name.
My parents died, and she was left to me.
I moved to care for her—but found instead
That nothing in that house is truly free."

"She speaks without a mouth. She sees too much.
She blinks, and you forget what year you're in.
She waits. She watches. No one ever leaves
Without her threading something deep within."

"She tried to take my love," the girl went on.
"She waved, and he approached, and that was all.
He disappeared. I found his scarf alone—
And heard her whisper just beyond the wall."

The man was pale. He shook. "What does she want?"
The girl looked down. "To share. Or to replace.
To trade her pain for something warm and soft—
A skin to wear. A mouth. A living face."

"She cannot walk, but wants to walk again.
She needs a host to make her grief stand tall.
And grief," she said, "has more than just one path.
It flows like blood, and drowns, and swells, and calls."

The man looked west—toward the woods again.
The house was waiting, lit with dying sun.
He didn't know what led his feet that way—
But still he walked, and knew he wasn't done.

Part II

He crossed the field again beneath the dusk.
The trees stood stiff, like soldiers out of breath.
The sky hung close, too heavy with its dark,
And something in the air now hinted death.

The gate was open. Ivy curled its teeth
Around the posts, like veins around a bone.
The steps were warped, the porch half-caved with time.
But still he walked, and still he walked alone.

He knocked. The door, half-rotted, gave a groan.
The hinges cried like children left outside.
The hall beyond was filled with velvet dark—
The kind that swells, and pulses when it hides.

He stepped inside. The boards beneath him bowed.
The smell was thick—of dust and skin and ash.
A lamp burned low beside a broken chair,
Its flame a little tongue that licked the past.

The walls were lined with pictures framed in mold.
Each face was blurred as if the glass could breathe.
The house was quiet—not the quiet of sleep,
But of a place that waits, and won't forgive.

A stairway led to blackness sharp as ink.
He did not climb. He wandered left instead.
The parlour swam with yellow, dying light,
And smelled of violets drowned and long since dead.

A clock stood still, its hands both pointing down.
A rug lay half-unraveled on the floor.
A single teacup sat upon a plate—
And something breathed behind the cellar door.

He did not move. He didn't even blink.
The shadows pressed like fingers on his skin.
And then he heard the creak of distant wheels—
And knew the woman wheeled herself within.

But no one wheeled her now. She moved alone.
He didn't see her—but he heard her breath.
It rasped like cloth dragged over shattered glass—
A rattle full of something worse than death.

She didn't speak. She didn't need to speak.
Her presence filled the corners like a flood.
She poured across the walls and in his mind—
And scraped her nails along the floor of blood.

He turned—and she was there, not in the chair,
But standing tall, her gown a blackened shroud.
Her legs were wrong—they jerked and cracked like sticks—
Her eyes were grey and blank and far too loud.

She stared into his soul and let him see.
She blinked—and time collapsed around her face.
He saw a well, a child, a cry too faint—
And saw the village turn away in grace.

They let her lose her child. They turned their backs.
They blamed her grief. They locked their doors and prayed.
And when she begged, they called her mad, possessed.
They said she led the boy to death that day.

She did not speak. But still her thoughts were sharp.
They pierced his skull like sewing needles fast.
He saw her mourning twist into a thing—
A beast of shadow, forged from all her past.

And now she needed. Not to weep or die.
But to continue. She had learned to wear
The living like a cloak, to fill their lungs—
To stretch herself through grief into the air.

"You dream of home," the voice inside him hissed.
"You want the quiet hearth, the softened bed.
Then take it—stay. I'll walk in you, and see
The world again, with beating in the head."

He backed away. The house began to moan.
The walls expanded, breathing out her name.
The mirror in the hall began to drip—
Its glass like flesh, reflective but inflamed.

He turned to flee—but found the door was gone.
The foyer stretched. The parlour spun around.
The house was not a house—it was a mouth.
And he was now the warmth it long had found.

A thousand whispers poured into his ear.
They called him father, brother, lover, son.
They promised healing, peace, a second chance—
And still he knew: it wouldn't be undone.

A portrait fell. The canvas tore like skin.
It showed a man—his own face in the frame.
He screamed—but silence ate the sound too quick.
And through the wall, she murmured "You are named."

He struck the mirror—shards rained at his feet.
And in their glass, her figure stayed intact.
She raised her hand—five fingers white with frost—
And through the shards, her grin began to crack.

She stepped. The carpet bruised beneath her weight.
Her bones clicked out of rhythm with her pace.
She reached toward him—not to choke or kill—
But gently touch the outline of his face.

He staggered back. His breath came thin and dry.
The air grew thick with soot and blooming mold.
His teeth felt loose. His heartbeat slowed to thuds.
And all around, the house began to scold.

"You came to take me," said the voice again.
"You dreamed of owning me—but I own you.
You want to fix me, scrape away the past—
But houses keep the things that men undo."

The girl burst in—her face alight with fear.
She threw a vial that shattered on the floor.
A stink of salt and burning roots arose—
And shrieks like knives spilled out from every door.

The woman froze. The house began to shake.
The girl screamed "RUN!" and yanked him by the coat.
They leapt through shadows curled like living ropes—
While walls cracked open, choking on their throats.

They reached the gate. The hinges split in half.
The girl fell hard. He grabbed her by the wrist.
The house let out a final, wordless groan—
Then swallowed up the path in crawling mist.

They ran. They didn't stop until the hill
Was far behind and stars returned to sky.
She wept against a stone, and wouldn't speak—
And all he did was breathe and wonder why.

"You're marked," she said. "She's in you now. She is."
"You looked too long. You saw too much. You stayed.
She needs a vessel—but she waits to move.
And when you're weakest, that's when she will trade."

He touched his chest. His heartbeat missed a beat.
He touched his face—it felt too still, too thin.
He opened up his mouth—but heard her sigh—
A sound that didn't come from deep within.

"I'll help," she said. "I've learned a way to bind.
A tether made from grief and blood and rhyme.
But it won't hold if you don't want it to.
She only wins when longing kills your spine."

He nodded. "Do it. Anything," he said.
And so she took a splinter from the stair,
A thread from off his coat, a lock of hair—
And sang a song no one was meant to hear.

It wasn't sweet. It wasn't kind or clean.
It sounded like a dying bird in frost.
But when it ended, he could feel the air
Return, if barely—like a line uncrossed.

"Go now," she said. "Don't dream of her again.
Don't walk that path. Don't speak her sacred name.
She's bound, for now. But time eats through all walls.
And grief, once born, becomes its own domain."

He nodded once. He didn't ask the cost.
He walked away, half-man and half a ghost.
And though the trees began to breathe again,
He knew he'd left the best of him inside that host.

The house remains. Its window sometimes burns.
The chair still waits in dust behind the glass.
But now the girl sits silent in its shade—
Her face too young to wear such ancient wrath.

They say she walks alone beneath the trees.
They say she hums a lullaby off-key.
They say the boy returned—but wrong, somehow.
His eyes too black. His hands too old to be.

And sometimes, when the moon is thin and cold,
A hand will wave from deep behind the pane.
And those who wave back feel their body shift—
And never quite return to flesh again.

The man has vanished. Some say he moved on.
But others saw him muttering at the sea.
His coat was wet. His eyes too wide with light—
He told the wind, "The house remembers me."

The path regrows, no matter how it's razed.
The vines return. The moss renews its floor.
And grief—the house, the woman, all the rest—
Will wait forever, just behind the door.

Part III

The woods were not the same once he had gone.
They whispered more, and held their leaves too long.
The crows flew lower, circling just one tree,
And thorns grew twice as fast, and twice as strong.

The girl remained, the house now hers in name.
But names don't mean a thing to what's beneath.
She swept the halls and lit the oil lamp,
And watched the shadows gather at her feet.

She spoke to none. She barely left the gate.
The town avoided passing near the bend.
They said she walked in sleep, her mouth ajar,
Her hair undone, her fingers stiff to bend.

The priest came once, with salt and sacred oil.
She watched him pray. She watched the candle flare.
And when he left, he whispered, "She is two."
And never stepped again beyond the stair.

The baker's son, who laughed at such old tales,
Dared tap upon her window late one night.
He never came to work the week that followed—
They found his shoes beside the quarry's light.

And then the dreams began to cross the town.
They shared a shape: the woman in the chair.
Her hands would rise, too slow for natural flesh,
And wave them forward from her room of air.

Some saw her blink, and felt their lungs collapse.
Some heard her breathe and woke with hair turned white.
A child drew her face in soot and chalk—
And whispered, "She comes knocking in the night."

The girl began to change. Her step was strained.
Her spine grew curved. Her skin turned grey and cold.
She'd sometimes mutter fragments of old songs—
And once was seen to dance like something old.

The house would moan in hours past the dark.
Its shutters banged, though every breeze was still.
One villager said he saw her climb—
Though none recalled her standing by her will.

Still she lived. She smiled, but once a week.
She kept the garden filled with thistle bloom.
She spoke to birds, and sometimes called a name—
And when she wept, it echoed through the rooms.

A postman vanished bringing news one dawn.
His sack was found beside the crooked stile.
Inside the house, a single letter burned—
A blackened edge, still curling with a smile.

The trees grew thick with vines that oozed red sap.
The path grew darker though no canopy
Had changed. And always, from that upper room,
A dim light pulsed in slow solemnity.

The girl would sometimes sit beneath the glass,
Her face against the pane, her fingers pale.
She'd watch the wind and mouth a nameless prayer—
And tap her nail upon the windowsill.

The man was seen—or someone with his shape.
A figure near the cliffside where he'd fled.
He wore a coat too large, a hat too low,
And when he passed, the birds all dropped like lead.

One farmer saw him digging in the field.
Not planting. No—the man was pulling things.
A length of cloth. A broken porcelain doll.
A jawbone bound in silver wedding rings.

The girl, one dusk, received a single box.
She didn't sign. The postman left it bare.
She brought it in with gloves and locked the door—
And ever since, she's walked with twisted air.

They say she dreams of someone locked inside.
A double-self, a copy full of need.
They say she whispers names that rot the ear,
And bleeds without a wound, and smiles at weeds.

One night, the house went silent as a grave.
The light went out. The path was overgrown.
A child swore she saw two figures leave—
One walked. One rolled. They wandered all alone.

The child drew pictures, many in a row.
Each one more dark, more warped with evil grace.
In every sketch, the girl grew pale and thin—
Until she wore the old ghost's ancient face.

The house was sealed. A padlock shut the door.
But still, the windows glowed from time to time.
A shadow crossed, then vanished in a blink—
And crows would gather, perfectly in line.

No one dared knock. No one dared say her name.
She'd left the square, but never left the glass.
Some said the woman traded places now—
And which one lived was anyone to guess.

And then, a letter came. No stamp or seal.
Just left upon the chapel's twisted pew.
It read: She's patient. She will walk again.
And when she does, she'll look exactly like you.

The priest resigned. The shopkeep sold and fled.
The mayor left without a word or cause.
The woods fell thick with mildew and with flies.
And silence ruled the town with sharpened claws.

The girl was seen again—just once, at dawn.
She fed a dog that barked and licked her hand.
She smiled, then frowned, then whispered to the air—
The dog lay down, and turned to stone, and sand.

She painted shutters black. She locked the well.
She placed small dolls in rows along the stair.
Each doll was dressed the same: a crimson dress,
And stitched across the chest—her maiden hair.

The townsfolk dreamed of fire they couldn't quench.
Of sobbing heard beneath the garden bed.
Of voices chanting songs in ancient tongues—
And every voice belonged to someone dead.

The crows grew bold and pecked the windowsills.
The frogs crawled far beyond the marsh and pool.
The river split its banks to flee the wood—
And still the house stood still, as still as rule.

The girl wrote notes and nailed them to a tree:
The soul returns. The mouth is never closed.
If she can wave, she can be seen again.
If she can blink, then something still is posed.

A stranger passed and scoffed at all the fear.
He walked the path and laughed at tales of death.
They found his boots beside the oldest stump—
The rest of him was nowhere, not a breath.

The town grew small. The borders closed in tight.
A schoolhouse shut. The grocer left his store.
And once a month, a knock would strike at doors—
But no one answered. Not like once before.

Part IV

The girl was seen again one moonless night,
Her dress too loose, her arms too stiff with cold.
She walked in circles through the hollow field,
Then sat and whispered secrets to the mold.

A hunter claimed he saw her drag the chair
With no one in it, down the forest path.
She spoke to it. It answered with a hiss.
He ran, and died that night inside his bath.

The weather turned. The clouds forgot to move.
The trees leaned in and listened without wind.
The lake refused to thaw despite the sun—
And something old was stirring from within.

Then came the knock. Three times, too slow, too soft.
A widow opened—she had been alone.
They found her sitting, smiling at the wall,
Her voice repeating, "Now the house has grown."

A shepherd heard a lullaby by dusk—
The tune a child might hum to soothe a toy.
It led him through the woods until he found
A field of teeth where once had lived a boy.

The girl began to vanish from her shape.
Her skin was pale, but sometimes turned to bark.
Her nails grew long. Her pupils lost their round—
And when she laughed, the corners bent too dark.

At times she'd speak, but only backward words.
At times she'd hum, but no one knew the song.
She once walked straight into the church and knelt—
Then grinned and said, "You left her there too long."

And far away, along the coastal road,
A man returned—his coat a shade too light.
He walked with limbs that twitched at every turn,
And muttered, "Grief becomes a house at night."

He came back not as saviour, but as sign.
He bore the stain of having once survived.
He felt the call that hummed through stone and trees—
The pulse of what should never be alive.

The village saw him. None dared speak aloud.
His eyes were dull, his hands were stiff and raw.
He walked the path as if beneath the dirt—
And paused before the gate with hanging jaw.

The girl looked out. She did not speak or blink.
She watched him stare. She tilted once her head.
And then she wheeled the empty chair outside—
And placed it down where he had once been led.

"You left," she said. "But something stayed behind."
"You broke the house—but never shut the door."
He fell upon his knees and begged the dark—
"I didn't know what grief was waiting for."

She didn't move. The silence was too sharp.
The leaves turned black, the air too thick to breathe.
The chair began to rock without a touch—
And something hissed from underneath the eaves.

She reached into her coat and pulled a shard—
A piece of glass once cracked from hallway frame.
"Your face," she said. "It still remains in here."
"And now you'll help me learn to say her name."

The man rose slow. He took the glass with care.
The mirror showed him not as he had been,
But older, hollowed, carved by years of guilt—
A ghost that lived in skin no longer thin.

And in the glass, behind his ruined shape,
The woman stood—the one who never died.
Her gown was stitched with eyes, her hair a net,
Her mouth was red but never opened wide.

He raised the shard. It trembled in his grip.
He looked to her—the girl now made of grief.
He cried, "I'll end this, even if I burn!"
She smiled and said, "You never had belief."

He threw the glass. It shattered in the grass.
The sky turned red. The trees began to howl.
The house itself began to crack and pulse—
A beating heart beneath its shingled cowl.

The chair rolled forward, empty but alive.
It circled him, then stopped beside his knees.
He reached to touch it once—and felt the dark
Slip straight into his spine and seize his teeth.

His body froze. His breath became a fog.
His mouth fell slack. His shadow left the ground.
He heard the girl begin to speak in tones
That bent the air and turned it inside-out.

"Your grief was weak," she said. "But ripe with guilt."
"She needs more strength. She needs a proper frame."
She placed her palm against his stuttering chest—
And through his ribs she breathed the woman's name.

The wind reversed. The soil began to steam.
The birds flew backward into trees that wept.
The air grew hot. The grass began to boil—
And still the man stood still, and still he slept.

She blinked—and when her eyes were open next,
They burned with light not born of any sun.
She took the man's last breath between her teeth—
And said, "Now we are two. And we are one."

The house began to move—its beams to shift.
It stretched and cracked, then pulled its roots up slow.
The porch began to slither through the mud.
The windows glared like lanterns filled with woe.

It left the bend. It shuffled through the trees.
The girl walked just behind, her face serene.
She dragged the chair in which no one now sat—
And sang the song that once had fed the scene.

The village woke to thunder in the dark.
The woods had changed. The trails were all unknown.
A path had split the graveyard left to right—
And from it came a sound too near to moan.

The church bells rang. The candles all went black.
The wheat grew brown. The milk turned into stone.
And at the well, a little boy knelt still—
And whispered, "Now she walks. And not alone."

The girl approached the mayor's yellow door.
She tapped three times. No more. Just like before.
But when he answered, she was not the same—
Her hands were not her hands. Her name no more.

She entered calm. The house stood just behind.
It loomed and sighed and crouched beside the hill.
Its chimney turned to bone. Its roof to flesh.
Its shutters blinked. Its door grew sharp and still.

The girl sat down. The chair was placed beside.
The mayor wept. The walls began to drip.
The girl leaned in and touched him on the brow—
And filled his mouth with darkness at her lip.

They found him next day, seated by the fire.
His eyes were open, empty of the flame.
He rocked and hummed, and smiled at nothing near—
And called the girl "my daughter's mother's name."

The village cracked. The fabric split in threads.
The crows built nests upon the schoolhouse beams.
The dogs grew mute. The horses would not blink—
And none could tell the waking from the dreams.

And in the centre stood the house itself.
It had no plot. It moved when none could see.
It watched. It breathed. It grew a second floor—
And no one knew what grew inside but three.

The girl was two. The woman now was none.
The man no more, but etched beneath her spine.
They watched the town through lace and shadowed glass—
And every soul began to fall in line.

Some disappeared. Some turned their clothes to ash.
Some walked in circles, muttering of names.
And when they saw the window's lamp at dusk—
They waved in slow, mechanical refrains.

The girl now speaks to things behind the trees.
She plants no flowers, only broken teeth.
She writes in chalk along the chapel walls—
And speaks of birth, and death, and what's beneath.

They tried to burn the house. It only smiled.
They prayed. It echoed louder through the floor.
They fled. But found the woods had wound in knots—
And every trail returned them to its door.

And still she waves. Each night at exactly ten.
The hand so slow, the movement barely made.
But when you see it, something in you breaks—
And longs to join her in the garden shade.

She does not knock. Not anymore. She waits.
She watches for the one who turned away.
And when she finds him—wherever he may crawl—
She'll show him how the house has learned to stay.

The girl once more grew thin and hard to see.
She flickered in and out of morning's hue.
And once, a boy went looking for the well—
They found him dressed in thorns and speaking true.

Part V

The ground grew soft. The seasons lost their sense.
The summer snowed. The autumn would not fall.
And all around, the house stood firm and wide,
Its windows blank, its shadows ten feet tall.

The girl was rarely seen, but still she was.
At times she walked, her feet not touching ground.
At times she stared, and all the birds turned back.
At times she hummed, and milk turned into sound.

They tried again. A circle made of priests.
A ring of salt. A prayer in bleeding tongue.
They chanted loud, and rang a hundred bells—
But every single bell came off unstrung.

The house grew arms—its roots like fingers spread.
The bricks would sigh when no one was around.
The chimney wept a black and bitter soot.
The door would laugh, a warm and muffled sound.

One mother wept. She'd lost her youngest son.
He'd wandered off, they said, into the green.
She swore she heard him knocking late that night—
And in her dreams, he sat upon the screen.

Then came the man. A stranger none had known.
He wore a coat with candles stitched inside.
His voice was low, and full of winter's breath.
He said, "I've come to meet what others hide."

He walked the path. The woods fell into hush.
The trees leaned back. The moss unwrapped his feet.
He found the house and nodded once in thought—
And whispered, "Yes. The grief is near complete."

He knocked once only. No one answered him.
The door unlatched and swung with patient groan.
The hall was warm. The parlour smelt of dust.
The walls were lined with portraits drawn in bone.

He stepped inside. The air grew strangely sweet.
He saw the chair, alone, and draped in black.
And by the fire, the girl stood calm and still—
But all her eyes were watching from her back.

"You've come," she said, in voices not her own.
"A witness. Maybe more. Or maybe less."
He bowed and placed a box upon the floor—
And said, "I bring her name, and bring her dress."

He opened it. The box let out a sound.
A little coo, like child not yet grown.
The dress inside was red with stitched-up tears.
The name was carved in buttons, dried and sewn.

The girl stepped close. Her hands began to shake.
Her pupils shrank. Her teeth began to grind.
The house let out a groan beneath the floor—
And every mirror cracked in double time.

"You bring me back," she said. "But not to save.
To bind. To cage. To take away my song."
He nodded once. "You've sung enough," he said.
"Your grief has walked the world too loud, too long."

The woman blinked. The girl began to cough.
The chair rolled forward, creaking as it wheeled.
The fire turned to frost. The air grew sharp.
The floor became a web no foot could feel.

"You'll join me, then?" she asked. "You'll wear it too?"
"You've touched the grief—you cannot walk away."
He drew a thread and tied it round his wrist.
He said, "I've lived in grief since my first day."

She paused. She grinned. "Then sit. We'll talk awhile."
She waved her hand. The table split in two.
A hundred cups appeared, all filled with breath.
A hundred chairs for all the past she knew.

He sat. She sat. The house began to chant.
The walls drew in. The floor let out a sigh.
And from the hearth, a scream began to bloom—
A scream not made to end, or even die.

They spoke in quiet voices none could hear.
The tea grew cold. The light began to fail.
And when they rose, the table was no more—
And in its place, a tiny wooden jail.

He placed the dress inside and closed the lid.
He sealed it tight with ash and folded thread.
The girl stepped back, her eyes returned to green—
And from the walls, the woman's presence bled.

"You held her long," he said. "You played her well."
The girl just wept. "She was me, more than me."
"She fed on what I lost and could not fix.
She drank my heart. She chewed my memory."

They turned and watched the house begin to pale.
Its bricks turned soft. Its windows lost their glass.
Its beams grew thin. Its door became a breath—
And then it sank beneath the yellow grass.

The woods returned. The moss grew clean and green.
The path became a path again, not wound.
The wind resumed its song among the leaves.
The trees unbent. The roots went deeper down.

The village, slow, began to lift its eyes.
The bells were fixed. The well was clear and deep.
The priest returned, and dared again to sing.
The dogs came back. The children learned to sleep.

But still they keep the border trimmed and bare.
No house may grow beyond a certain line.
And once a year, the girl walks to the hill—
And leaves a rose where grass refused to shine.

The stranger left, and took the box with him.
He whispered, "She is not the only one."
"They bloom in pain, and walk when we forget.
Grief makes a hundred ghosts from every son."

They say he walks where haunted places sleep.
That he can sense when sorrow turns to shape.
That he can feel the blink behind the glass—
And knows the steps the haunted dare to take.

The girl still hears her sometimes, in the breeze.
A song half-formed, a rattle in the bone.
But now she knows not to respond or speak—
For ghosts return to those who answer home.

The woods are green. The grass has left its ash.
The leaves no longer whisper when you pass.
But should you see a flicker at the bend—
You must not wave. That's how it starts again.

She'll raise her hand. So slow it chills the breath.
She'll blink once more. Her eyes too full of need.
And once you see her face, you'll find your dreams
Will rot in roots, and bear her bitter seed.

The village thrives. The path is seldom tread.
The girl now teaches how to speak of death.
She warns of kindness offered to the wrong,
And sings to grief beneath her careful breath.

And if you pass that road at eventide,
You may see nothing. You may feel no dread.
But something deep beneath the trees will pause—
And mark your face, in case it must be fed.

For once a house has known the taste of hope,
It does not starve. It waits for sorrow's swell.
It waits for those who long for something more—
And opens when they knock, and knows them well.

She dreams, sometimes, of fire without heat.
Of crying from a room that holds no wall.
Of reaching for a child she never bore—
Of walking where the rain will never fall.

But morning comes. She opens all the blinds.
She breathes the day. She cuts the overgrowth.
She plants no flowers red. She sweeps no ash.
She lives—but lives with memory of both.

And still she keeps the mirror in a drawer.
The one that showed the woman at her side.
She does not look—but once a year she lifts
The cloth, and sees her blinking deep inside.

She does not wave. She does not smile or cry.
She nods once gently, wraps it up again.
And stores the grief where it can do no harm—
Unless, of course, it's spoken of by men.

The chair remains, beneath a sheet upstairs.
No one has touched it since the final fall.
It creaks at times, and shifts a leg at night.
But no one speaks of what may one day call.

The final lesson carved above the gate:
Do not respond to grief that wears a name.
Do not return the wave of what was lost.
Do not rebuild what sorrow built in flame.

For though the house is buried by the years,
And though the girl has lived beyond her pain,
The past is long, and roots are longer still—
And some things grow when watered by the rain.

So if you walk the path, keep eyes ahead.
Ignore the lights that flicker through the green.
Ignore the voice that asks if you are cold—
Ignore the face that's watching, half unseen.

And if you smell a bloom that has no source,
Or hear the wheels of something just behind,
Then pray that you can find your way back out—
And leave no piece of longing left behind.

For grief survives. It learns. It walks. It waves.
It takes the shape of what we cannot mend.
And if you let it enter through your door—
It builds a room that never knows an end.

The girl is old. Her hands are worn and wise.
She keeps a journal sealed with iron string.
And when she dies, she leaves behind one page:
"The house was me. And I was everything."

The villagers will read it, slow and hushed.
They'll pass it down. They'll whisper it in schools.
They'll build no home too near the forest's hush—
They'll mark their maps with shadows and with rules.

But somewhere far beyond the wooded bend,
A child will see a flicker in the leaves.
And feel the urge to knock, to help, to heal—
And take the path that no one else believes.

And somewhere else, a girl will hum again.
Her song too faint for grown-ups to discern.
And all at once, a chair will start to rock—
And every lamp will blink, and slowly burn.

And somewhere deep inside the buried frame,
A heartbeat will begin that once was still.
And grief will find a voice, a mouth, a face—
And teach the next to weep, and take its fill.

You cannot kill what sorrow made to last.
You only hide it, hush it, bind its name.
But once you speak of what was not your loss—
The grief returns. The grief returns the same.

The field remains. The grass is soft and wild.
The wind is sweet. The world appears at peace.
But walk too far and feel the silence shift—
And know the house has only changed its lease.

The girl once said, "We are not meant to fix.
Some broken things must break until they end."
But grief is patient. Grief can wait for years.
And when it knocks, it will not call you friend.

So if you find a window lit too late,
And see a figure waving ever slow—
Do not respond. Do not approach the gate.
There are some truths you're never meant to know.

And if you do—then carve your name in stone.
And write a will. And plant no flowers red.
For once you've waved, she knows you from the rest—
And she will come to tuck you into bed.

And should you dream of wheels upon the floor,
Or feel a breath too close and not your own,
Then you'll recall the house that called to you—
And understand you're hers, and hers alone.

You'll see her eyes in puddles, glass, and sleep.
You'll feel her gaze when no one's at your back.
You'll wonder when the world began to fade—
And never find the moment that you cracked.

The door is gone. The key was lost in flame.
The walls dissolved into the hungry ground.
But still she waves. And still the house remains—
In anyone who lets the grief resound.

And if you write about her—if you dare—
Then mind the rhyme. Don't speak the name too loud.
For ink and meter give her shape again,
And every poem becomes her nesting shroud.

So end it here. The tale is told and done.
Let no one read these lines beside a flame.
Let no one seek the house beyond the trees—
Let no one bring new sorrow to her name.

And yet, I fear, the rhythm has her pulse.
The meter fits her steps. The rhyme, her breath.
The way the tale began is how she lives—
And how she steps again from out her death.

So hush the child who walks too near the bend.
And close the blinds before the dark is deep.
And if she waves, do not return the sign—
Just hold your breath, and pray the house still sleeps.

For grief is not a ghost you can outrun.
It waits. It learns. It knocks, and finds your floor.
And once you open up to let it in—
It builds itself a room behind your door.

www.ingramcontent.com/pod-product-compliance
Lightning Source LLC
Chambersburg PA
CBHW020825160426
43192CB00007B/533